Foreword by Gore Vidal

A Bush & Botox World

Saul Landau

CounterPunch

Foreword by Gore Vidal

A Bush
& Botox
World

Saul Landau

CounterPunch
PETROLIA

AK
PRESS

First published by
CounterPunch and AK Press 2007
© CounterPunch 2007
All rights reserved

CounterPunch
PO Box 228 Petrolia, California, 95558

AK Press
674A 23rd St, Oakland, California 94612-1163

ISBN 978-1-904859-61-1

Library of Congress Control Number: 2006933527

A catalog record for this book is available from the Library of Congress

Typeset in *Tyfa*, designed by Frantisek Storm for The Storm Type Foundry, and *Stainless*, Designed by Cyrus Highsmith for The Font Bureau, Inc. Cover and Title Page also use *Amplitude*, designed by Christian Schwartz for The Font Bureau, Inc.

Printed and bound in Canada.

Design and typography by Tiffany Wardle.

Cover Design by Tiffany Wardle.

Contents

Acknowledgements

T HANKS TO P J PATEL, EMILY LUTZ AND TORI BARRETO, WHO helped me edit and clarify some of the essays in the book. I also want to acknowledge the progresoweekly. com website that five years ago inspired me to start writing regular commentaries. Marc Raskin, my colleague and friend for decades, gave me useful and insightful comments on several of the essays. My other colleagues at the Institute for Policy Studies educate me on a daily basis. Similarly, my Cal Poly Pomona colleagues have helped me maintain my critical edge and I thank them. Special thanks to Tiffany Wardle, who designed the cover and the layout.

I owe an enormous debt to Rebecca Switzer, who provided key critical and brilliant comments, and kept me from making a fool of myself on more than one occasion. Farrah Hassen did more than help me. She became an organic part of this book-writing process and co-wrote the essay, "Paradise Now or Never—Movie or Life?" I am deeply grateful to her, for her astute writing and editing talents and her commitment to ordering these essays into book form.

Foreword by Gore Vidal

I HAVE SPENT PROBABLY TOO MUCH TIME IN THE COURSE OF A LONG life examining the American main-line media and, whenever possible, its antidotes in the form of progressive publications like *The Nation* as well as the foreign press. In the course of this media saturation I have seldom, if ever, come across a story in praise of another country's internal arrangements. Sweden: Yes, they have better schools and medicine for everyone as well as daycare centers for the children of working mothers. But, they all practice free love as they drink themselves to death, usually by suicide. President Eisenhower's eyes would go wide as he brooded upon the infamy of a state so free of crime, poverty, potholes that the residents would rather kill themselves than continue to stay alive under such non-faith-based regimes. Luckily, for a skeptic like myself, there are a handful of American filmmakers and writers who over the years (in the case of Saul Landau forty years) who have brought us the truth about how ripped off the average American is as well as the true glimpses of certain aspects of those nations constantly demonized by our masters in our (i.e. their) media. It was Landau who gave us our first good look at Fidel Castro in a PBS documentary film, FIDEL. A longtime director of digital media programs at California State Polytechnic University, he has opened many windows for the rest of us: parts of the world, where we are not usually allowed to know about except to be told how wretched they are. Only Landau could remind us that Cuba has more doctors abroad than the World Health Organization while its own doctor-patient ratio is similar to that of Beverly Hills. The Bushites, in the event of Castro's death, are planning to privatize Cuba in order to benefit our AMA, pharmaceutical, healthcare entities which have done such a bang-up job for, if not us, companies and the like.

Now in *A Bush and Botox World* Landau surveys the great mess that the Bushites have made of the United States. Did I mention that Landau is a witty writer who has found his—alas, our—subject the sort of mess that Bush and his tax exempt one percent of the nation have made of our economy, our military, our politics, as he plunges from war to war? Landau, like the narrator in *The Great Gatsby*, marvels at how the rich so joyously make messes secure in the knowledge that others will clean up. But what if, one day, they don't? Can't? Read Saul Landau.

Title Explanation

P.T. BARNUM, THE 19TH CENTURY CIRCUS ENTREPRENEUR, GETS credit for saying "there's a sucker born every minute." He probably didn't say it, but whoever did should receive eternal acknowledgment as George W. Bush's only important teacher—with the exception of the docent who had him memorize only the first three words of the Golden Rule.

In the 1930s, people sang "it's a Barnum and Bailey world, just as phony as it can be." In 2005-7, most people don't know those lyrics. But they do sense that after Bush took them to war in Iraq in 2003 and went AWOL during the aftermath of 2005's disastrous Hurricane Katrina, the man in the White House played them for suckers. He offered voters the equivalent of a cheap circus act. Instead of the sword swallower, Bush offered voters the "I'm just one the good old boys" act.

He has maintained his three ring performance by playing dress up throughout his presidency, appearing in a fighter pilot's jacket on an aircraft carrier in 2003, a plaid shirt, jeans and cowboy hat while vacationing at his lush Texas estate and in a windbreaker as a hard working guy after—well after—Hurricane Katrina hit the Gulf Coast. He used the costumes and his penchant for destroying English syntax to obscure his real character: a man unable to deal with suffering and death, the most difficult parts of life.

On September 13, 2005, President Bush made a pretense of atoning. "I accept responsibility," he said in an address to the nation, but not "I made a terrible mistake." He told a few lies about what a good job his Federal Emergency Management Agency (FEMA) appointee Michael Brown had done. "Brownie, you did a heck of a job." Then, Bush fired him—after the media revealed the facts of "Brownie's" gross incompetence. Bush simultaneously tried to cover up the negligence by appointing loyal insiders to investigate.

Just as Botox erases wrinkles—for a short time—Bush's Botox approach to politics, like badly wrinkled skin, also revealed itself as something getting old very fast. Hence the title, A BUSH AND BOTOX WORLD.

Introduction

GOD BLESS AMERICA SAID THE BUMPER STICKER ON INVESTMENT banker Jack Ryan's fancy car. In 2004, he vied for an Illinois Senate seat with Barack Obama, his Democratic challenger, as he simultaneously fought his wife in court for custody of their ten year old son. She claimed that he forced her to frequent sex clubs to watch others indulge and engage themselves before eager spectators. He said she exaggerated, but had to drop out of the race. The scandal distracted potential voters.

It has become difficult to separate the headlines of sex and sin from the serious political issues of our time—war, poverty, environmental degradation. Ryan's story—not related to the private who was saved during World War II—dramatized the confusion created by the informing media's desire to attract audiences through libidinous lures and its traditional role as a Fourth estate that protects the public against the inevitable excesses of the political class.

When politics and culture merge in sex and scandal, as they do on a daily basis, the President invariably repeats variations on the old saw that ours is the best civilization money can buy. US foreign policy stands on a spiritual sales pitch: the rest of the world should buy US products, which will lead them to enjoy our values as well. By absorbing shopping culture, they will through virtual osmosis save their godless souls and convert their material and spiritual poverty into the kind of happiness enjoyed by the Ryan family.

But the entertainment industry doesn't export the Kinky Ryans as the typical upwardly bound striving American couple. Instead, the rest of the word gets offered a romanticized vision of suburban life. In it, multiple-car families commute happily on unclogged freeways, kids not on drugs or booze merrily drive their Hummers five blocks to the local high school and on weekends the harmonious family spends creative time and lots of money at shopping malls. The pre-menopausal Mom alternates her days between driving kids in SUVs to soccer fields while speaking on her cell phone, and then shuttling the uniformed offspring to munch on Carl's Jr. low-carb burgers.

The real soccer Mom, however, might also have to save time for worrying that the weekly Botox injection won't really remove the wrinkles. The real kids might have tried, or even gotten hooked on, crystal meth, the drug of choice among suburban and urban youngsters.

The real—and deeply shallow—US culture does get exported. Danish kids get pierced and tattooed, hip hop reverberates through tapas bars and tweaking teeny boppers in Moscow find tovarich dealers on the street.

The culture of immediate experience, of techno-multi tasking, has replaced centuries of directed development. No longer is one's future writ large in one's family tradition. As "rust belt" factory jobs have all but vanished to "less developed" (low wage) countries, the new US working class culture has become immersed in gadget-ownership, a condition in which technology replaces reading and writing as a cognitive foundation. This new culture screams with artificially manufactured music or at least electronic sounds and rapidly flashing images on plasma screens.

The Aristotelian meld of beauty and ugliness, good and evil, makes little sense as a universal aesthetic in a society whose moral poles have drifted far from righteousness. The red and blue states, culture and politics, religion and paganism, republican and democrat, repression and pornography defy any principle of harmony—despite President George W. Bush's messianic urge to export them.

Just as European empires imposed their values on their colonies, so too does the informal US empire reshape—or tries to—older cultures with different notions of good and good looking. Reality TV, for example, plays nightly in Iraq!

US reality, however, has remained elusive for the US public. Most Americans, for example, will state without hesitation that their nation possesses the most powerful military in world history. Yet, few think about their country as an empire or their government as imperial. Rather, they accept, as the Pledge of Allegiance assures us, that the flag stands for the republic. A republic that, in 2005, possessed some 800 bases abroad.

When he invaded Afghanistan in 2001 and Iraq in 2003, Bush crossed the metaphorical Rubicon into overwhelming imperial status. In the name of stopping terrorism and spreading democracy to the Middle East, he dropped whatever camouflage had previously covered the imperial features of the US system.

The military component of empire went hand in glove with the zealous and aggressive export of the US political and economic order and its culture and entertainment. From the 1960s on, in the Western Hemisphere alone, US troops or CIA covert operators invaded Guatemala, Cuba, the Dominican Republic, Brazil, Chile, Nicaragua, Panama and Haiti. They even invaded the miniscule island of Grenada. In each case the president invoked the magical words, "national security," without ever defining the term.

The real objective of these policies had little to do with "national security." In 1954, a Guatemalan peasant who received a parcel of unused United Fruit Company land hardly jeopardized US national interests. But corporations like the United Fruit Company and the banks who financed their operations did not want interference with their overseas operations. They had made a partnership with a willing US government, which promoted their products through overseas sales, opened markets and worked to circumvent taxes, labor and environmental regulations and work place safety standards by "deregulating." The media obediently labeled this promotion of corporate interests "free trade."

In the technically compelling and substance-deprived TV and cinema products, one can often find inherent notions of virtue shown in modern US culture: shopping, anorexia, egoism, insensitivity and violence.

Such values seem a far cry from those of the austere Puritans who landed at Massachusetts Bay almost four centuries ago and those of the Founding Fathers in the 1770s. In the passing centuries, the ever growing empire has eroded republican principles. Somehow, politicians finessed the tensions between the needs of a republic and those of an empire; indeed, a prime feature of American uniqueness.

One means of achieving the stability in the face of conflicting republican and imperial forms lay in the continued ignorance of the public. Few Americans have read their history or know it from oral traditions. This ignorance has made them into suckers—people who fall for gimmicks, advertising slogans and false promises of improving their imperfections, even those that come from aging and dying.

Thus, the ubiquitous "sucker" has stood for almost two centuries as a guidepost for marketers and politicians. The salesman has found the ultimate mark in the TV addict who lets the slickster into his or her bedroom—even at midnight—to push used cars, cleavage enhancing bras, anti-constipation medicine and Prozac. The current sales force benefits from the inundation of the public. TV and radio, internet and e-mail, old fashioned newspapers and magazines floods the public with messages implying that each individual receiving the message is the most important person in the world—and therefore must improve his or her figure, clothes, car, bank loans etc., by buying something.

The thrust of the message world denies both the necessity of aging and death. Small wonder that the discovery of botulism toxin—it will "cure" wrinkles—found an immediate market—for those who could afford it! Indeed, the truly rich could die without aging. And if they lived long enough, modern science might find a cure for death as well—or at least make it seem as if it didn't happen.

The rich lessons of history, philosophy and art pale before the possibilities of technology, whose commercial perpetrators hold out the ultimate reward of eternal life—and 24/7 shopping. Commercial messages in public spaces distract citizens from public consciousness and direct behavior in coded and abbreviated language toward some personal obligation. What a culture! And what sophisticated politics!

"Eat a Whopper" and "Support Our Troops" bumper stickers, next to American flag and "I Love Jesus" decals, characterize our age. Logos, brands and vicarious identification have sucked reason from the modern consumer brain. As science penetrates the genetic code and masters the physics of instant global communication technology, fanatical bible thumpers advocate medieval crusades to spread a zany religious and culturally sick order into the Islamic world. If theology contained reason in the past, its modern expounders have rationalized it away. The programmed Christians whose artificial smiles serve as a coat of armor against disturbing sensations or thoughts have become political soldiers in the cause of corporate reaction. They call it God and freedom. The army of Christ has become the most hawkish force in the world. In the name of the Prince of Peace, the Lords of War in Washington bombed and invaded Afghanistan and Iraq.

Along with the Bible citers, the professional military walk in the cultural front lines. Once relegated to cellar status where it belonged, military culture since World War II has become both prestigious and pervasive. Like corporate brands and logos, the marching band and the rifle drill team have all but married professional and college sports. Military color guards carry the flag before important games and military bands "entertain" crowds during halftimes as squadrons of air force jets fly over the stadiums housing the World Series and Super Bowl. Digital games abound with military technology. "Be all that you can be," not by studying and going to law or medical school, but by joining the army that turns normal individuals into trained killers—who pray several times a day.

In this 21st Century Barnum world—with suckers abounding—the very people who strive to make the consuming public feel deeply inadequate have concocted the sure-selling remedy for the effects of time. Botox wipes away not only signs of aging, but the signs of time passing; indeed, the very notion of time.

This book is not about the shallowness of one president or the culture of corruption that he embodies. It is an appeal for citizens to re-address their reality, stop allowing the message senders to keep us in the sucker role and instead play a role during the course of our short passages in the long historical drama.

I. The Bush Culture:
Nothing Succeeds Like Failure

God and Botox:
Spirituality through Shopping

"Nature is a woman, with lots of wrinkles."—Anonymous

"In 2001, more than 1.6 million people received Botox injections, an increase of 46 percent over the previous year. More popular than breast enhancement surgery and a potential blockbuster, Botox is regarded by some as the ultimate fountain of youth. Botox injections are the fastest-growing cosmetic procedure in the industry, according to the American Society for Aesthetic Plastic Surgery (ASAPS)."
—Carol Lewis, Botox Cosmetic: A Look at Looking Good

"My Mama never told me that there would be more than 3 billion people without enough food, clean water and access to medical care. She should have seen the traffic jams in Los Angeles and the good people worrying about wrinkles."—Forrest Shlump

SOME AMERICANS RELY EXCLUSIVELY ON PRAYER TO RELIEVE stress and the emotional emptiness that accompanies their work life. Others have discovered that more "scientific" ways help them cope with the dubious aesthetic results of daily strain. The official Botox website offers highlights designed to relive the suburban professional couple's nightmarish existence.

"Meetings . . . deadlines . . . chauffeuring the kids . . . picking up something to eat on your way home—you've got a lot going on. But you know you have to make time for yourself, too."[1]

In the linguistic world of advertising, the enunciation of worries and woes means that you can find remedies. For example, "you've decided to try Botox Cosmetic. To help you get started, here's some help with the first step: selecting a doctor."[2]

That's right, some of the very people who have endured the vicissitudes of medical school can now supervise (and get wealthy quickly from) treating the ultimate in medical science—or at least its appearance: stopping outward signs of aging.

"Could this be what you've been looking for—a procedure that can smooth those moderate to severe frown lines between your brows with no surgery and no recovery time? An improvement can be seen within days, lasting for up to 4 months."[3] Curing death may be just around the scientific corner!

To make sure, while on earth, two Botoxing parents of my daughter's friend attend church, teach their children to follow the Lord's word and even vote Republican because it's the more godly party. And then try to "improve" on God's design by having venomous botulism toxin injected into their skin, for the purpose of placing the façade of youth over their maturing faces.

They inwardly achieve the wisdom that comes with aging, but that insight outwardly clashes with the obvious signs of the process of acquiring: wrinkles. The advertisers who push Botox occupy the same or nearby offices with those that offer daily illustrations of how the undernourished look signifies beauty, usually equated with good or goods. Youth is beautiful and—with the right product—it can be eternal.

Signs of un-youth are, by contrast, disgusting. What good is wisdom if it means ugly lines on your face, you ask? Wisdom in the fast-paced professional business world translates into not giving away any secrets—including those about how old you are or how miserable you might feel. For God's chosen people, honesty has become a professional and social anathema.

Lest any potential customer think that Botox belongs only to the feminine mystique, the website clarifies that it "is certainly *not just for women*. Women may talk about their looks more often, but men are concerned about their appearance as well."[4]

A friend admitted that 90% of the professional women she knows have "had alterations done" in their post-40 lives. The

Botox manufacturer understands the fear of aging and, thanks to the advertising geniuses who peddle the skin presser, it can proudly claim that Botox does not discriminate against men.

"A man who has pronounced lines between his brows may be perceived as angry or stressed—and he doesn't want to look that way. That's why it's not surprising that men are also choosing Botox."5

Nor am I surprised that the media cast its inquisitive and ever trivial eye on the youthful-looking (for his age) Senator John Kerry who, of course, denied rumors that his new, "shinier" visage came from Botox. Teresa Heinz Kerry, however, admitted to taking the wrinkle removing injections. Indeed, Teresa told *Elle* magazine, "I need another one. Soon."

But who would have expected the cadaverous Dick Cheney— beyond Botox help—to re-plant the Kerry rumor? At the March 7, 2004 *Daily Standard* Gridiron dinner, Cheney told *Associated Press'* Terry Hunt that then Deputy Secretary of Defense Paul Wolfowitz had advised him on the matter and "The Administration takes this development seriously. Botox, of course, is related to the botulism toxin, which can be processed into high-grade biological weapons. We have dispatched Dr. David Kay ... to search for the bio-warfare agents we believe hidden in Senator Kerry's forehead. If Senator Kerry has used Botox as part of a wrinkle enrichment program, he is in violation of U.N. Resolution 752. Upon receiving Dr. Kay's report, the weapons of mass destruction that Senator Kerry so adamantly insists do not exist ... may well be above his very nose."6

If you're not a billionaire and worry about losing work time, the website assures the wrinkle-faced client that "such treatment requires little time out of the office. So, it's possible to have the procedure done during a lunch hour and head right back to the office."7

After reading those words I thought of the story of the amiable but homely man who at his wife's urging undergoes plastic surgery and emerges as a handsome old lion. But as he leaves the hospital with his new comely face, a taxi runs him over. He confronts God, in Heaven, pleading: "You could have put the brakes on that cab. After all, I've been a pious man all of my life. Why didn't you let me enjoy my new face for at least one day?"

God replies: "Honestly, I didn't recognize you."

Indeed, did God create Botulinum, a protein complex produced by the bacterium *Clostridium botulinum,* to cause food poisoning or did he really intend it to be injected under the skin to erase frown lines? Mary Schwallenberg, "a pharmaceutical sales representative who is excited about her next round of injections, says she wants to look her best for her job. 'That's corporate America for you,' she says. 'I have a lot of energy and I just wanted to look good.'"[8]

In some particularly anxious but less than totally affluent circles Botox parties, seminars, evenings and socials take place. At these soirees, attendees can get reduced-price Botox treatments and simultaneously calm their apprehensions by creating group confidence that the toxin injections won't kill you or cause chronic diarrhea.

Over forty coeds nervously imbibe in a common area until their names are called, one by one. They proceed to an examination area where a doctor collects his fee and the patient signs the consent form. Sometimes the plastic surgeon will provide a local anesthetic, but usually a tranquilizer will suffice. The injector of eternal youth then squirts a few ccs of the Ponce de Leon drug into the facial muscles, usually in the forehead. The newly inoculated one then rejoins the not yet youthified.

Dr. Scott A. Greenberg, in Winter Park, Florida, told Carol Lewis that since April 2003, when the FDA approved the face ironer, he regularly hosts "Botox Happy Hours" in his office. For Greenberg, the Botox parties "are an opportunity to treat a lot of people at one time in a relaxed but professional atmosphere."

Indeed, Botox not only performs magic on wrinkles, it makes you sexier by treating—as if it was a disease—severe underarm perspiration.

One website assures those who suffer from sweat in the pits, which can turn off even the horniest potential lover that "Botox is FDA approved for severe underarm sweating that is not adequately managed with topical agents. Botox treatment helps control this condition by temporarily blocking the chemical signals from the nerves that stimulate the sweat glands. When the sweat glands don't receive chemical signals, the severe sweating stops."9

People can even make Botox the social center of their lives and meet others who have used this internal poison to enrich their external facade and stop the sweat from leaking out from their arm pits. They can enter a contest and get a free consultation to boot, if they win (the odds look good).

"You can register now for your chance to win a luxury spa vacation for 2 to the Fairmont Southampton in Bermuda + 1 free BOTOX Cosmetic Treatment Consultation valued at $150."10

How does one's brain integrate such events in a world where 3 billion people fear starvation? When Hollywood and Madison Avenue mount their next pitch for America before and after the next war with Iran, North Korea, Syria, Cuba, you pick it, will they include Botox treatments as one of the selling items, alongside reruns of "Jerry Springer" and "Who Wants to be a Millionaire?"

Instead of having to endure starving children in the Sudan, the natives could experience vicariously the thrills and tribulations of teenagers being filmed in life-style experiments: Reality TV. Now, that's exporting culture!

In Iraq, some ex-Ba'athists (Saddam Hussein's Party), have produced a hit show, "a version of extreme home make-over called *Labor and Materials*," according to Mark Dunn.11 The show involves "rebuilding battle-scarred homes and filling residences with new furnishings." What a wonderful idea! The United States military destroys homes and a new TV show is born to rebuild them! Now that's the entertainment equivalent of applying Botox to aging (destroyed) skin.

George W. Bush "Won" Another Disputed Election in 2004

WHAT'S WRONG WITH THE VOTING PUBLIC? OR IS IT ME? FOR five plus years, I watched Bush on TV, which conjured up the image of a spoiled rich kid, a fool who thoughtlessly led the country into a bloody mess in Iraq, screwed up the economy and devastated the environment. Instead of pursuing the terrorists who attacked on 9/11, he made war on Iraq, which had no links to the 9/11 fiends. Yet, millions of soccer moms and pious working people obviously saw in him a candidate who would command with wisdom and protect them from terror. I wouldn't have bought a used car from this guy, much less a baseball team.[12]

Instead of watching a dry drunk mouth empty platitudes on TV, almost 60 million Americans saw Bush as either the lesser of two evils or the guy who would teach their children proper Christian values. Such a thought almost impelled me to try to make my fortune selling the Brooklyn Bridge in the South and Midwest.

One quiet conversation, however, disturbed me more than all the rhetorical ranting during the 2004 election campaign. An intelligent, sensitive and caring woman said her gut feeling made her trust Bush more than Democratic Massachusetts Senator John Kerry; a coded message that the abortion issue would guide her vote. Indeed, the gut and not the head may have made the electoral difference—hardly a new phenomenon. The tendency of millions of Americans to vote against their own economic interests didn't begin in 2004.

For almost a century and a half, politicians have used distracting issues to manipulate voters. After the Civil War, mountebanks used race and immigration to turn white workers against blacks and Asians. The industrialists and bankers gloated; the union movement was weakened.

In the 21st Century, as technology and science surround us, tens of millions still cling to the irrational, those "faith" issues that politicians use like stale songs to divide working people from their common interests. Racial slurs have evolved into clever euphemisms and subliminal forms of expression, ways of referring to the present and past that avoid any direct reference to race.

In a Mississippi university classroom, a professor lectured about the meaning of the Civil War. A student raised her hand and her voice filled with confusion, asked: "Sir, are you referring to the war of Northern aggression?"

Likewise, immigration remains a hot topic, along with abortion, guns, prayer in schools and gay marriages. Worse, charlatans have converted these subjects into matters of faith or passion. Indeed, how does one discuss matters that defy rational discourse? The absence of political coherence frightens me. Five years ago, I debated an extreme right winger who insisted that the government should ban abortion and stop subsidizing the poor for food, medical care, shelter and transportation. "The unborn are innocent," he bleated, "and deserve our love."

"Yes," I replied, "and under your philosophy as soon as they are born they get what's coming to them. The government should only intervene to make sure a fetus gets born, but not help the tiny baby get nutrition, medical care or any other necessity—and you'd then execute them at age eight if they get really naughty."

The debate deteriorated at that point as he called me and my ilk murderers, because fetuses constituted actual human beings. I retorted with the old cultural differences line. "Where I grew up," I said, "a fetus didn't become a genuine human being until it graduated from medical school."

One does not convince pro-lifers on the abortion issue; rather, one tries to get an agreement to keep it out of the legislative agenda. Women got abortions before it became legal and many died as a result.

Similarly, the very notion of gay marriage threatened one woman at my university. "It's beyond disgusting," she said. "The whole institution of marriage has been put into jeopardy because of this liberal tolerance toward outright sin."

Did gay marriage cause Rush Limbaugh's third marriage to fall apart in 2004? Do half the Californians who marry divorce within a decade because they live in daily fear that gays will marry? Yet, a sizeable part of the electorate considered this issue as a major factor in their decision to vote for Bush.

In political science classes, I learned that people tend to vote for their economic interests. From life experience, I deduced that the rich want lower taxes and fewer problems with their servants. Bush certainly fit that bill for them. But in 1980 and 1984, Ronald Reagan won the votes of millions of poor, working class and middle class citizens—registered Democrats. They liked Ronald Reagan, a regular guy who promised to lower everyone's taxes, meaning he would lower his best friends taxes (the richest) and reduce government services for the rest of the people. The voters liked him better than Jimmy Carter and Walter Mondale.

Like Reagan, Bush possessed an appeal that defied my sensibilities. Fifty-five million found Bush attractive as a political leader, despite his destructive policies. Bush has extended the power of the executive beyond the worst nightmares of liberals and conservatives, attacking not only the Bill of Rights but the Magna Carta: detained suspects, including US citizens, no longer have a right to hear charges against them (Jose Padilla case, among others), or have routine legal counsel or a speedy trial.

Bush has waged war against the environment by promoting drilling in wildlife areas, scoffing at the emission controls (called for by the Kyoto accords, which are hardly tough), waging aggressive war in Iraq, justifying torture while denying its existence and tapping the phone conversations of US citizens without warrants. He has all but erased the line between church and state and distributed wealth upwards at an alarming rate. He has built the nation's largest debt and deficit—and shows no signs of amending any of these frightening ways.

How do progressive people begin to rethink political education?

Bush Invests National Treasure in Death and Destruction

I FEEL CERTAIN THAT HISTORIANS WILL JUDGE GEORGE W. BUSH AS the worst president in US history—not just for lying the nation into war with Iraq, but for spending its treasure on instruments of war. During Bush's first term, a toady media, a fundamentalist clergy and a group of astute right wing political manipulators extolled him as the liberator of Iraq and savior of the United States from Iraqi strongman Saddam Hussein's threat (weapons of mass destruction and links to the terrorist Al Qaeda).

But no weapons materialized. So, Bush petulantly told an Oak Ridge, Tennessee crowd in mid July, 2004: "So I had a choice to make. Either take the word of a madman or defend America. Given that choice I will defend America."[13] By defend, Bush might have meant "spend it to death."

Since he advertises himself as a religious man, he should at least have heard of Jesus teaching Matthew.

"For where your treasure is, there will your heart be also," Jesus said in Matthew 6:19-21. The United States, the most Christian nation on earth, has placed its treasure in destruction and death. As *Associated Press'* Dan Morgan reports, the Pentagon "plans to spend well over $1 trillion in the next decade on an arsenal of futuristic planes, ships and weapons with little direct connection to the Iraq war or the global war on terrorism."[14]

These ultra high-tech weapons would allow the US to "preempt an attack by a nation or a terrorist group using weapons of mass destruction" and includes "the option of using nuclear arms to destroy known enemy stockpiles of nuclear, biological or chemical weapons."[15] Such language and the defense budget itself have made the word "defense" into a joke: $600 billion plus (counting the CIA), $50 billion higher than 2004. The Congressional Budget Office estimated that over the next ten years, the armada of aircraft, ships and killer toys will cost upwards of $770 billion more than Bush's projection for long-term defense.[16]

Morgan reports that Bush wants "$68 billion for research and development—20 percent above the peak levels of President Reagan's historic defense buildup. Tens of billions more out of a proposed $76 billion hardware account will go for big-ticket weapons systems to combat some as-yet-unknown adversary comparable to the former Soviet Union."

The mantra heard in Congress to support such outrageous spending, "we can't show weakness in the face of terrorism," failed to take into account the fact that when the 9/11 hijackers struck, the U.S. military—the strongest in the world—did not prevent the attacks, albeit some intelligence officials foresaw them.[17] So, logically one should ask, how does a futuristic jet fighter defend against contemporary enemies, like US-born jihadists who could smuggle explosives in backpacks into a train station or crowded shopping mall?

Rather than facing the nasty facts of cancerous corruption, which translates immediately as war profiteering in Iraq,[18] the political class accepted "defense uber alles" as its political foundation. Following the President's lead, Congress hardened the American heart by making weapons a clear priority over housing, health, education and jobs. When Congress squanders the taxpayers' money and America's heart on useless weapons of mass destruction, it also fills the already fat wallets of defense corporate executives.

Each year billions go to General Dynamics, Lockheed and the other household names of mass weapons production. And the top executives kvell.

Think of the fortunes made by the schnorrers who sold SDI to the late President Reagan! Or how Reagan took money from the hungry and homeless: he said "it's their choice," as he handed taxpayers' money to the fakirs who pretended they could intercept incoming missiles.[19]

The Bush presidency has taken military spending (wasting) to new heights (depths). More frightening, a military culture has emerged over the past decade that includes military language in everyday speech—yes sir. The military that until World War II carried low social prestige has become a highly respected institution. Its recruiters have become as ubiquitous on high school and college campuses as ivy on the walls. At graduation ceremonies, some high school administrators even don military garb alongside those with traditional black robes. But, wait a minute! In a republic, a professional military merits minimal status. Indeed, republics need citizens' militias, not standing armies at a time when a foreign state poses no immediate threat to U.S. security.

Vice President Dick Cheney, a self-confessed draft dodger—"I had better things to do" than serve in Vietnam[20]—represents the new and cold heart of the nation. Flying in the face of known evidence, he has continued to insist that Saddam Hussein possessed weapons of mass destruction and links to Al Qaeda[21] and has kept secret his minutes (executive privilege) with the dishonest Enron officials, one of whom laughs about "fucking [overcharging] those poor grandmothers" in California. Former California Attorney General Bill Lockyer planned to use such statements, recorded on tape, to prosecute Enron officials for rigging energy prices in 2002 to bilk Californians out of billions of dollars. "This is further evidence of the arrogance that was so fundamental to the business practices of Enron and the other energy pirates who acted so rapaciously,"[22] said Lockyer.

For Cheney, rapaciousness is as American as apple pie. He belongs in Ripley's *Believe It or Not*: the first man who suffered several heart attacks and does not possess a heart. Cheney stands as an allegorical reference to the nation's morality in the early 21st Century.

Although he denies this, Cheney has looked out for the interests of his former company. As CEO of Halliburton from 1995-2000, Cheney made his and the company's fortune in the national security-energy arena, which he removed from accountability on "national security" grounds. Congress no longer has clear oversight over hundreds of billions of military dollars. Ten billion dollars, for example, get allocated simply for "missile defense." Behind such an authorization, the military demands: "trust us."[23] The Founding Fathers would have scoffed at anyone uttering these two words—especially in reference to money.

With the sounds of Enron, World Com, Adelphia and other huge company scandals of tens of billions of dollars still reverberating in the public's ear, why would Congress cede its accountability function to the Pentagon officials? The military apparatus, a killing machine by its very nature, stands for heartlessness. And the Bush Administration and its military spokespeople have even given prevaricating and cronyism bad reputations. From the President down to key cabinet members, the Bushies link dissembling with leadership, like the proverbial horse and carriage.

Under Bush's rule, lying has grown institutional roots. On April 29, 2004, the State Department released a report on the "Patterns of Global Terrorism." In it, Department researchers claimed that in 2003 terrorist attacks had fallen to only 190, their lowest since 1969. In fact, as anyone who could count knew, the number of attacks had risen dramatically.

"It's a very big mistake," acknowledged then Secretary of State Colin Powell on June 13 to ABC's *This Week*. "And we are not happy about this big mistake." Powell predictably denied that political motives lay behind this rosy report, which could have served to support Bush's claim that he was winning the "war on terrorism." "Nobody was out to cook the books," Powell said.

But Powell himself had misled the UN Security Council. On February 5, 2003 he presented a power point lecture of misinformation about the location of Iraqi WMDs, claiming incontrovertible evidence for every fib he uttered. On September 9, 2005, Powell admitted to Barbara Walters that he now considered his fraudulent Security Council presentation a "painful blot" on his record.[24]

The "urgent" military demands of the Iraq and Afghan Wars have obscured the crying needs of this age. The arch Christian George W. Bush, who exalts the "value of human life" in his campaigns to prevent stem cell research and abortion, also directs Congress to pour the nation's treasury into destruction and death budgets. He offers little to alleviate starvation, homelessness and disease and he alternately mocks, ignores or exacerbates the deterioration of the environment.

How will the meek inherit the earth if they starve to death, die of exposure, bomb shrapnel or environmental toxicity? Or does Bush think inheriting the earth means getting buried six feet under it?

The Reagan Legacy: Bush Inherits, World Grows Poorer

SPOT PROPOSED BY ONE OF THE EAGER, YOUNG STAFFERS AT THE Republican National Committee—still being considered for possible use.

"Welfare Mothers for Bush"*

Rashida: "I'm sick and tired of getting these government checks that I use only to buy vodka and drugs while the kids go hungry."

Kenyana: "Yes, let's voluntarily give up the pittance that we get and get good jobs stocking shelves at Wal-Mart or making beds at Days Inn."

Rashida: "We could drop off the kids at the fundamentalist church where Reverend Righteous could indoctrinate them in the principle of individual responsibility—not at the Catholic Church, where those no-good priests check the little boys for hernias and hemorrhoids."

Kenyana: "I'm so grateful to President Bush for making me understand that poverty is my own fault, not part of a system that enslaved and segregated my ancestors for 300 years."

*Paid for by the Republican National Committee's special branch to "Win Black Votes and Bury the Last Vestiges of the New Deal."

In his five years, Bush surpassed Reagan's eight years in his presidential accomplishments. In some ways, Reagan served as Bush's mentor. Both presented the world in uncomplicated truisms. The corporation is inherently good, so abide by the corporate wish list. Don't spend money on anything that doesn't yield corporate profits because that would empower government, which is bad.

Bush went further. He even looked beyond earth's environment to Mars, where he wants to launch settlements. He also surpassed Reagan in diminishing meaningful parts of government: public education, health, transportation, protection of the environment and helping citizens after disaster strikes.

Does Reagan deserve some credit for these "accomplishments?" On June 11, 2004, when Reagan's seemingly interminable funeral ended, I said to myself that the public now won't have The Gipper to kick around until, of course, the fifth, tenth and twenty-fifth anniversaries of his death.

The funeral could have served as a news event in which the media reminded what Reagan's deeds had done to the nation, the environment and the world. Instead, pundits, politicians and preachers offered nostalgic, fact-less eulogies, exalting the virtues of a President who taught history by telling charming anecdotes and who equated facts with tales that others told him.

Who could not marvel at Reagan's proclamations? "We stole the Panama Canal and it's ours." Few Panamanians guffawed. Or, "The Sandinistas are a two day march from Harlingen, Texas." Well, the ill-humored residents of Harlingen and Nicaragua didn't laugh! One statesmanlike line, "The Contras are the moral equivalent of our Founding Fathers," confused even the most meticulous scholars. Did he not know, asked professors, that the Contras tortured and murdered civilians as instructed by their CIA manuals? Or did he mean that the Founding Fathers advocated murder and torture? Or was he just kidding around?

It didn't seem to matter. Like George W. Bush, Reagan also believed first and foremost in loyalty. "He's getting a raw deal," he said in 1985 of Guatemalan President, General Efrain Rios Montt, accused of having authorized the slaughter of thousands of Guatemalans, with massive evidence to support the charges. He also pardoned Iran-Contra felons from his own Administration including Elliot Abrams and John Poindexter, who ran into scandal again.[25] Well intentioned guys!

No matter! Memorial service speakers celebrated the virtues of this backward-looking actor. Some wag, however, characterized Reagan's behavior in the White House as following half of Benjamin Franklin's advice: "early to bed."

No wonder he looked so well-rested, so willing to flash that Hollywood smile. At an amusement park, my son and daughter posed for a photo with the late President, with his arms around them. The smiling figure in the middle is just a realistic cardboard cut out. We took the photo as a joke.

Reagan, like Bush (43), was a joker, or maybe a sick political joke. Not too bad. After all, humor offers release. I admit that the tumultuous sexual activities of the Clinton years made me occasionally nostalgic for the Reagan era, when sleeping with the President meant attending a Cabinet meeting. Reagan also knew how to explain the ills of our time in words we could all grasp. In his 1980 campaign, for example, he denied that the big logging and chemical companies held any responsibility for air contamination. Instead, he blamed trees for causing pollution. After all, they emitted 93 percent of nitrogen oxide.

Like those "killer trees," the behavior of the homeless also came under Reagan's scrutiny. They preferred their idiosyncratic life style to one with a roof on it. In support of cutting funds for school lunches, he blithely labeled ketchup as a vegetable.

Reagan's cavalier delegation of parts of traditional presidential prerogatives to special interest groups has proven less than a healthy remedy for what ails the nation. His economic policies—

Reaganomics—raised the cost of living, more than canceling out any tax breaks he offered for the poor and middle classes. Reagan also hated abortion, loved guns and wanted more prayer, even in schools. Nevertheless, this less than brilliant grade B actor became the greatest political educator of the late 20th Century. Along with his pal, Margaret Thatcher in England, he taught people to hate their government and therefore not pay taxes to support it—except for the virtuous police and military, of course, which merited full backing.[26]

I admired Reagan's wit: "Government's view of the economy could be summed up in a few short phrases: If it moves, tax it. If it keeps moving, regulate it. And if it stops moving, subsidize it." Except for his amusing one and two liners, Reagan slept his way through the presidency. He left governance to those who understood it.

He actually increased the federal budget significantly, albeit he did slightly slow its rate of growth. Reagan also increased the federal work force by more than 60,000. But his supporters seemed not to care about these details (Clinton, ironically, cut 370,000 jobs from the federal payroll).

Reagan learned from political mistakes. When his ideologues convinced him in 1981-2 to try to cut Social Security, his party lost 26 House seats in the 1982 midterm elections, largely as a result of this attempt to overachieve. The Great Somnambulist them reversed himself and bailed out the Social Security system with a $165 billion payment. So what that it meant a hike in payroll taxes and finally taxed the Social Security benefits only of upper-income recipients!

Clearly, the majority of voters found in Reagan their regular guy, a man who didn't know much about most subjects and told jokes of dubious taste: "My fellow Americans. I'm pleased to announce that I've signed legislation outlawing the Soviet Union. We begin bombing in five minutes."[27] He told this gag during a microphone test at a radio broadcast.

Bush unquestioningly follows in Reagan's rhetorical voice-steps, without of course possessing the Great Prevaricator's poise or wit. He did come close to Reaganese oratory—simplifying the complex—when he described the 9/11 fiends as terrorists who "hate our freedoms."28

Bush also overshadowed Reagan as the President who has done most to hurt the poor. In his eight years, Reagan oversaw the increase of numbers of families living below the poverty line by one-third. Bush has worked hard to match that figure. Between 2003 and 2004, 1.1 million new people fell into the poverty index.29 Indeed, in one year, Bush diverted more than $22 billion dollars in federal money to "homeland security." The Bushies took $2 billion of that amount from the Department of Housing and Urban Development's (HUD) budget that previously helped fund both homeless shelters and housing for America's poorest of renters and transferred the funds assets to Homeland Security.30

On May 20, 2004, typical of the ungrateful citizens who don't appreciate all that Bush has done, a crowd of Los Angeles protesters denounced proposals to diminish the federal government's Section 8 housing program. The protestors claimed that the cuts would displace some 13,000 low-income area families. Similarly, the Boston HUD office sent out 650 eviction notices to tenants. Other metropolitan areas suffered similar affronts.31

Reagan, even in his most aggressive mode, did not match such audacity. Nor will his record rival Bush's 2001 $1.35 trillion tax cut, which produced sighs of contentment from the excessively rich that border on the orgiastic.

Finally, Bush has also outdone Reagan in his scorn for international law. Reagan began his presidency in 1981 by rejecting the Law of the Sea Treaty. His attitude toward international cooperation became even more dramatically hostile when he withdrew the United States from UNESCO in late 1983 and of course taught the UN a major lesson by cutting the US contribution to that organization.

Reagan explained that UNESCO "politicized virtually every subject it deals with, has exhibited hostility toward the basic institutions of a free society, especially a free market and a free press, and has demonstrated unrestrained budgetary expansion."[32] On December 29, 1984, the State Department concluded "that continued US membership in UNESCO will not benefit the country." Reagan admonished Americans to uphold the law, but he didn't recognize the International Court of Justice's jurisdiction when on June 27, 1986 it ruled against Washington for mining Nicaraguan harbors.

Bush backed down from Reagan's tough anti-UN stance only after his advisers convinced him that he would temporarily need the world body in the wake of the 9/11 events.

He announced the US reentry into UNESCO on September 12, 2002, the very day he addressed the General Assembly. He also used that opportunity to label Iraq's government "a grave and gathering danger." One step forward, two steps back?

In March 2003, Bush, however, returned to the Reagan anti-UN line, but only after US arm twisting and attempts to bribe failed to win enough votes to push his "invade Iraq" resolution through the Security Council. Bush invaded anyway, heaping scorn on the UN, whose earlier resolution on Iraqi arms prohibitions he solemnly proclaimed he was duty bound to enforce.

Since the Iraqi war and his dramatic passivity following Hurricane Katrina, Bush's natural and world stature has diminished. I suggest that he redeem himself by stealing from Reagan. If Arial Sharon recovers from his coma,[33] he could say, cameras rolling, his head tilted back, a slight twitch of emotion in his face: "Mr. Sharon! Tear Down That Wall."[34]

If you believe he'll do something like that then you'll also probably think there's a chance that Bush will convert to socialism.

Reagan's Last Funeral in a Calgary Coffeeshop

Television executives ordered crews

To film endless funeral
scenes I watched silently
At the breakfast emporium
Two Germans ate sausages
Talked about deals profits
Counted percentages chewed loudly
Old men stooped over
Grease not feeling grief
Young men bearing flags
On sleeves stopped gazed
At a former leader
While experts hypocrites charlatans
Took turns quoting Yeats
Byron other dead white
Poets who had thought
About words designed to
Satisfy their premature deaths

English poets had not
Altered the destiny of
Central Americans nor thought
of proposing to eliminate
Nuclear weapons accusing trees
Of responsibility for pollution
Basking in their ignorance

A Bush & Botox World

Smiling at unpleasant facts
Confusing their deeds with
Lines said in movies
Zat is ze bottom
Line concluded a German
A camera zoomed in
On the casket and
Somber voices intoned before
The celebrated became entombed.
His last TV appearance
Until the news slows

Karl Rove as Strategist: Roy Cohn Lives On in Bush White House

L IKE THE LATE SENATOR JOSEPH McCARTHY (R-WI) IN THE early 1950s, George W. Bush has transformed American politics by abandoning the traditional rules in the 21st Century. In 1950, McCarthy earned his fame magnet when he claimed that the State Department housed large numbers of "Communists." He became instantly famous. His subsequent "witch hunts" to "expose the subversives" terrified not only his potential victims on the left, but the vast liberal population that had only recently acceded to the creation of a national security state. The supposed enemy posed such a serious and immediate threat that the nation's security required a new (non-elected) elite to keep secrets and manage a nuclear system. McCarthy took advantage of the climate of fear and used the "Communist menace" to accuse thousands of people from all over the country of belonging to subversive groups. He offered no proof, but got lots of headlines. He also gave no chance for the accused to defend themselves.

On June 9, 1954, after much of the Establishment agreed that the junior Senator from Wisconsin had gone too far, a lawyer for the Army exposed his ridiculous assertions at a televised congressional hearing.[35]

Roy Cohn, a young and ambitious lawyer, had helped prosecute the Rosenbergs—he made illegal calls to the trial judge to feed him "inside" information—for giving atomic secrets to the Soviet Union. The couple was convicted and electrocuted. Cohn became McCarthy's hatchet man and Senate staff attorney. From 1951 to 1954, Cohn relished his role as persecutor of those hauled before the sub-committee as "red infiltrators;" or, he leaked names to the press, and caused people to lose jobs and reputations. Cohn's lover, G. David Schine, also worked for Joseph McCarthy's Committee. Cohn showed chutzpah by humiliating other homosexuals in televised hearings.

Bush's key strategist, Karl Rove, also used homosexuals to advance his boss's image. During Bush's first term, some very high White House official issued instant press credentials to Jeff "Bucky" Gannon, a.k.a. James Guckert. For two years, this ultra right-wing "reporter" for a Republican Party Web site (owned by a Texas millionaire) got called on regularly by White House press aide Scott McClellan and by Bush. Gannon, predictably, asked loaded, pro-Administration questions.

"While the Democrats are challenging the Ohio results on Capitol Hill, Democrats in Washington State have disqualified any number of military votes in order to win that gubernatorial election there. Considering that American soldiers are in Iraq fighting to give those people there the right to vote, the right to free and fair elections, don't you think we owe it to them to make sure their votes are counted back home?"

The Secret Service knew about Guckert's homo-erotic Web sites. A web designer admitted he had "designed a gay escort site for Gannon and had posted naked pictures of Gannon at the client's request."[36]

On his website "USMCPT" with the eagle and other Marine military symbolism, "Bucky," who describes himself as "military, masculine and very discreet," also assured potential clients that he "won't ask, won't tell." The photo shows a well endowed, naked (except for his combat boots) hunk, with a shaved crotch, offering himself as "personal trainer, body guard, escort."

He advertised himself as "aggressive, verbal dominant type" and cutely added, "I don't leave marks, only impressions." In case you didn't understand, at the bottom of the website, Gannon-Guckert makes sure you get the point: "Hot Male Escorts."[37]

When high White House officials placed Gannon-Guckert in the press pool and fed him stories, which he leaked as a supposed reporter for a Republican-owned web zine, the cynical God-fearing manipulators chuckled. Some of the "news" tripe they dangled actually got swallowed by the mass media. Well, in pursuit of American freedom, the White House manipulators might have rationalized, one should take advantage of any tactic that God makes available—including Kinky Gannon.

"I was rejected for a White House press pass at the start of the Bush administration," protested *NY Times* columnist Maureen Dowd. "But someone with an alias, a tax evasion problem [he owed $20,700 in income taxes] and Internet pictures where he posed like the "Barberini Faun" is credentialed to cover a White House that won a second term by mining homophobia and preaching family values?"

"No one called me back," Dowd complained after repeatedly seeking renewal of her credentials. "After a new Secret Service background check that stretched for several months," she got them.[38]

As Dowd cleared the new "security hurdles," the shadier-than-thou Guckert slipped through the "increased security" cracks and received his daily press card. A former federal policeman assured me that "only a direct order from very high up could have gotten him that close to the President."

It didn't take Sam Spade to deduce which prankster dreamed up the Gannon-Guckert ploy. Karl Rove, the Roy Cohn of the 21st Century, plays the same power game as McCarthy's chief plotter.

In the early 1950s, Cohn helped McCarthy grab headlines as a way to become powerful by throwing fear. Within months after McCarthy's bogus "revelation" about the number of Reds in the State Department (he changed the number several times), he and Cohn, his human pit bull, learned that fighting dirty got results. They discovered the press would convert the silliest scare charges into urgent headlines: "Today we are engaged in a final, all-out battle between communistic atheism and Christianity," intoned McCarthy in a 1950 speech. "I have in my hand fifty-seven cases of individuals who would appear to be either card-carrying members or certainly loyal to the Communist Party, but who nevertheless are still helping to shape our foreign policy."

Such ranting got McCarthy a picture on *Time* magazine's cover. His sneering voice became familiar on radio news. As McCarthy's chief counsel, Cohn became a master at using implication to smear his liberal-pink targets. To taint the Voice of America's French desk chief, Cohn stated that communists don't believe in the family and advocate collectivism. Since the VOA's French desk chief "tried to recruit an employee for a collective ...[he] must be a communist." Or, "Communists are atheists; the head of the VOA's religious programming doesn't believe in God ... therefore, that VOA employee must be a communist."

Cohn used God and country as weapons, thrusting on the accused the burden of "proving they did believe in God and were patriotic."[39] In that tradition of bending logic and rules, Rove apparently also utilized the available Guckert to promote Bush's causes and attack his enemies. Bloggers found that Guckert leaked the "Shock and Awe" story hours before Bush announced his March 2003 invasion of Iraq. John Aravosis of Americablog. org said "Guckert delivered other "scoops" to "friendly" news outlets, [like Fox's Sean Hannity] including details concerning the Dan Rather/CBS memo scandal."[40]

The urgent tone given to the Rather scandal, along with the ever "breaking news" about Michael Jackson, Kobe Bryant, Robert Blake and Phil Spector, creates public distraction. Far more Americans know the gory details about life in Michael Jackson's Neverland Ranch than about how neo conservative policy geeks like then Deputy Defense Secretary, now World Bank President Paul Wolfowitz and former Defense Advisory Chair Richard Perle (whose political thinking seems close if not identical to that of Ariel Sharon) have begun to restructure the Middle East.

The "moral values" crowd also demands adherence to abstinence on sex and substances. They seek to blanket the country in religious symbols and punish a sinful network that traumatized a hundred million Americans by showing Janet Jackson's breast at the 2004 Super Bowl.[41] They seem unconcerned over less spiritual issues, like millions of yearly deaths from preventable diseases.

Some public spokespeople for fundamentalist morality have demonstrated a farcical distance between preaching and doing: radio loudmouth Rush Limbaugh said that "if people are violating the law by doing drugs, they ought to be accused and they ought to be convicted and they ought to be sent up."[42] Until he got arrested for illegally buying and using prescription drugs (Oxycontin or rural heroine)! Then, he asked for understanding.[43] Ah, the pain!

Should we also sympathize with Fox's Bill O'Reilly, author of children's morality books? According to a legal complaint, O'Reilly phoned an associate producer and suggested she "purchase a vibrator and name it, and that he had one 'shaped like a cock with a little battery in it.'... It became clear that Defendant was masturbating as he spoke."[44]

Newt Gingrich, the rhetorical champion of marriage and family values, left his wife as she lay dying of cancer—to marry a younger and healthier bride, whom he later divorced.

It doesn't matter what you do, only how aggressive you sound. In late February 2005, in Roy Cohn's angry tradition, Bush backer Sam Johnson (R-TX) told a church congregation that Bush should nuke Syria because it was evil. The flock applauded.

Similarly, Cohn won applause from the McCarthyites when he used aggressive language to link liberal targets to homosexual illusions or he used sexual secrets to blackmail potential informants. Ironically, Cohn's homosexuality was an open secret. Although he drank at gay bars and often left with gay men, Cohn opposed New York City's gay rights law and tried to ban homosexuals from becoming school teachers. He died of AIDS in 1986, still in adamant denial.

Cohn's earlier counterparts, Nazi Party members in the late 1920s and early 30s, projected sexual repression into daily politics. Emerging from the embrace of male lovers, some Nazis would search for non-Nazi homosexuals to kill. Indeed, until 1934, when Hitler turned on and killed his homosexual friend Ernst Roehm and his followers, some of the most brutal "repressors" (Storm Troopers) were homosexuals.

Psychiatrist Wilhelm Reich suggested that political repression ties into sexual repression (homo or hetero). Does this provide insight into Kinky O'Reilly or fundamentalist preachers, like Jim Bakker and Ted Haggard, who seemed addicted to hookers? They preach sexual and political repression—for others! For enjoying sex, Clinton became a hated scoundrel; mass murderers Rumsfeld, Cheney and Kissinger, serve as role models.

The Patriot Act, passed in the wake of 9/11, embodied the repression that Joe McCarthy tried to institutionalize under the pretext of fighting communism. Although the sexually repressed have not yet been able to produce organized psychic terror for the society—unless you're Muslim[45]—they have that Act, which looms as the most convenient instrument for those who seek to repress others because they cannot repress their own most loathsome impulses. Repressed individuals, from Roy Cohn to Karl Rove, like to organize campaigns to persecute or to wield power—always in the faces of the "weak" Democrats.

Leakgate: The Screenplay

OPENING: THE SCREEN PRINTS LINES FROM A *NY Times* Op-ed (July 6, 2003) by former Ambassador Joseph Wilson that reveals the bogus nature of the story that the Bush Administration circulated about Saddam Hussein trying to buy yellowcake uranium in Niger.

CHENEY: (throwing the *Times* into the trash basket) Interesting that Joe Wilson is running off his mouth in public about how we concocted the story of Iraq trying to buy yellow cake uranium from Niger. Did you know that Wilson's wife worked at the C.I.A. in the counter proliferation division?[46]

LEWIS "SCOOTER" LIBBY: (Speaking to Vice President Dick Cheney and Karl Rove in a White House office). No, sir. So you're saying Wilson's a tool of the old guard at the CIA? For Christ sake, everyone knew that the Iraq-Niger-uranium story was bogus. So the pissed off losers at the CIA sent him there to "investigate." That's an attack on you, boss (points to Cheney). After all, you used this claim in speeches and even fed it to the President. We have to do something to sons of bitches like Wilson, show them they can't attack us with impunity.

FLASHBACK: Bush's State Of the Union Address, January 2003

BUSH: The British government has learned that Saddam Hussein recently sought significant quantities of uranium from Africa.

DISSOLVE BACK TO MEETING

KARL ROVE: Look, CIA officials played dirty. They used that son of a bitch Wilson to publicize what Washington insiders already knew. Who in his right mind would believe that ridiculous Niger story? I think we got one of those second rate neo-con assholes from Georgetown to help plant the phony documents. But embarrassing us like that? They want to play dirty. We'll show them dirty! Let's get Novak or one of those other press toadies to expose the woman, ruin Valerie Plame's career. That'll show a pussy whipped guy like Wilson what hard ball really means.

FADE TO 2003 LIBBY MEETING WITH JUDY MILLER

LIBBY: *(flirtatiously)* I know you're the best in the business at this investigative reporting, and a mighty foxy scent you're wearing too (She smiles seductively). But you can't use me as a source. I'll give this to you as an exclusive. If the *Times* won't run it, you can make sure someone else gets it (Judy has her pen poised over her reporter's notebook). Wilson's wife sent him on the mission where he did practically nothing but talk to some of the naysayers and his so-called information taught us nothing. By the way, I should mention that she's a covert op at CIA. Valerie Plame.

Miller writes in notebook "'Valerie Flame'—source former Hill Staffer."

DISSOLVE: ROVE ON PHONE WITH NOVAK

ROVE: Yes, Bob, I hear that his wife is a CIA cover op. That's what I hear. Call some other sources of yours. You'll get her name.

CUT TO LIBBY PICKING UP PHONE:

LIBBY: Yes, Bob. I heard the same thing. Check with Judy Miller or the *Time* magazine guy if you don't believe me.

NOVAK COLUMN APPEARS ON SCREEN NAMING VALERIE PLAME AS COVERT CIA OPERATIVE

HEADLINES FOLLOW: "SPECIAL PROSEUCTOR TO INVESTIGATE LEAK"

"WILSON ACCUSES ROVE"

FADE TO BUSH ON SCREEN AT PRESS CONFERENCE:

If someone committed a crime they will no longer work in my administration.

DISSOLVE

TO BUSH AT PRESS CONFERENCE AUGUST 2004:

We may still find weapons. We haven't found them yet. ... Let me just say this to you: knowing what I know today, we still would have gone into Iraq.

LIBBY WITH CHENEY AND ROVE:

Well, we got the twit to say it again. Now, do you think we could get Judy Miller to convince those boobs who edit the *NY Times* to run a story that starts with "reliable intelligence source verifies existence of hidden nukes in Iraq?" We have to do something to keep people from focusing on the leak and instead pay attention to Saddam accumulating WMD.

ROVE: Scooter, it may be too late. The shopping seasons are too far ahead. And that damned special prosecutor Fitzgerald is already sniffing around about the leak. Do you think any of the toady reporters we talked to will rat us out?

FADE TO BLACK

OCTOBER 2005:

Footage showing police arresting Libby.

CUT TO: Fitzgerald holding a press conference explaining how Libby lied, obstructed and connived to cover up a leak.

CUT TO: Shots of Bush brooding. He snaps at an aide who tells him 7 more Americans died in Iraq today.

CHENEY MEETING WITH ROVE IN CHENEY'S OFFICE:

This is the last time we'll meet until this thing blows over. I've had to let Scooter go. He must know that by keeping his mouth shut he will assure himself of a pardon. He must not mention my presence at any of the conversations. Is that clear?

ROVE: Sir, they're also after me.

CHENEY: Discipline, son. We're playing for big stakes. The world. Don't blow it because they threaten you with a little jail time. The CIA spooks are getting their revenge because we took their toys away and used them. Intelligence is meant to serve power, not some abstraction like truth, whatever the hell that means. You taught everyone that lesson, Karl. Don't blow it by opening your mouth. The press will tire of this leak crap and we'll distract them with flu vaccines and other issues.

CUT TO LAWRENCE WILKERSON, FORMER CHIEF OF STAFF TO FORMER SECRETARY OF STATE COLIN POWELL REPORT TO NEW AMERICA FOUNDATION (OCTOBER 2005):

"What I saw was a cabal between the vice-president of the United States, Richard Cheney, and the secretary of defense, Donald Rumsfeld, on critical issues that made decisions that the bureaucracy did not know were being made."

HEADLINES: COVERUP, SCANDAL, COMPARISONS TO WATERGATE—MONI-CAGATE

Cut to shredding machines with documents being eaten

DISSOLVE TO BUSH FAMILY: GEORGE H., W., BARBARA AND EXTENDED FAMILY. THEY ARE LISTENING TO A MINISTER IN A KENNEBUNKPORT CHURCH

"The wicked flee when no one pursues. Wickedness keeps a person restless and unsettled. The guilty conscience worries about being caught at any moment and sees every person as the one who will uncover secret sin." (Proverbs 28:1)

BUSH THE ELDER TALKING TO HIS SON, WHO LOOKS NERVOUS:

It's loyalty that counts in the end. Remember that.

FADE TO archival footage of Justice Clarence Thomas at Senate confirmation hearings as Anita Hill describes how he came on to her with his "pubic hair in the Coke can" ploy.

HEADLINES: THOMAS APPROVED BY SENATE FOR SUPREME COURT SEAT 1991

SUPREME COURT STOPS VOTE COUNT IN FLORIDA 2000

RETURN TO THE BUSH FAMILY MEETING:

THE ELDER BUSH: Loyalty begets loyalty, but disloyalty on the other hand, meaning public disagreement with policies, means treason.

CUT TO: Cabinet meeting in Bush's first administration. Paul O'Neill, then Treasury Secretary, questions the priority of invading Iraq. "It has no justification and will cost a lot." Bush looks distracted. O'Neill tries to get the attention of "a blind man in a roomful of deaf people."[47]

DISSOLVE to O'Neill celebrating the release of his biography, *The Price of Loyalty*, written by Ron Suskind

ROVE ON PHONE: I want O'Neill accused of leaking classified documents.

HEADLINES: "O'NEILL USED CLASSIFIED MATERIAL IN BOOK" (FEBRUARY 2004)

O'Neill looks older, troubled and fearful.

FLASH FORWARD: ROVE AND LIBBY IN A SECLUDED BOOTH OF A WASHING-TON BAR, EARLY NOVEMBER 2005

LIBBY: I can't tolerate the fools who could not accept the harmonious matrimony we carefully arranged. Who could have imagined a coalition including anti Semitic Fundamentalist nuts and Catholic fanatics bonding with neo-con Jews like me, who worship Ariel Sharon and Israel? (HE SIPS HIS MARTINI) It took strategists like you, Karl, to illicit from every member of the Bush wedding coalition its own excuse for going to war with Iraq.

ROVE: Thanks, Scooter (HE TAKES A GULP OF HIS SHIRLEY TEMPLE). Right now we both need good lawyers. But don't rat just to save your pampered hide (THEY BOTH DRINK AND SNORT, SEMI LAUGHS). I don't know if I'm ready to serve a couple of years in a white collar prison before getting a presidential pardon. Remember what old man Bush did?

CUT TO ARCHIVAL FOOTAGE OF BUSH PARDONING HIS CRIMINAL CRONIES IN DECEMBER 1992 BEFORE LEAVING OFFICE:

"BUSH PARDONS 6 IN IRAN AFFAIR, ABORTING A WEINBERGER TRIAL; PROSECUTOR ASSAILS 'COVER-UP'"

LIBBY: Whatever happens, we had some good times (HE DOWNS HIS MARTINI).

ROVE: You know, exercising power is more than an aphrodisiac, as Kissinger called it. It's like the most explosive orgasm ever, especially when you get to punish those who dared dissent, those who implied moral superiority and accused us of making errors. You know Scooter, I don't give a shit for those who died and all the destruction. That's the way of history. We showed the world what it means to have power. So what we didn't realize one successful program—save for enriching the already endowed. Well, we're not finished yet. I have a couple of tricks left in my playbook.

CUT TO WASHINGTON DC ON HALLOWEEN NIGHT

Costumed trick or treaters prance through neighborhoods.

A TELEPHONE RINGS AND A HAND PICKS IT UP. REVEREND PAT ROBERTSON FROWNS: "Yes, I still think we ought to close Halloween down. Do you want your children to dress up as witches? The Druids used to dress up like this when they were doing human sacrifice... Your children are acting out Satanic rituals & participating in it, and don't even realize it."[48]

ROVE: I'm glad to see you haven't let the winds of liberal change affect you.

ROBERTSON: "Many of those people involved with Adolph Hitler were Satanists, many of them were homosexuals the two things seem to go together."[49]

ROVE LAUGHS: Pat, I heard that Fitzgerald might be a homo. It comes from a well-placed source. Maybe you could inquire with your, how shall I say it, higher sources? I'm sure He'll confirm what I heard. The ball's in your court."

CUT TO THE OVAL OFFICE: Cheney is talking to Bush

CHENEY: The *NY Times* will release the story on our wiretapping. The liberals will have a shit fit. And shout civil liberties and the Constitution and all that bullshit. We will say it is to get the terrorists. Just hang in there. It's only three more years.

Globalization and Its Discontents

"More than any other time in history, mankind faces a crossroads. One path leads to despair and utter hopelessness; the other, to total extinction. Let us pray we have the wisdom to choose correctly."—Woody Allen

O N JULY 7, 2005, FOUR SUICIDE BOMBERS, THREE BRITISH and one Jamaican born, detonated themselves to kill civilians on London public transport. In so doing, they dramatized the globalization of resistance and the futility of Bush's war against terrorism. Their numbers may still not be very large, wrote Patrick Cockburn, "but they are numerous enough to create mayhem in Iraq and anywhere else they strike, be it in London or Sharm el Sheikh."[50]

Beneath headlines, however, lurks Sir Isaac Newton's third law: "For every action, there is an equal and opposite reaction." Bush ignored basic physics before deciding to invade and occupy Iraq. His goals of pursuing democracy and instigating regime change required violence and non violent manipulation. The resistance to his action—the other side of the Newtonian equation—also contains both violent and non violent elements.

The non violent sector took to the streets to oppose the war as well as policies of the WTO, IMF and the free trade treaties. People from all over the world came to Seattle, Washington DC and other places where the rich and powerful made decisions affecting how the rest of the world lived. They demanded a voice in the decision-making process that affects their and the rest of the world's lives.

This diverse movement of Muslims, Christians and Jews, anti-establishment students, small European farmers, U.S.

factory workers and indigenous Latin American peasants represent the non-violent response to corporate globalization. The other side struck in New York on 9/11 and more recently in Iraq, Afghanistan, Bali, Madrid, London and Egypt. Grotesque, suicidal violence answered violent state policies.

The July 7 London suicide bombers, the irrational side of resistance to imperial globalization, did not share the moral values of the leaders of their countries of birth: England and Jamaica.

In the value and idea clash between corporate globalists and their opponents, pundits like Thomas Friedman defend the new order. In his moralistic *NY Times* columns, his 1999 book, *The Lexus and the Olive Tree*, and his 2005 update, *The World is Flat*, Friedman hails the new world of lightning fast markets, money, information, and rapid transformations of politics and culture. Friedman sees the march of globalization as both positive and inevitable.

Friedman accepts that those who benefit most directly from this process, which includes outsourcing by multinational companies from the U.S., Britain and other wealthy and modern nations, also share a symbiotic relationship with militarism. McDonald's, he writes, needs McDonald Douglas, which stands for the military industrial complex, to enforce property rules, and insure expanded markets even to places where they're not wanted: "rogue states" neither accept nor obey the rules of the new transnational corporate order.

Ronald McDonald and the three-fingered, de-sexed Mickey and Minnie Mouse hardly reveal, however, the savagery with which the Bush Administration has pursued the extension of the new order that Friedman extols. The residents of devastated Falluja and tens of thousands of families of dead Iraqi and Afghan civilians can testify to that. Paul Bremer, Bush's man in Iraq for the first two years of occupation, forced the privatization clause into the Iraqi constitution "so as to put the real US stamp on the invasion." Imposing the Friedman-Bush vision of American open, consumer culture in Baghdad has already cost more blood and destruction than anticipated.

McDonald's, however, transcends icon-for-America status. Fast food belongs in the category of Friedman's beloved technologies. These chains and gadgets suck labor out of human beings. Along with microwave ovens, McDonald's allows women to supersize their families in minutes and thus spend more time in offices and factories.

Friedman's adoration of change has outpaced even his own prescience. Since techno-change occurs now in weeks, a question that Friedman used in 1999 as an illustration—"How fast is your modem?"—has become obsolete. Concepts of time and space, thanks to the internet and e-mail, have changed as well. But Friedman gets carried away with the possibilities of technology without analyzing the darker side—the hidden hand inside the glove of progress.

Few people think about how the bar code replaced millions who once did inventory, how e-mail and robot phones have taken the place of millions of women who once toiled as secretaries and switchboard operators. Where did these workers go?

Much of recent "progress" has meant either replacing workers with machines or exporting production (jobs) to places like Mexico, Honduras and China and its neighbors with drastically lower labor costs, no environmental regulation or workplace oversight and no taxes

Fiber optic and digital innovations along with satellite communications have also increased productivity. This word of economic measurement refers not only to line workers, but also to salesmen and executives, repair personnel and technicians who no longer enjoy "down time" and work more intensely and for longer hours on their shifts.

The new technology has brought with it a new level of cultural trivia and the sad state of institutionalized loneliness.

Advertisers offer consumers new "toys" like video camera-cell phones, laptops on which to watch movies, Blackberrys and I-pods—commodities to replace people as partners in new experiences.

In fact, these "fun" gadgets do make people more productive—and more stressed. Millions of individuals experience the solitude of hours in their cars stuck in daily traffic jams. They talk with the "office" on the cell; at home, kids lock their doors and play video and computer games. The glories of modern life!

Friedman sees development possibilities in the spread of technology. Capital can invest around the world in nanoseconds—without restrictions. These new opportunities have also removed limits on greed. Without considering consequences, speculators can ruin or make economies, which Friedman converts in his morally relativistic sensibility into a process that "turns the whole world into a parliamentary system, in which every government lives under the fear of a no-confidence vote."[51] Indeed, Latin American governments have fallen, e.g. Argentina, thanks to such economic activities! More importantly, speculators saw profits in buying public property like water in Bolivia and Detroit, forcing up the price of a human necessity—as if it were a luxury item.

Those who seek ever more comfort and convenience also tend to discard history as unworthy sentimentalism. For Friedman, the "olive tree" signifies a tradition whose time has passed. Think of laboratory created olive oil! Old cultures had their historical era, Friedman implies, and should move quietly like ancient elephants to the burial ground.

The olive tree side of the world has indeed sunk deeper into poverty as globalization violently skews world income distribution. On July 26, 2005, UPI reported that the hunger crisis in Niger has also had an impact on neighboring nations, affecting at least 2.5 million people in Mali, Burkina Faso and Mauritania.

Similarly, Friedman tends to gloss over the pounding given to the environment by the increase in fossil fuel burning. Scientists monitoring a glacier in Greenland issued urgent warnings over the dramatic shrinking of a glacier's boundary probably because of melting brought about by climate change. Experts believe any change in the rate at which the glacier transports ice from the ice sheet into the ocean has important implications for increases in sea levels around the world. If the entire Greenland ice sheet were to melt into the ocean it would raise sea levels by up to 23ft, inundating vast areas of low-lying land, including London and much of eastern England.[52]

Friedman does, however, accurately foresee that the transfer of the old world order to the new will not occur peacefully. As the bombings of civilian targets of US allies show, suicide has become a weapon of resistance. Friedman sees these sacrificial bombers as reactionary and ignorant, trying to hold back the inevitable.

Compare the fanaticism of the Palestinian, Iraqi and London suicide bombers with Friedman's ethnocentrism. While Friedman balances a Lexus with an olive tree, most of the world has no access to a Lexus and lives in fear that their version of olive trees will disappear. Indeed, most of the nearly 7 billion people in the world will not own a fancy car; nor will they inherit their father's olive trees—or corn patches. Indeed, Israelis—new order people—routinely bulldoze the trees of old order Palestinians.

Friedman, the pithy salesman for mega corporate progress, thinks that our own society has reached the proper balance. "America at its best takes the needs of markets, individuals and communities all utterly seriously. And that's why America, at its best, is not just a country. It's a spiritual value and role model—the nation that invented cyberspace and the backyard barbecue, the Internet and the social safety net, the SEC and the ACLU."[53]

His America does not coincide with mine, where shopping has become the only spiritual value. Maybe add flag waving and barbecues! But globalization means spreading a culture of corporate brand names and 24/7 sales pitches. Rogue states who refuse to embrace this order become targets of regime change. But if Cuba and Syria, for examples, adapt to the demands of the McDonald's-Disney order they will not become like us. They will simply lose their cultures, become poorer and more stressed.

Those resisting corporate globalizing violently and non-violently don't yet have clear alternatives, but they are absolutely justified in saying BASTA YA!

Reagan and Bottled Water

"If this irresponsible outside power is to be controlled in the interest of the general public, it can be controlled in only one way—by giving adequate power of control to...the National Government."—Theodore Roosevelt, State of the Union Address, December 8, 1908

"Big government cannot and will not solve the multitude of problems confronting our nation...because big government is the problem."—Senator Jesse Helms, speech to the North Carolina Legislature, May 27, 1997

WHEN I SEE PEOPLE DRINKING WATER FROM BOTTLES I THINK of Ronald Reagan and how he destroyed the New Deal. Go back to 1936, when I was born and the first New Deal ended. From 1933-35, President Roosevelt tried to revitalize the economy by paying farmers not to produce while millions went hungry (Agricultural Adjustment Act) and by using government as a broker between industry and labor (National Recovery Act). The second New Deal, 1935-7, however, turned the federal government into an entity that cushioned poor people as they fell from the ledge of misery toward the pavement of disaster.

The grossly underpaid and mistreated workers' population found solace in the 1935 National Labor Relations Act (Wagner Act), which strengthened protection of collective bargaining. The Social Security Act offered working people a chance to have modest pensions when they could no longer earn wages. The Act also established unemployment insurance payments and a rudimentary welfare system, allowing dependent children and handicapped people to get government help. New Deal legislation convinced poor Americans to believe in their government, including its word that civil servants would monitor the contents of water running from the tap.

In my youth, I don't recall people drinking from plastic bottles. We used public fountains. Before privatization, bottled water couldn't have competed with tap water. I attribute the triumph of expensive bottled (contents unknown) over cheap tap water (contents monitored regularly) to the steady decline of the political alliance between the poor majority and the government. The New Deal established an informal pact between labor unions and other groups of poor people and their representatives in national office. In the mid 1960s, this alliance included civil rights and it inspired the only other meaningful American reform of the 20th Century: the Great Society Program.

Lyndon Johnson's Great Society expanded the New Deal. Between 1964 and 1966, he pushed through The Civil Rights Act and Equal Opportunity Act of 1964, the Elementary and Secondary Education Act, the Medicare Act and Voting Rights Act of 1965, plus programs like Head Start to help poor children of pre-school age, and laws giving legal and medical help to the needy.

The most activist sectors of the corporate world responded. In 1963, extreme anti-liberal Richard Mellon Scaife began funding the American Enterprise Institute (AEI). Other inheritors of fortunes, like Lynde and Harry Bradley and Joseph Coors, used their "charitable" foundations to form the Heritage Foundation and other think tanks. They hired well-paid "conservative" intellectuals to undo the momentum generated by three decades of liberalism. This anti-New Deal campaign selected its villains as "big labor," which was painted as crime-ridden and non-representative of its members, and "big government," which they painted as the corrupt waster of taxpayer money.

The vilification of the federal government, they formulated, was the first step to returning power to citizens. Ironically, weakening the government hardly returns more control to the citizenry. Instead, as government regulations decrease, the large corporations and banks become stronger. Arthur Schlesinger Jr. called it, "Getting government off the back of business simply means putting business on the back of government."[54]

The well-endowed right wing propaganda mills cranked out sophisticated tracts against liberalism, the New Deal and Great Society programs. Their hired intellectual guns performed on radio and TV shows. Their themes: hate unions and especially the government—and don't pay taxes to it. Instead, respect the virtuous private sector (Military and police remained, of course, good branches of government).

By 1976, this aggressive and unanswered campaign had pushed the Democratic Party to the right, so that even its candidate, Jimmy Carter, adopted anti-government rhetoric. In 1978, California voters bought the hate government rhetoric and passed Proposition 13, a tax revolt that drastically limited the State Legislature's ability to raise property taxes and placed limits on spending for public education as well. The results: rich people paid minimal taxes; poor and middle class home owners saved a few hundred or even a few thousand dollars.

California schools, number one before voters passed Prop 13, plummeted. But working class voters failed to see that the massive propaganda campaign had swayed them to vote against their own interests. Indeed, in 1980, the blue collar voters tipped the scales of the 1980 presidential election as well.

Ronald Reagan drove the decisive nail into the coffin of modern liberalism. In his campaigns for California governor during the 1970s he underlined the theme of government as the enemy of the people. In 1976, stumping for the Republican nomination for president, he talked about a "welfare queen," who drove a Cadillac and stole $150,000 from the government using 80 aliases, 30 addresses, a dozen social security cards and four fictional dead husbands. Reporters wanted to interview this "welfare cheat," but discovered that she didn't exist.

In the 1980 presidential campaign, Reagan satirized Carter as running for the presidency on a platform calling for "national economic planning." Then he added, sarcastically, "I'm sure they meant well—liberals usually do. But our economy was one of the great wonders of the world. It didn't need master planners. It worked because it operated on principles of freedom, millions of free decisions, how they wanted to work and live, how they wanted to spend their money, while reaping the rewards of their individual labor."

In a 1984 "Good Morning America" appearance, Reagan went further. "Those people who are sleeping on the grates...the homeless...are homeless, you might say, by choice." Thanks to a steady campaign of lies and distortions about the people who received welfare, the majority of voting Americans began to believe that their tax dollars went to support lazy black women taking drugs, drinking and having wanton sex. Some even fell for the idea that federal support for housing intruded on one's personal choice.

Right wing "think tanks" churned out Reagan lessons like shining but rancid butter. They equated hating government and not paying taxes with both patriotism and practical self interest. Simultaneously, Reagan and his minions extolled the virtues of the private sector, which he promised would more efficiently meet peoples' basic needs.

New right ideology sought to reverse the negative connotations that business had earned by centuries of screwing workers, consumers and the poor. The right wing even managed to dominate the world of literary criticism. The 1930s business villains of John Steinbeck's *Grapes of Wrath* and Clifford Odets' plays gave way to capitalist-loving heroes in Ayn Rand's novels.

Privatization became the White House leitmotif, creating the atmosphere for the plastic water bottle, which appeared en masse in the 1980s. By the 1990s, corporations like Bechtel had even obtained the right to run Bolivia's water supply. Needless to say, the price of this basic need skyrocketed—as Bolivians discovered, before forcing their government to undo the privatization in 2004.

U.S. blue-collar workers, however, remained under the rhetorical magic that convinced them to vote against their interests. Citizens who once automatically voted Democrat and trusted their government became skeptical and opted for Bush. Did their political choice connect to the notion that private water was safer than what flowed from the government regulated tap?

At movie theaters, 16 ounces of PepsiCo's Aqua Fina cost $3.50. At my university, students pay $1.50 and keep one in their backpacks. Previously, they drank from pubic fountains in school corridors. Now those fountains appear as arcane sculpture. Students pay for a little convenience.

Dining at people's homes, I receive assurances from hosts that they filter tap water, even though scientists have tested and declared it perfectly healthy. Behind this change of water choice hides a key political axiom of our time. Americans don't trust their government and pay private companies whose bottles don't reveal the bacterial and other germ content of their product.

Globally, according to Tom Standage, bottled water is now a $46 billion industry.[55] Yet, tests show that tasters can't distinguish between bottled and tap water. Standage also points to an *Archives of Family Medicine* report in which researchers from Cleveland found that nearly a quarter of the samples of bottled water had significantly higher levels of bacteria than tap water. The scientists concluded that "use of bottled water on the assumption of purity can be misguided."

Indeed, most cities monitor tap water content far more extensively than making fortunes selling the bottles. New York City water was tested 430,600 times during 2004 alone. Ken Blomberg, who directs the Wisconsin Rural Water Association that offers less-expensive bottled municipal water for sale, claims that almost 70 percent of commercially bottled water comes from a municipal tap.

Omnipresent commercial water bottles have come to symbolize more than a convenient hydration source. When I look at the bottles' labels, I see a right wing cultural victory, one that will take more than liberal electoral victories to reverse. Can government prove again that it works? Will liberals have energy to re-educate this generation in lessons their grandparents learned during the New Deal? The November 2006 Democratic victory, reclaiming both houses, offers the test.

Bush, God and Katrina

IN LITERATURE, GOD SENT WARNINGS. HERMAN MELVILLE'S Captain Ahab refuses to recognize God's limits. Moby Dick, the white whale (God's instrument?), chews off Ahab's leg in his first attempt to capture the mighty creature. Instead of respecting this admonition, the commander of the commercial whaling vessel sought revenge; i.e., domination of a large animal. Ahab felt compelled to show who possessed ultimate power.

In life, George Bush froze—unscripted—when world-shaking issues fell onto his morally weak shoulders. Suffering and death confound him. Perhaps Barbara traumatized her seven-year-old boy when little sister died of leukemia? The day after the funeral, the Bushes played a round of golf—how the proper set deal with death. Barbara, according to Dr. Justin Frank, had trouble connecting emotionally with her son. W's father also played a role in shaping his son's character pathology: "emotional and physical absence during his son's youth triggered feelings of both adoration and revenge." The President suffers from "grandiosity" and "megalomania." He sees himself, America and God as interchangeable.[56]

Indeed, as U.S. troops invaded Iraq, Commerce Secretary Don Evans said that "Bush believes he was called by God to lead the nation at this time."[57] W's spiritual adviser Rev. James Robison said that Bush told him: "I feel like God wants me to run for President. I can't explain it, but I sense my country is going to need me. Something is going to happen... I know it won't be easy on me or my family, but God wants me to do it."[58]

On 9/11, something big happened. But W didn't disentangle himself from the plot of "My Pet Goat," which he continued to read to Florida second graders for seven minutes after aides told him a jet had flow into the Twin Towers. A day later, he emerged from his daze. He didn't appear at the scene of the tragedy until September 14. Likewise, when Katrina struck four plus years later, God apparently didn't order Bush to visit the tragedy site. The Prez remained on vacation, jogged, did fundraisers and other religious work. After five days, Bush finally visited the crater. Was anyone less qualified to love thy neighbor as thyself?

Unable to overcome his emotional learning disability, manifested by insensitivity to human tragedy, he posed for photo ops instead. Hugging women didn't tax his psyche. Then, to mask his discomfort about the distressful situation in the once Big Easy, he joked about his drinking days in "N'Oleans."

"Very funny," said the diseased and half dead. Bush's unease with proximity to real pain led him to seek out Trent Lott, about whom he spoke with sincerity. Senator Lott (R-MS)—a multi millionaire—had also lost a house. But Bush optimistically predicted that he would replace it with "a fantastic house—and I'm looking forward to sitting on the porch."

How better could God humble the world's most powerful nation then to saddle it with Bush in the midst of a tragedy? How best to show limits to arrogant Americans then by placing in charge a bungler incapable of responding to other people's sorrow?

White House handlers scripted return visits to the disaster sites. But deep inside, W wanted to return to Crawford, his Eden, a place to ride bikes and jog. Momma Barbara had, after all, reassured him—and the nation—that since "so many of the people in the arena here, you know, were underprivileged anyway, so this-this [she emits a chuckle referring to government programs] is working very well for them."

She saw the evacuation of people to Houston as an example of her boy's successful administration. "What I'm hearing which is sort of scary is they all want to stay in Texas. Everyone is so overwhelmed by the hospitality. Almost everyone I've talked to says we're going to move to Houston."[59]

Bush had described himself as a leader and "leaders lead." But God did not suddenly imbue W with take-charge qualities when thousands felt anguish over disease, death and home loss. Indeed, Bush doesn't grasp even moderately difficult situations and therefore can't see how to deal with them.

He looked down from Air Force One at the broken 17th Street levee through which water flooded New Orleans. Then W landed and spoke about the urgent need to control lawlessness, not suffering and death. He probably forgot Defense Secretary Rumsfeld's wisdom on looting. Rummy had ordered U.S. troops not to crack down "on looting in Iraq because it might alienate the Iraqi people they are trying to win over." Rumsfeld understood looting as part of a process. "U.S. forces should not be blamed for the lawlessness and looting in Baghdad as it is a natural consequence of the transition from a dictatorship to a free country."[60]

After his initial display of unconcern, Bush returned to Louisiana and toured with Senator Mary Landrieu, who initially believed he was making "a real and significant effort to get a handle on a major cause of this catastrophe." But when she flew over the same "critical spot again this morning, less than 24 hours later," she realized it had been nothing more than "a hastily prepared stage set for a Presidential photo opportunity; and the desperately needed resources we saw were this morning reduced to a single, lonely piece of equipment. The ... people of southeast Louisiana and the Gulf Coast ... deserve far better from their national government..."[61]

As a religious man, Bush knew that God created man and then woman. Intelligent design? But Bush did not delve into God's subsequent ambivalence toward his creations. After they committed their initial sin, from which of course they received

knowledge and guile and got tossed out of Eden for their disobedience, they lacked a collective brain. So, Adam and Eve and
their progeny began a long process of destroying His perfect
environment. Think of the millennia in which He watched
people systematically erode His sculpture.

With the industrial revolution, the attack on His intelligent
design became downright ferocious. Assaults on thousands of
His species, the ozone layers and the air, water and soil might
well have offended even the most patient of gods. Massive green
house gas emission altered the very framework of His opus.

Did God vindictively choose Bush to administer at times of
great catastrophes? He knew that the Bush family chose its servants on the basis of loyalty. So, He must have smiled smugly
when Bush chose Michael Brown to run the Federal Emergency
Management Agency (FEMA). Brown lost his previous position
as head of the Arabian Horse Association by apparently not
properly organizing horse shows. But for the Bushes, subservi-
ence was the perfect trait for servants. Bush picked him first
as deputy director and then head of FEMA when the director
resigned.

Brown shared Bush's ignorance of suffering and how to deal
with disaster. After Katrina struck, however, Kate Hale, former
Miami-Dade emergency management chief, said "Brownie" had
"done a hell of a job, because I'm not aware of any Arabian
horses being killed in this storm."

Brown apparently didn't understand that Congress created
FEMA, his agency, to handle disasters. "The U.S. Forest Service
had water-tanker aircraft available to help douse the fires raging
on our riverfront," said Senator Landrieu, "but FEMA has yet
to accept the aid. When Amtrak offered trains to evacuate significant numbers of victims—far more efficiently than buses—
FEMA again dragged its feet. Offers of medicine, communications equipment, and other desperately needed items continue
to flow in, only to be ignored by the agency."[62]

Brown admitted to CNN's Paula Zahn that "The federal government did not even know about the convention center people until today [days after people took shelter there]."

"I think the other thing that really caught me by surprise," he said, "was the fact that there were so many people, and I'm not laying blame, but either chose not to evacuate or could not evacuate. And as we began to do the evacuations from the Superdome, all of a sudden, literally thousands of other people started showing up in other places, and we were not prepared for that. We were surprised by that." While corpses floated in the waters that filled New Orleans, Brown patted himself on the back. "Considering the dire circumstances that we have in New Orleans—virtually a city that has been destroyed—things are going relatively well."63

Harsh critics of Bush's handling of Katrina assume that citizens deserve efficiency and compassion from the federal government. But Bush responded, judging from his behavior during the Katrina aftermath, as punisher—of the poor, not the rich—not rescuer. Less than a week after the media revealed just some of FEMA's gross incompetence, Brownie resigned—and was replaced by R. David Paulison, who previously advised Americans to use duct tape in case of a chemical or biological attack.

In 1785, Thomas Jefferson, reflected on slavery. "I tremble for my country when I reflect that God is just. His justice cannot sleep forever." Was Jefferson's God defining justice as sardonic revenge—not only by inflicting us with Katrina, but placing George W. Bush as chief administrator of its aftermath?

An Oily Religious Dream

N SEPTEMBER 2005, THE BODY COUNT AND PROPERTY DAMAGE assessment mounted steadily along the Gulf Coast. After watching TV news images of the carnage, the Rev. Jerry Pat Flatulence had one of his many epiphanies—after eating his dinner in his home in Lynchemhighburg, Virginia. Millions of religious broadcast watchers knew Jerry Pat's fleshy cheeks, impish eyes and beatific smile. Over the decades, he had saved countless souls for Christ and coincidentally collected hundreds of millions of dollars in Jesus' name.

Even before becoming one of George W. Bush's spiritual advisers, Jerry Pat worked TV miracle cures, helping the blind to see and the lame to walk. Cynics said he used actors instead of real people, but true believers maintained their faith: "Hallelujah!"

Indeed, Bush himself took the Reverend's cure for alcoholism: abstinence, physical exercise, video golf and prayer—infinitely preferable to going forever to AA meetings. Most of those "recovering alcoholics" did not exactly fit into the president's family circle.

Like Bush, Jerry Pat claimed that God had spoken to him. When catastrophic events occurred, Jerry Pat orated to his flock at the Absolute Baptist Church. The TV audience watched the same sermon.

"God has punished the USA, which has become a haven for homosexuality, atheism, and false religions," Jerry Pat said he got this from God, who had also inflicted the events of 9/11 on New Yorkers because they had an unusually high level of devil's advocates. "The ACLU has more members there than in all of southern Virginia," he announced. No one inquired about the source of his figures.

Indeed, Jerry Pat had made a worldwide reputation for saying unpleasant things about others—especially Muslims. Logically, his fame spread to Israel, although it disturbed him that the bearded, black-clad men who applauded enthusiastically also talked to each other or slept through his entire sermon. But they did contribute handsomely to his various causes. He did, after all, support Israel 100% even though he had warned his flock to be cautious before doing business with "those people whose prayers God does not hear."

On this September day, the TV news images had upset him. Bleeding bodies from suicide bombings in the Middle East and bloated ones floating in the flood waters of Louisiana and Texas sent Jerry Pat to the dinner table, a place to calm upset nerves. He consumed three portions of his wife's extra fried chicken, two sides of baked oyster pie with cream and two helpings of whiskey pudding.

Coping with indigestion, he prayed in his study. He requested the Good Lord for stomach relief because the Alka Seltzer didn't seem to help. As he mumbled his final prayers, he dropped into a heavy sleep on his comfortable couch. Soon, he began to dream...

A stormy black cloud formed over his head, followed by blinding rays of lightning and deafening thunder. Wait!

The thunder disguised a booming voice, a basso profundo exhorting. "Follow the oily brick road," it said. "Then shall you know your transgressions."

In the dream, he stared at the cloud, waiting for more explanation. In the past, he had not exactly had such direct conversations with God. Rather, he reconstructed what he thought God should have said to him. Jerry Pat was not the kind of man to quibble over small details.

But this dream frightened him and he could not force himself to wake up. The big voice belched loudly again. "The oily brick road. Your president has lied in order to wage war in my name. Your disciple in the White House has raised my ire. Now I have shown him what I can do to his oil. Talk to him."

The dream took on nightmarish qualities. He awakened with a start. Did the Lord mean he had sent Hurricanes Katrina and Rita to wreak havoc on the Louisiana and Texas coasts because the oil industry does its major drilling and refining there?

In the dream, The Lord never mentioned abortion, gay marriage, carnality or any of Jerry Pat's favorite Godly themes. Only that echoing phrase, "The oily brick road."

Jerry Pat's aching stomach took second place on his bio-discomfort list to his throbbing brain. He picked up the phone and dialed the special number W had given him in case urgent messages from above came through.

After a brief and unpleasant round with Karl Rove, who screened all religious hot line calls, the familiar voice resonated in the earpiece.

"Flatty," W said. "How y'doin?" The Reverend Jerry Pat Flatulence shuddered over the nickname, but he also knew that you can take Texas out of the boy, but you can't take the boy out of Texas—or whatever.

"Mr. President," he said hesitatingly, "I have just received a very disturbing message, one that I believe requires your urgent attention."

"Is this for real?"

"Mr. President," Jerry Pat sad gravely, "this is truly serious."

Jerry Pat phoned his pilot and his private jet took him to Washington. Within minutes, Secret Service agents ushered him into the Oval Office.

The two men fell to their knees and prayed silently. Jerry Pat's prayer involved a request: "Please God, don't appear ever again in my dream or give me any real messages. Please let me just keep interpreting what I think you should be telling me rather than what you really told me in that last dream."

Bush prayed silently for peace. "Please God, give me a little peace from that resentful Cindy Sheehan whose son died in Iraq and now nags the heck out of me not to send other mothers' sons over there. God, you know how difficult it is for me to deal with death and suffering. Well, strong angry women are even worse. I also beg you not to hit us with any more hurricanes—at least until I'm out of office. I really hate going into those places with lots of poor people, dirty, some 'em diseased—especially while I'm on vacation. Well, you know what I mean God and I await your message, which I hope will come as months of good weather and success on the battlefields of Iraq and Afghanistan."

They shook hands after praying and sipped Diet Pepsi. Jerry Pat related his dream. "This message could not have been clearer," he told Bush.

"Heck, Flatty," Bush responded, "that's just one dream. And knowing you, it probably came after you ate too much of your wife's home cooking."

"But, really," Jerry Pat pleaded, "the oily brick road message, I couldn't have invented something like that."

"Flatty, we didn't go to war for oil. Even though I'm practically sure God told me to invade Iraq and tell the folks at home that it was about weapons of mass destruction and all that. He knew that Saddam was sitting on all that oil and that Saddam didn't deserve all that oil and that we good Christians did. So, go on home and relax, Flatty. And tell the folks out in TV land that they should keep the pressure up on those liberals and Democrats on abortion and taxes and homosexual marriages."

The Reverend Flatulence returned to Lynchemhighburg. Depressed about his inability to convince Bush, he feasted on his wife's cooking and again he dreamed. This time an even angrier bass voice burst through the dark cloud.

"You have failed me," it said. "You and your disciple who says the stupidest prayers in the world will slip on the oily brick road. It will lead you to your doom."

Jerry Pat woke up, frightened. He consulted with Robbem "Robby" Paterson, a fellow televangelist, who shared his elite status—at the bank, anyway. Robby had become a realist after getting caught on several occasions with underage hookers. After the third bust he vowed to God never to get caught again.

Robby had a way of putting Jerry Pat at ease. "Flatty," he said, imitating the President, "what you gonna believe, all the money you got in the bank or a bad dream about oil? If God wanted to send you a message, your stock would go down. If he wants to send Bush a message, his approval ratings would go down."

"But they have gone down."

"Yes, but if He really wanted to send Bush a message, He'd put those twin girls of his in the centerfold of *Playboy*. If God wanted to take his anger out on Bush, the cover of *Playboy* would read 'A Tale of Two Bushes'—heh, heh." Jerry Pat smiled. He thanked Robby and then phoned the White House. "Mr. President, things are alright. You don't have to follow the oily brick road. I mean..." He thought. "I mean watch your daugh..." He hung up. He no longer knew what he meant. It was all so oily.

Different Americas:
New Year's 2007

EORGE W. BUSH, LIKE EUROPEAN MONARCHS, CLAIMED HE POSsessed inherent rights and implied that those who question such prerogatives might have treasonous motives. "As President and Commander-in-Chief, I have the constitutional responsibility and the constitutional authority to protect our country," Bush responded to those who thought he shouldn't have authorized wiretaps on US citizens without getting legal permission. Bush then turned on the leakers.

"It was a shameful act for someone to disclose this very important program in a time of war," said Bush. "The fact that we're discussing this program is helping the enemy." Bush did not apparently recall that he assured the public that "a wiretap requires a court order... It's important for our fellow citizens to understand, when you think Patriot Act, constitutional guarantees are in the place..."64

W doesn't seem bothered by contradictions between what he says and does. For example, he denied that the US practiced torture just as the press revealed that US officials spawned torture at Guantanamo, Cuba, Abu Ghraib, Iraq and at secret CIA-run prisons throughout the world. He also scolded the media for reporting on US agents kidnapping suspected terrorists and shipping them elsewhere (rendition) for torture and interrogation. The Bush family does not think such issues merit discussion—certainly not during the holidays.

A week earlier he had snapped at a reporter who raised the constitutional question. "I don't give a goddamn. I'm the President and the Commander-in-Chief. Do it my way."

One aide apparently said. "There is a valid case that the provisions in this law undermine the Constitution."

"Stop throwing the Constitution in my face," Bush screamed back. "It's just a goddamned piece of paper!"[65]

A Democratic Member of Congress told me that Bush's display of arrogant power exceeded Nixon. "Bush justified his violation of laws by referring to a Congressional resolution to fight al-Qaeda, passed after 9/11, that he claims transcends the Fourth Amendment, the right to spy on US citizens because Presidents have inherent powers to fight wars that Congress did not declare.

Bush's imperial managers invoke "national security"—without defining other than as "combating terrorism"—to justify circumvention of court warrants and congressional oversight. W defined wire tapping US citizens without warrants as "fully consistent" with his "constitutional responsibilities and authorities."[66]

The "important" people, however, bank presidents and corporate CEOs, ignore such trivia. They had deciphered Bush's feeble "compassionate conservative" code before he ran for the presidency. They assured their stockholders that the Bush Administration aimed above all else to enhance the worldly proprietary interests of the super rich.

Bush has allowed an atmosphere of tolerance in awarding defense contracts, coincidentally, many of them to corporations that had also heavily contributed to the Bush political coffers or had close ties to the Administration. (Vice President Cheney's old company, Halliburton, got no-bid contracts in Iraq.) "Executives at some companies with military contracts have increased their salaries by 200 percent since 9/11," wrote Sarah Anderson.[67]

The big oil companies also got huge windfall profits after Bush invaded Iraq. The 2005 film "Syriana" dramatizes oil tycoons and other corporate bosses paying fortunes to lobbyists to get the powerful to support Middle East war. The rest of the business elite takes for granted—as it normally does—that the government will protect the interests of the very propertied classes. The moguls therefore seem uninterested when the Bushies disregard traditional rules and abdicate conventional responsibility.

In Oakland, California, part of that public, some not yet of voting age, struts down a street where the faces are black, Asian or Hispanic. Many do not speak English. The teenagers dressed in baggy pants, grew up in these grey streets, flanked by decaying warehouses, garages, body shops and taquerias. A group of Central American day laborers wait for work on a corner where old newspapers blow and empty plastic soda cups litter the sidewalk. Occasional cars stop and drivers hire some of them to help move furniture or clean a back yard. The Central Americans ignore the black teenage posse.

A passing patrol car slows down. The cops stare at the men on the corner—illegals?—and at the swaggering teenagers. If the boys change their choreography to indicate that cops intimidate them it would amount to surrender. So they maintain hip hop rhythms. The cops ooze by, then speed up. A radio alert to stop a real crime? Two boys run combs through their carefully coiffed hair, as if to call attention to the expensive sculpting on the tops of their heads. Several turn up the volume on their digital music players so they can parade in rhythm to the hip hop.

The kids don't demonstrate any overt acknowledgement that they might have won a very minor stare-down skirmish in their never-ending struggle for respect. Later, they will probably discuss it at length. On the street, however, they maintain the cool façade, based on protocols that predate them.

They will retreat to someone's house, smoke weed, or crack and talk shit about possible future crimes and fantasies of owning expensive cars. No one will mention Bush or his policies, which have curtailed their access to medical care and cut down on the food stamps their mothers can obtain.

Their street lives focus on the enemy gangs and the ubiquitous cops. When cops stop them, it means automatic search. If cops find drugs or drug paraphernalia, it means Juvie. A Public Defender usually won't have time to prepare a case, so the kid serves time. That's American life.

In Piedmont's hills, teenagers don't walk the streets in groups. They drive expensive cars and wear whatever their expensive tastes dictate. They don't achieve identity, respect and self-esteem through things. They've always had everything they wanted.

Unlike the teenagers in the flats, the Piedmonters understand that the primary job of police is to protect them and their property in case larcenously intentioned kids from the flats should wander up there. The Piedmont kids drink and use drugs, just like the gang bangers. But the police stop them only if they're driving out of control—for their own protection. When a rare bust occurs for DUI or possession, high priced lawyers convince judges to offer their young clients probation—or find technicalities on which to get them released.

Such class segregation, with a heavy racial component, has existed for centuries. So, what's new? Some African Americans have acquired wealth and even own houses in Piedmont. Millions more have joined the middle classes. But the destiny of the majority, the poor black, the Hispanic and Native American people, remains unchanged.

In Washington, the Bushies hope the political class will forget or overlook the policy peccadilloes and instead count their money made from tax cuts and the loose atmosphere provided by Bush's incompetent regulators to get rich on insider trading.

The boys in Oakland have little to trade. Many will not graduate from high school and will find their way into the California prison system. "The majority of inmates come from the poorest sectors and are mainly Hispanic and black," said a nurse who has worked at two California state prisons. "In the Youth Authority [men between 18 and 25] at Chino lots of the guys expect to join their fathers and grandfathers at Folsom and San Quentin [state prisons]."

Two of the baggy pants wearers tell me, smiling, that they have friends and family in the system [prison]. One considers joining the army "and going to Iraq or wherever." The others laugh when a boy yells: "Someone gonna put a cap in your ass over there."

The Piedmont kids will go to expensive colleges, graduate and become CEOs and professionals—like their parents. On New Year's Eve, both sets enjoyed parties, booze and drugs, sex and making resolutions. They, like the Bushies, were F. Scott Fitzgerald's "careless people." In *The Great Gatsby*, Fitzgerald described how "...they smashed up things and creatures and retreated back into their money or their vast carelessness ... and let other people clean up the mess they had made." And what a mess Bush has made!

II. Mission Accomplished: Iraq Is Broken

Who We Really Are

GEORGE W. BUSH RETURNED FROM A BRIEF BUT DIFFICULT November 2005 learning foray in Latin America: "Wow, Brazil is big." Meanwhile, U.S. citizens grew impatient with his performance. CBS polls rated him at 35% approval in early November. Even his supporters acknowledge that Bush's policies have created enormous ill will throughout the world. More ethically worrisome, cried his critics, those policies don't represent who we really are.

Most Americans, for example, abhor torture. So, on November 7, Bush flatly declared: "We don't torture"—just as front page stories appeared with details of how the Pentagon charged five U.S members of an elite Army unit with kicking and punching detainees in Iraq.

Few Washington insiders expressed shock over Bush's not having heard of the massive evidence compiled by the Center for Constitutional Rights, Amnesty International and the Red Cross about routine U.S. military and CIA torture of prisoners in Guantanamo and Abu Ghraib. Nor did he seem upset over reports of secret prisons set up by the CIA in other countries in which methods that the United States and most other nations had agreed by treaty to never practice. The CIA had stashed prisoners in a series of secret, "black-site" prisons around the world, where U.S. officials "punished" them in ways prohibited by the U.N. Convention Against Torture and Other Cruel, Inhuman or Degrading Treatment or Punishment.[68]

CIA interrogators abroad used "Enhanced Interrogation Techniques," banned by both the U.N. and by U.S. military law, such as "waterboarding," making a prisoner believe he or she is drowning.[69]

The *Washington Post* also claimed that "a small circle of White House and Justice Department lawyers and officials "approved this policy" and tried to affirm that "Congress may no more regulate the president's ability to detain and interrogate enemy combatants than it may regulate his ability to direct troop movements on the battlefield."

On November 7, Bush said he didn't want the enemy to know what might happen to them. "There's an enemy that lurks and plots and plans and wants to hurt America again. And so, you bet we will aggressively pursue them. But we will do so under the law."[70]

Bush dodged military service and Cheney had "better things to do" than risk his life in Vietnam. Senator John McCain, on the other hand, who experienced torture, led the fight to ban it.

"Subjecting prisoners to abuse leads to bad intelligence because under torture a detainee will tell his interrogator anything to make the pain stop," McCain said. "Second, mistreatment of our prisoners endangers U.S. troops who might be captured by the enemy. ... And third, prisoner abuses exact on us a terrible toll in the war of ideas because inevitably these abuses become public."

On October 7, 2005, 89 other senators joined McCain in condemning torture, nine voted for it. Radio bigmouth Rush Limbaugh said the torturers were just "having a good time," getting "emotional release." In his May 4, 2004 show, a caller commented to Rush: "It was like a college fraternity prank that stacked up naked men."

LIMBAUGH: Exactly my point! This is no different than what happens at the Skull and Bones initiation and we're going to ruin people's lives over it and we're going to hamper our military effort, and then we are going to really hammer them because they had a good time. You know, these people are being fired at every day. I'm talking about people having a good time, these people, you ever heard of emotional release? You ever heard of need to blow some steam off?

One day before, Limbaugh called the women soldiers accused of abusing Iraqi prisoners "babes." Why, the published photos of this alleged mistreatment looked like something "you'd see Madonna, or Britney Spears do on stage."

The outspoken radio host even satirized the tortures scandal as something you'd "get an NEA grant for... something that you can see on stage at Lincoln Center...maybe on 'Sex in the City'—the movie. I mean..."

This is not who we are? Was the 19th Century torture and massacre of Indians just a bit of venting by frustrated U.S. troops? Did the murder and torture of Filipinos between 1892 and 1932 represent no more than a fraternity hazing party?

Why, journalists should have asked, did Bush want to exempt the CIA from the torture ban? To claim he didn't want enemy prisoners to know what might happen to them appears contradictory to his public statement: "we don't torture." "They," Bush declared, "use violence and torture." We're free and democratic.

In June 2005 in Istanbul, I heard a group of students challenge a U.S. academic to explain how democratic people could elect Bush. "Bush doesn't really represent the American people," the American academic replied. The Turkish students pressed him about the Iraqi invasion for oil and demanded to know how Americans could have possibly voted for "the butcher of Baghdad."

"That's not who we are," he assured them.

It's not? Decent people have repeated that line to distance themselves from atrocious crimes since the 17th Century. Henry David Thoreau and Harriet Beecher Stowe insisted that slavery and the massacre of Indians did not define us. After reports that the U.S. firebombed German and Japanese cities and dropped two nuclear bombs on Japan, many citizens said: That's not who we are.

Supreme Court Justice Robert Jackson went to Nuremberg to try to ban future wars. "We must not allow ourselves to be drawn into a trial of the causes of war, for out position is that no grievances or policies will justify resort to aggressive war. It is utterly renounced and condemned as an instrument of policy."[71]

Other legal scholars drafted the UN Charter to maintain peace and helped revise President Franklin Roosevelt's Four Freedoms (speech and expression, religion; freedom from fear and want) into the UN Covenants on Human Rights.

Meanwhile, other U.S. officials carried out nuclear weapons tests for use in future wars and helped circumvent the actual Senate ratification of the covenants.

Law vies with lawlessness. The Bush Administration tried to get legal UN cover for its invasion of Iraq before breaking both international codes and Justice Jackson's denunciation of aggressive war. Then he painted a rhetorical veneer of democracy over his naked aggression.

In late September 2005, to show the Middle Easterner who we really are, Bush dispatched Karen Hughes, to promote the real U.S. image in Saudi Arabia, Egypt and Turkey.

Hughes found it tough to sell democracy and human rights as reports surfaced of systematic, routine U.S. torture of prisoners in Iraq and Afghanistan. The armed forces tried and convicted more than 200 bottom level personnel. Not a single general or civilian official, including those who authorized torture has faced trial.

As Karen Hughes "sold" Bush's America, alternate salespeople on Al Jazeera highlighted the U.S.' rising deficit and towering debt and featured stories on how poor blacks continue to get the short end of every government stick.

Americans believe they live in a model of freedom, opportunity and prosperity not available in older cultures. The 37 million living under the poverty line shocked them. As do the three-plus million millionaires.

The typical white family has $80,000 in assets; the average black family about $6,000. Some 46 million can't afford health insurance, 18,000 of them will die prematurely because of it.

The U.S. ranks 43rd in world infant mortality ratings. Beijing babies have far greater chances of reaching their first birthdays those born in Washington. The survivors face rotten schools. Reading and math tests for 15-year-olds placed the U.S. 24th out of 29 rich nations.

Meanwhile, 18 corporate executives went to prison for corporate accounting fraud and looting. Bush's Enron pals will also soon face trial for practicing their "greed-is-good" culture.

The war costs $6 billion a month. In five years the conflict will have cost each American family $11,300. Bush will cut programs for the poor to pay for the war, but not reverse his tax cuts.

Throughout U.S. history, truly pious and sensible down-home Americans have shared church space with zealous nuts and bigots. Cotton Mather, the Puritan witch hunter and Roger Williams who pleaded for religious freedom in the 17th Century have as their warped descendent Pat Robertson and Jerry Falwell who gloat over having one of their own kind running the country. On the democracy and freedom side, William Sloan Coffin and the Berrigan brothers decry imperial aggression and suppression of liberties.

Threads of racism and imperial aggression characterize U.S. growth and expansion from 13 colonies to the world's greatest power. So does democracy. This inextricably interwoven love of freedom developed hand in glove with racism and imperialism.

Who are we? Racists, imperialists and democrats. The struggle now, as in the past, pits those who want the democracy element to prevail and bury the evil that has emanated for the other two threads of our history.

Breaking Falluja: The 21st Century Guernica—Where was Picasso?

ON NOVEMBER 12, 2004, U.S. JETS BOMBED FALLUJA FOR the ninth straight day. On that same day, a Redwood City California jury found Scott Peterson guilty of murdering his wife and unborn child. That macabre theme involving adultery captured headlines and dominated conversation throughout workplaces and homes.

Indeed, Peterson "news" all but drowned out the U.S. military's claim that successful bombing and shelling of a city of 300,000 residents had struck only sites where "insurgents" had holed up. On November 15, a BBC newsman embedded with a marine detachment claimed that the unofficial death toll estimate had risen to well over 2,000, many of them civilians.

As Iraqi eyewitnesses told other BBC reporters that they had seen bombs hitting residential targets, Americans exchanged kinky jokes about Peterson. One photographer captured a Falluja man holding his dead son, one of two kids he lost to U.S. bombers. He could not get medical help to stop his boy's bleeding.

A November 14 *Reuters* reporter wrote that residents told him that "U.S. bombardments hit a clinic inside the Sunni Muslim city, killing doctors, nurses and patients." The U.S. military denied the reports. Such stories did not make headlines. Civilian casualties in aggressive U.S. wars don't sell media space.

Editors love shots of anguished GI Joes, however. The November 12, 2004 *Los Angeles Times'* front page carried a photo of a soldier with mud smeared face and cigarette dangling from his lips. The GI complained he was out of "smokes." This image captured the "suffering" of Falluja.

The young man doing his "duty to free Falluja" stood in stark contrast to the nightmare of Falluja. "Smoke is everywhere," an Iraqi told the BBC. "The house some doors from mine was hit during the bombardment on Wednesday night. A 13-year-old boy was killed. His name was Ghazi. A row of palm trees used to run along the street outside my house—now only the trunks are left... There are more and more dead bodies on the streets and the stench is unbearable."[72]

Another eyewitness said that "a 9-year-old boy was hit in the stomach by a piece of shrapnel. His parents said they couldn't get him to hospital because of the fighting, so they wrapped sheets around his stomach to try to stem the bleeding. He died hours later of blood loss and was buried in the garden."[73]

U.S. embedded reporters—presstitutes?[74]— accepted uncritically the Pentagon's spin that many thousands of Iraqi "insurgents," including the demonized outsiders led by Abu Musab al-Zarqawi, who had joined the anti-U.S. jihad, had dug in to defend their vital base. After the armored and air assault began and the ground troops advanced, reports filtered out that the marines and the new Iraqi army that trailed behind them had faced only light resistance. Meanwhile, uprisings broke out in Mosul and other cities. For the combatants, however, Falluja was Hell.

Hell for what? Retired Marine Corps General Bernard Trainor declared that: militarily, "Falluja is not going to be much of a plus at all." He admitted that "we've knocked the hell out of this city, and the only insurgents we really got were the nutcases and zealots, the smart ones left behind the guys who really want to die for Allah." While Pentagon spin doctors boasted of a U.S. "victory, Trainor pointed out that the "terrorists remain at large."

The media accepts axiomatically that U.S. troops wear the "white hats" in this conflict. They do not address the obvious: Washington illegally invaded and occupied Iraq and "re-conquered" Falluja—for no serious military purpose. Logically, the media should call Iraqi "militants" patriots who resisted illegal occupation.

Instead, the press implied that the "insurgents" even fought dirty, using improvised explosive devices and booby traps to kill our innocent soldiers, who use clean weapons like F16s, helicopter gun ships, tanks and heavy artillery.

Washington even promised to rebuild the city that its military just destroyed. Bush committed the taxpayers to debts worth hundreds of millions of dollars, which Bechtel, Halliburton and the other corporate beneficiaries of war will use for "rebuilding"—if they ever get around to it. By February 2006, Bush had forgotten about his Falluja reconstruction promises. Indeed, billions of Iraqi reconstruction money had gone to thieves appointed by the Administration.[75]

Banality and corruption arise from the epic evil of this war, one that has involved massive civilian death and the destruction of ancient cities. That has been the essence of modern war for 100 years.

Using experiences from the Russian Japanese War of 1904-05 and from World War I, Nazi General Erich Luderndorff argued in his *The Total War*[76] that modern war encompasses all of society; thus, the military should spare no one. The Fascist Italian General Giulio Douhet echoed this theme. By targeting civilians, he said, an army could advance more rapidly. "Air-delivered terror" effectively removes civilian obstacles.

That doctrine took on new meaning. In April 1937, Nazi pilots dropped their bombs on Guernica, the ancient Basque capital. A year earlier, in 1936, the Spanish Civil War had erupted. General Francisco Franco, supported by fascist governments in Italy and Germany, led an armed uprising against the Republic. When the residents of Guernica resisted, Franco asked his Nazi partners to punish these stubborn people who had withstood his army's assault.

The people of Guernica had no anti-aircraft guns, much less fighter planes to defend their city. The Nazi pilots knew that at 4:30 in the afternoon of market day, the city's center would be jammed with shoppers from all around the areas.

Before flying on their "heroic mission," the German pilots had shared a toast with their Spanish counterparts in a language that both could understand: "Viva la muerte," they shouted as their raised their *copas de vino*. The bombing of Guernica introduced a concept in which the military would make no distinction between civilians and combatants. Death to all!

Almost 1,700 people died that day and some 900 lay wounded. Franco denied that the raid ever took place and blamed the destruction of Guernica on those who defended it, much as the U.S. military intimates that the "insurgents" forced the savage attack by daring to defend their city and then hide inside their mosques. Did the public in 1937 face the equivalent of the Peterson case that commanded their attention?

Where is the new Picasso who will offer a dramatic painting to help the 21st Century public understand that what the U.S. Air Force and army artillery just did to the people of Falluja resembles what the Nazis did to Guernica?

In Germany and Italy in 1937, the media focused on the vicissitudes suffered by those pilots who were sacrificing for the ideals of their country by combating a "threat." The U.S. media prattles about the difficulties encountered by the marines. It never calls them bullies who occupy another people's country and kill civilians and destroy their homes and mosques, or accuses them of subduing patriots with superior technology.

On November 15, an embedded NBC cameraman filmed a U.S. soldier murdering a wounded Iraqi prisoner in cold blood. As CNN showed the tape, its reporter offered "extenuating circumstances" for the assassination we had witnessed. The wounded man might have booby-trapped himself as other "insurgents" had done. After all, these marines had gone through hell in the last week.

The reporting smacks of older imperial wars, Andrew Greely reminded us. "The United States has fought unjust wars before— Mexican American, the Indian Wars, Spanish American, the Filipino Insurrection, Vietnam. Our hands are not clean. They are covered with blood, and there'll be more blood this time."[77]

Falluja should serve as the symbol of this war of atrocity against the Iraqi people, our Guernica. But, as comedian Chris Rock insightfully points out, George W. Bush has distracted us. That's why he killed Laci Peterson, why he snuck that young boy into Michael Jackson's bedroom and the young woman into Kobe Bryant's hotel room. He wants us not to think of the war in Iraq. We need a new Picasso mural, "Falluja," to help citizens focus on the themes of our time, not the travails of the Peterson case to divert us.

The Bush Administration sensed the danger of such a painting. Shortly before Colin Powell's February 5, 2003 UN Security Council power point presentation, where he made the case for invading Iraq, UN officials, at U.S. request, placed a curtain over a tapestry of Picasso's "Guernica," located at the entrance to the Security Council chambers. As a TV backdrop, the anti-war mural would contradict the spirit of the Secretary of State's case for war in Iraq. Did the dead painter somehow know that his mural would foreshadow another Guernica, called Falluja?

Bush was not the first President to offer zany explanations for going to war.

Listening and Talking to God About Invading Other Countries

"I went down on my knees and prayed Almighty God for light and guidance more than one night. And one night late it came to me...:(1) That we could not give them [the Philippines] back to Spain—that would be cowardly and dishonorable; (2) that we could not turn them over to France and Germany—our commercial rivals in the Orient—that would be bad business and discreditable; (3) that we could not leave them to themselves—they were unfit for self-government—and they would soon have anarchy and misrule over there worse than Spain's was; and (4) that there was nothing left for us to do but to take them all, and to educate the Filipinos, and uplift and civilize and Christianize them, and by God's grace do the very best we could by them, as our fellow-men for whom Christ also died. And then I went to bed, and went to sleep, and slept soundly, and the next morning I sent for the ... War Department map-maker, and I told him to put the Philippines on the map of the United States (pointing to a large wall map), and there they are, and there they will stay while I am President!"[78]

PRESIDENT WILLIAM McKINLEY'S WORDS SHOULD ECHO WITH President Bush and his Evangelical zealots. Like the Republican who initiated U.S. overseas military expansion, the current President also talks to God and hears His words. Like McKinley, Bush understands that the stars and stripes stand for inseparable U.S. commercial interests and pious purposes.

Until 1933, 120,000 U.S. troops occupied the Philippines. "Pacifying" those "heathens" took longer than McKinley thought and brought out the brute in the soul of U.S. Christian soldiers.

Long before troops destroyed the Vietnamese village "to save it" in the 1960s, and a century plus before GIs decimated Falluja and killed thousands of its residents to bring democracy to Iraq, their predecessors committed atrocities in the Philippines.

One frustrated U.S. general even ordered troops to kill every Philippine male over age ten. Fortunately, that order was not carried out, but U.S. troops did slay up to 200,000 Philippine men and women in three years, until overwhelming superiority in weapons and sheer ruthlessness overcame local resistance forces. Two thousand U.S. servicemen died as well.

One critical citizen satirized McKinley's war: "G is for guns/ That McKinley has sent/ To teach Filipinos/ What Jesus Christ meant."

The bible thumpers of the time praised McKinley's will in overcoming Satan (Filipinos, not Arabs) with military force. Now, 108 years later, as scientists map the human genetic structure and discover secrets of the galaxy, the descendents of the religious zealots that counseled McKinley try to win court battles to validate creationism and push Armageddon and Rapture as practical themes of U.S. Middle East policy.

How can educated people—using high technology and science—believe that God revealed His Middle East plan to Pat Robertson and Jerry Falwell?

In October 2004, Robertson, the aging Baptist Maharishi, told some 4,000-plus pilgrims in Jerusalem's convention center that devious Muslims intended to foil "God's plan" to let Israel hold on to its lands.

Robertson interpreted Islam's intention "to destroy Israel and take the land from the Jews and give East Jerusalem to Yasser Arafat, [the Palestinian Authority Chairman who died in November 2004]... as Satan's plan to prevent the return of Jesus Christ the Lord."[79]

Robertson's fellow Baptist preacher Jerry Falwell has proclaimed strong support for Israel and simultaneously evinced blatant anti-Semitism.

"A few of you don't like the Jews and I know why," Falwell sanctimoniously told his congregation. "They can make more money accidentally than you can on purpose."[80]

Too bad such accidents don't happen to me, I thought. The Biblicists have placed me inside a contradictory construction. As a Jew I remain an object of their scorn, since I descended from the tribe that betrayed Jesus. But I could move to Israel and convert to rabid Zionism that calls for shooting Arabs as part of the Lord's work. I would then become an instrument of the Lord in removing pagan Palestinians from their lands so Jews can occupy it. Then God can orchestrate the final wars in that region (which will involve the whole world) so that Robertson, Falwell and company can enjoy their own special rapture. Whew!

Imagine Falwell and his pious congregation dropping acid amidst velveteen paintings of Jesus, as the clean-cut Liberty Baptist Church of Lynchburg, Virginia sings "Jesus Is All the World to Me."

The support Israel dogma—especially its extremists—has reached deep into the White House. President Bush even called Ariel Sharon "a man of peace."[81] Sharon should have sued Bush for slander for casting doubt on his record as an unrelenting warrior. At least Sharon could have retaliated by calling Bush "a great intellectual."

Israeli extremists don't seem to mind that the most fervent supporters of "a greater Israel" make anti-Semitic comments. "God does not hear the prayer of Jews," I heard one Texas TV preacher announce in 1980. To prove his love for Israel, however, he showed a Star of David that he hung from a chain on his neck. "A present from Menachem Begin [former Israeli Prime Minister]," he announced. He agreed in principle with Begin that "all Jews should be in Israel."

The preacher denied he was anti-Semitic. "An anti-Semite," he explained, "hates Jews more than he's supposed to." Would Jesus have endorsed such flummery? "Would Jesus wear a pinky ring, would he drive a fancy car? Would Jesus wear a Rolex on his television show?" asked country satirist Ray Stevens.

Life outstrips satire, however, when it comes to Robertson's intimate relationship with God, especially as He dictates political moves. Using God's name, Robertson sent "notice" to Osama bin Laden and Palestinian militant groups that "you will not frustrate God's plan" to have Jews rule the Holy Land until the Second Coming of Jesus."

"God alone," Robertson declared, "should decide if Israel should give up the Gaza Strip and the West Bank, captured in the 1967 Arab-Israeli War." According to Robertson, "God says, 'I'm going to judge those who carve up the West Bank and Gaza Strip.'" He continued reciting God's words. "'It's my land and keep your hands off it.'" Israeli officials and Knesset members gleefully attended the October gatherings of Robertson's pilgrims in Jerusalem.[82] Robertson and Falwell claim that the Bible predicts the Messiah's return to the Holy Land at the time the Jews defeat the pagans.

I understand that Israelis need the pilgrims' tourist dollars, but many Jews laugh at "Messiah babble." A Jew tells his wife that after months of unemployment the elders hired him to stand outside the village gate and greet the Messiah when he comes—but for only 2 kopeks a month.

"You'll work for such low pay?" his wife asked incredulously.

"Don't worry," he reassured her, "it's a lifetime job."

Shortly after the birth of Israel a New Yorker told his wife to pack their belongings. "The rabbis said that all Jews must move to Israel to greet the Messiah."

"Are you crazy," his wife replied. "After spending all that money fixing up the house, I'm not moving."

The Israeli government, however, has submerged humor and forged close alliances with fundamentalist Christians. In return, evangelicals contribute big bucks to Israel and lobby for pro-Israeli policies.

However, Israeli officials turn blind eyes to Reverend Falwell's verbal transgressions. As recently as January 14, 1999, Jerry Falwell speculated on "the Anti-Christ."

"Is he alive and here today?" asked Falwell. "Probably. Because when he appears during the Tribulation period he will be a full-grown counterfeit of Christ. Of course he'll be Jewish and male."[83] I looked in the mirror when I read that statement. Could it be me? "Of course he'll pretend to be Christ." I breathed easier since I had no such pretensions. But what about other Jewish men? Well, most of them didn't vote for Bush, or believe that God spoke to him—or McKinley for that matter. Reasonable people don't think that God ordered Bush to bring freedom (free markets) to the Middle East. Indeed, as Lily Tomlin quipped, "Talking to God is prayer. God talking to you is schizophrenia."

Poor intelligence also contributed to the bloody mistakes made by former presidents, who followed triumphal rhetoric rather than fact-based analysis.

Lessons from Vietnam: Wars Kill Empires as Well as People

I N 2005, THE UNITED STATES BECAME COMMUNIST VIETNAM'S single-largest trading partner. Ironically, as Vietnam's products permeate U.S. stores, the "Vietnam War trauma" remains central to U.S. politics. Note how the Vietnam service record of presidential candidates arose as a contentious issue in the 2004 elections. People don't overcome traumas unless they understand them.

Since public education provides citizens with minimal context, we rely on mass media to reach into its collective attic and drag out "Fall of Saigon" stories. However, when the commercial press pushes the anniversary method of history teaching, the public tends to divorce rather than engage with its past connections.

Personal anecdotes overwhelm analysis. Relatives of dead soldiers weep at Washington's Vietnam Wall; others relive battles and deaths of comrades. Few media presentations offer the past as a way to learn for the future. Nor do they apply to the U.S. occupations of Iraq and Afghanistan the lessons of the Vietnam War. Vietnamese refer to that period between the early 1960s and April 1975 as "The American Phase," since they also suffered periods of foreign domination by Chinese, Japanese and French occupiers who, unlike the Americans, learned the painful lesson of trying to subdue and occupy that land.

U.S. leaders adamantly refuse to grasp the obvious: some people, like Koreans, Vietnamese and Iraqis, for examples, do not submit to force and brutality. How to teach that simple lesson?

Teachers will have shared the experience of trying to educate students who have not ingested their own history. Instead of absorbing historical context from first grade on, U.S. students learn a kind of patriotic mythology. Words like "unbiased" obfuscate history. Critiques of U.S. behavior in Vietnam, or Iraq, seem to require the presentation of the good side of torture, mass murder and the napalming of villages—or at least excuses for it.

A Voice of America reporter sympathized with U.S. historians who "have struggled for years to find a fair and balanced way to teach students about the Vietnam War—and the atrocities committed there by U.S. soldiers."[84]

"Fair and balanced" sound discordant in the era of Fox News and CNN. Teachers should show students news clips of the inglorious U.S. retreat from Saigon in April 1975. Military helicopters took off from the Embassy with desperate Vietnamese clients clinging to them and falling to the ground.

High school and many college texts don't tell that story. Steve Jackson, an Indiana University of Pennsylvania Political Science professor, found that students in his Introduction to American Politics course "have little if any knowledge about the Vietnam War and its lessons. He finds that appalling, especially in light of the U.S.'s current involvement in Iraq."[85]

Gore Vidal calls this syndrome "The United States of Amnesia." As memorials abounded and the media teemed with veterans recalling fallen comrades and anecdotes of combat, many school boards wanted history taught as simplistic lessons of right and wrong in which our leaders might make mistakes, but don't do evil.

As a result of such tampering with high school history teaching, my college students don't know that the U.S. military dropped more bombs on Southeast Asia than they did in World War Two. General Curtis LeMay even wanted to bomb Vietnam "back to the Stone Age." How Christian!

Despite overwhelming military superiority, the U.S. lost in Vietnam. When American forces departed in 1975, the U.S. puppet army in Saigon "had over three times as much artillery, twice as many tanks and armored cars, 1,400 aircraft and a virtual monopoly of the air and "a two-to-one superiority of combat troops."[86]

Seven years earlier, the North Vietnamese lost a major battle and won the war. In late January 1968, the armies of the North and National Liberation Front of the South staged an armed uprising during Tet, the Vietnamese holiday. General Vo Nguyen Giap and the other Hanoi leaders had decided that the levels of casualties exacted by massive U.S. artillery shelling and bombing had become intolerable. Giap's quick military victory plan called for coordinated attacks on targets near the South Vietnam border to lure U.S. troops away from the cities, where dramatic assaults would take place by Viet Cong (the pro Communist forces in the South and by regular North Vietnamese troops who had infiltrated South Vietnam's urban areas). Giap predicted that such bold and large scale initiatives would also inspire citizens to revolt against the puppet South Vietnamese government. The fall of this U.S.-backed regime would then remove the last pretext for occupation and the Americans would withdraw.

Giap achieved his goals, but his plan didn't work. The puppet government didn't fall. U.S. forces took about 1,100 casualties and many more wounded, but then retaliated, inflicting very heavy casualties on Giap's troops—some 35,000 killed and 60,000 wounded. But Giap's plan did lead to an unanticipated victory in the home front propaganda war. TV news clips showed Viet Cong fighting their way inside the heavily-guarded U.S. Embassy in Saigon, thus dramatizing the gap between official statements of optimism about the enemy's weakness and the real battlefield facts.

The fact that the Tet offensive took place after repeated official assurances of impending victory—seeing "light at the end of the tunnel," according to Defense Secretary McNamara—so undermined the war propagandists' efforts that public opinion swayed convincingly against the war.

Seven years after Tet, the TV public saw images of U.S. embassy officials burning documents and U.S. money to prevent the rapidly advancing Communists from getting them. These pictures and the commentaries that accompanied them induced disgust and serious doubt about the wisdom of U.S. leaders.

Three years later, if doubts persisted about the duplicity of U.S. officials, Daniel Ellsberg, a former national security official, released to the *New York Times* a massive archive of classified documents. The *Pentagon Papers,* as they were called, confirmed that Lyndon Johnson had lied and covered up important facts about the origins of the war. Worse, neither he nor any other official had devised a plan to end the war and leave. The credibility gap between government and people became unbridgeable.

Most Americans don't remember or know why the United States intervened and then got deeper into Vietnam. Its leaders had not learned from Korea, where another tough Asian foe fought U.S. troops to a bloody standstill. Bush has repeated the murderous and futile scenario in Iraq. In each war, the U.S. killing machine slaughtered many more natives than Americans. In Vietnam, Lyndon Johnson confessed to his National Security Adviser McGeorge Bundy that he didn't "think it's worth fighting for." But he neverhtless continued to send hundreds of thousands of troops to kill and die—and ultimately lose. Some of his advisers, like Walt Rostow, continued to provide him with optimistic scenarios that flew in the face of the facts.

In that same vein, Stephen J. Morris of Johns Hopkins University's School of Advanced International Studies blamed anti-war lobbying for convincing Congress to cut funding, thus assuring the Communist victory in Vietnam.[87] How many *NY Times* readers will recall the instant collapse of the militarily superior, U.S.-trained South Vietnamese army when they had to fight?

How many will remember that the United States invented South Vietnam in 1955 as a way to avert a national electoral victory by President Ho Chi Minh? Or that rampant corruption characterized all the U.S.-picked regimes there? How many will know that the U.S. chose Catholics to rule a predominantly Buddhist population? Morris' sour grapes scenario belies the facts: in early 1975, South Vietnam showed all the signs of decomposition.

The Times omitted historian Gabriel Kolko's vital lessons. "Successive administrations in Washington have no capacity whatsoever to learn from past errors. Total defeat in Vietnam 30 years ago should have been a warning to the U.S.: Wars are too complicated for any nation, even the most powerful, to undertake without grave risk. They are not simply military exercises in which equipment and firepower is decisive, but political, ideological, and economic challenges also. The events of South Vietnam 30 years ago should have proven that."[88]

In Iraq, Bush repeats Lyndon Johnson's sinful stupidity of wasting a surplus on military and security madness. Congress' 2005 budget froze domestic spending, but not military and "security" funding. Bush's advisers should read him Pat Buchanan's lines from *A Republic, Not an Empire*: "...all the empires had disappeared. How did they perish? By war—all of them."

Outsourcing War

IN THE FACULTY DINING ROOM AT THE CALIFORNIA STATE UNIVERSITY, a Mexican-American woman places the thin slice of turkey on the bread to make my sandwich. The stress lines that radiate down from her high cheekbones twitch as she tells me politely that she's fine. One of her sons is in Afghanistan, she reports. The other will leave tomorrow for Iraq. "I pray every day," she says, smearing the mayonnaise on the other slice of bread.

"Why did the kids join the military?"

"The older joined the National Guard," she informs me, with still a trace of an accent. "He thought he wouldn't see real action. The other one just wanted to fight overseas." She smiles, resigned to her lack of control over adolescents growing up in a combat culture. "He's a good boy, but believes what the whatcha' call 'em guys told him, you know, the ones that look for kids to join up?"

I ask how she feels.

"I ask God to return them to me," she says. "Do you think they'll be alright?

"I hope they will," I say. "But I don't know."

"What can I do to bring them home? I'm desperate."

Desperation describes the mood of hundreds of thousands of Latino parents whose kids serve in the war zones of Afghanistan and Iraq. It also describes the current behavior of the rich and confident managers of the US empire who have gotten almost 200,000 young men and women stuck in two quagmires without an exit strategy.

Bush's Middle East wars and the subsequent occupation of large countries by the US military and the National Guard, have not only divided the nation and fomented deep anti-American sentiment throughout the world. They have also strained the resources of the mighty Pentagon. The 2005-6 "Defense Budget" of $640+ billion—counting the Intelligence budget—came to almost twice what the rest of the world spent on "defense." For his 2007 Budget, Bush proposed $439.3 billion for defense (not counting Iraq and Afghanistan costs).

Until the 21st Century Middle East wars, the military casually filled its recruiting quota from amongst poor youth around the country. National Guard service appeared attractive since the chances of having to ever engage in an actual war seemed remote to hundreds of thousands of volunteers.

That all changed quickly after Bush invaded Afghanistan and Iraq and discovered that he did not have enough troops to occupy both places. So, he called up the Guard and launched an aggressive recruiting campaign. But news of the growing count of dead and wounded filtered through the Administration's optimistic spin and even the least informed and usually gullible teenagers began to think twice about "joining up."

In order to get the young flesh "to serve" without the draft in the almost 2 million strong armed forces, the Pentagon raised salaries and increased benefits. From top to bottom, military salaries jumped between three and four times in less than twenty years. In 1981, a private, the lowest rank, earned less than $4,500 a year. Today, that same rank comes with a salary of almost $15,000. A corporal, two short grades up, leaped from $5,000 to $22,000. In addition, he or she gets free food, housing and clothing—uniform—and discounts on most consumer goods.

Officers, many without post graduate levels of formal education, can earn up to $125,000 and enjoy the privileges of elite clubs, like ski resorts in the Alps, and have private jets at their service. High ranking officers have servants and other perks. For the first time in its history, the United States has a large, standing professional army.

Yet, by 2003, despite increases in salaries and bonuses—and other promises of free training and education—offered by the armed forces, the recruiters fell short of their quotas. In the past, the slogan "be all you can be in the army" might have lured the innocent, but now even the barely literate began to feel the sway of opposite stories, of how friends and family members got killed or permanently disabled by IEDs (improvised explosive devices). The body count and wounded numbers rose in the war zones. By January 2007, some 3000 US servicemen and women had died; estimates of more than 25,000 wounded.

The Iraq War had become so unpopular that H. L. Mencken's old phrase no longer applied. "No one ever went broke underestimating the intelligence of the American public."

"As dimwitted as American teenagers are," a Mexican-American army recruiter confessed to me in June 2005 in Pomona California, "they're not stupid enough to fall for the crap we're selling to get them to go to Iraq or Afghanistan. Don't quote me."

I'm quoting him, but omitting his name and rank. His parents came from Sinaloa and settled in San Bernardino, where he grew up and decided to make an army career after he dropped out of high school. "It pays OK and I don't work too hard. I'd rather be here than in Iraq or Afghanistan. I'll tell you that."

His partner, a young woman with sergeant stripes on her sleeve whispers to him in Spanish. *"Estas loco? No digas mas. No te chingas cabron."* He laughs.

Next to his recruiting table outside the university student center, some undergraduates had set up a "de-cruiting" table, offering prospective recruits "the facts about the US military," including the numbers of dead and wounded that the two wars had already exacted. In addition, the anti-military students "clarified" some of the army's promises about big loans and other supposed benefits, which they claimed were far less than the military had promised. They had statements from some returning wounded veterans to the effect that the army had docked their pay and cut their benefits.

The sergeant made no attempt to counter the students at the adjoining table. He handed out pamphlets, shook hands and laughed. "It's my job. I have a quota of kids to recruit, so what the Hell."

Hell, indeed. That word has spread even to those black and Latino communities that have traditionally supplied more than their share of youth for the US military's frequent overseas and violent excursions.

Faced with shortages of manpower, the ever inventive Pentagon began to look abroad for fresh meat to send to Iraq. The closest neighbors to the South make an ideal recruitment arena: widespread poverty and unemployment. The armed forces offer citizenship to "illegals" who enlist.

In addition, young Latin American men will cost the Pentagon much less than home-grown soldiers, just as they do when they work in the maquilas (foreign-owned factories that produce goods mainly for the US market) rather than in US factories.

Like the maquila owners, who engage contractors to find them workers for their factories, the Pentagon also hired companies—American of course—to find "outsourced mercenaries" for the Iraq occupation. Like the outsourcing of other jobs, third world people take positions once held by Americans at much lower wages—but higher than they could make at home.

For "illegal" Mexicans or those who want a quick route to citizenship, the military holds a strong attraction. Since Mexico provides the closest and most logical recruiting arena, Mexican "illegals" numerically outstrip all other Latin Americans living in the United States and in Iraq itself. Some 8,000 Mexicans have now volunteered for official military service.[89] Mexicans and those of Mexican descent make up more than half of the approximately 110,000 Latinos mostly, Puerto Ricans, Dominicans, and Central Americans currently serving in the U.S. military. In addition, almost 25,000 other Mexicans have enlisted as a means of obtaining US citizenship. Coyotes smuggled some of these Mexicans into the country as children who never had any "legal" documents.

The recruiters target high schools with heavy population of Mexican descent. The Marines have had particular success in their forceful publicity campaign. They claim that youth of Mexican origin make up 13% of the Corps. But that high percentage of Latinos also shows up in the high dead and wounded count.

If US corporations can outsource jobs, why can't the Pentagon outsource war? After all, role reversal has characterized the globalization period. The United States once imported cheap raw material from Latin America and made finished goods in its booming factories. Now, it exports raw materials and parts to Mexican and Central American maquilas where low wage Latinos and Latinas make clothing, auto parts, electric goods, computer and TV chases and finished wood products.

For much of the 19th and 20th Centuries, US troops invaded Latin America. Indeed, not one country in the Hemisphere has escaped the presence of uninvited US personnel. Now, the United States recruits Latin American troops to train in its homeland bases and then ships them to the Middle East.

In late February 2005, Salvadoran President Elias Antonio Saca unashamedly welcomed "his heroes," a unit of soldiers returning from Iraq. Then he thanked President Bush while school kids he recruited for the ceremony waved flags—US and Salvadoran.

These "coalition of the willing" troops represented the pay-off for bribes offered by Washington to the rest of Latin America. Most presidents did not bite. Those in Colombia, Costa Rica, the Dominican Republic, El Salvador, Honduras, Nicaragua and Panama did offer token forces. But most of the willing turned unwilling when the occupation of Iraq turned into a sticky situation and the elaborate promises made by Bush didn't materialize. El Salvador is the only Latin American country to remain in the coalition with some 340 soldiers troops left in Iraq.

As most other nations withdrew their troops and US National Guard members began serving longer tours of duty, much to the dismay of their families, recruiters found El Salvador a fertile recruiting ground.

"I guess the Central American wars of the 1980s paid off," laughed a mid level State Department official, who would speak to me only if I promised not to use his name. "Tens of thousands of soldiers, officers, cops and private security people got laid off when peace came. Now, we need them. Pretty ironic, huh?"

Indeed, private "contractors" working for the Pentagon hired some 700 Salvadoran "professionals" to provide food services, transportation, guard oil pipelines and refineries, diplomatic missions and anyone important enough to merit a bodyguard.[90]

By paying Latino Americans trained in firearms and other repressive skills up to $3,000 a month, the Pentagon's private recruiting companies flesh out its ranks in Iraq. They're "having no problem finding recruits," said Dan Briody, author of *The Halliburton Agenda: The Politics of Oil and Money* (2004). He estimates that the United States has hired more than one private security professional for every 10 American soldiers in Iraq.

Contractors and even subcontractors have also recruited in Chile, Colombia, Nicaragua and Guatemala. Because these countries have all trained huge numbers of young men in the "science" of killing and other police and military-related activities, they make ideal pools for Iraq head hunters.

But in May 2003, no one expected to outsource the war. Indeed, the White House heavies expected Iraqis to kiss and throw flowers at them; not have a prolonged occupation that turned into a mass graveyard and mutilation arena for US service men and women. Bush's triumphal "Mission Accomplished" speech on the aircraft carrier USS Abraham Lincoln did not prepare the nation for the sobering facts that gradually begin to leak into the media.

Even before the bloody November 2004 battle of Falluja which exacted a heavy toll, Mexican families began to feel the pain of war. The dead, the legless, armless, eyeless and brain dead wounded began to come home. On both sides of the Rio Grande, Mexican parents shared a common anguish.

122 Latinos were among the first 1000 U.S. casualties in Iraq. 70 of them were of Mexican descent.

On December 24, 2004, the day before Christmas, Sergio Diaz Varela died in Ramadi. His family and friends attended his funeral in Guadalajara, where "armed troops from Fort Hood, Texas led by General Ken Keene accompanied the young soldier to his final resting place, and U.S. ambassador Tony Garza commended the boy's soul to God."[91]

Similar funerals took place in San Luis de la Paz, Guanajuato and in the altos of Jalisco. On the invasion day, the first GI killed was Mexican-American. Fernando Suarez del Solar, father of Jesus, a resident of Escondido, California, spoke in Spanish. The 48 year old man, slight of build, said he had immigrated from Tijuana in 1997. He now works as cashier at a convenience store and delivers newspapers.

He began hesitatingly in Spanish. "Today I demand the immediate return of our troops," he told a student audience at the California State Polytechnic University in California. "I lost my son, my Aztec warrior, Jesus Alberto, because of negligence from the American command in Iraq in this illegal war full of lies by President Bush."

As he spoke he seemed to gain confidence and strength. "You know that my son died when he stepped on a 'friendly' grenade, a grenade put there the previous night by the Army who never advised my son's unit and gave them the order to advance and since my son was the explorer he stepped on one of them and he waited almost three hours to receive medial attention until a helicopter arrived with help. This is a death from our invincible army? This is a death from the protection that our kids are given?" A tear of grief or rage or both fell onto his cheek.

He got no answers from the Pentagon. So, he traveled to Iraq to find the truth about his son's death. He joined Military Families Speak Out. With other relatives of dead and wounded servicemen and women, he speaks and organizes against the war. But no such organization exists for the thousands of non-US-based Latin Americans that have also contracted to serve the US cause in Iraq.

Far from the recruiting tables on high school and college campuses, internet ads and word of mouth through the military and ex military clubs have led to the recruitment of Colombian gunmen for work in Iraq. The internet is loaded with such opportunities. "We are seeking talented individuals willing and capable of working as a Protective Security Specialist in a high risk environment. (Must be willing to deploy to Iraq or Afghanistan for 3mo., 6mo., and up to 1 year). Immediate Openings—Effective in September 2005 APPLY VIA OUR WEBSITE (www.hctactics.com). Skills required: Individuals with prior military, law enforcement and close protection/bodyguarding experience preferred."

Another ad under www.iraqijobcenter.com tells job seekers that "Your New career in IRAQ starts here. Posting your resume on Iraqi Job Center, you are taking the first step to a great new career! Post your profile and resume for FREE and find the perfect job!"

On May 15, 2005 in the "Jobs Wanted" section of Epi Security and Investigation Company's website, Pedro Buenaño of Ecuador described himself as "Mercenary, payed killer." He would accept work in Afghanistan, Iraq, Iran, Kuwait and of course the United Kingdom and the United States. He described his qualifications: "My experience dates from 25 years ago specialized in INFANTERY (sic) and handling of arms."

Manuel Alfonso Becerra Santillan of Peru posted his qualifications on July 10. "My desire is to work in security, Petroleum coast outside, in countries like Iraq, Nigeria, Afghanistan, Kuwait, and all country that is in hostile situation."

Epi is based in Manta, Ecuador and was managed by American Jeffrey Shippy, a US citizen. The website claims that Iraqijobcenter "is owned and run by the private Dutch company NOURAS. Iraqi job center offers its service for free for job seekers and employers."

46 year old Rafael Orlando of Ambato Ecuador lists his resume for a security job in the war zone. He offers extensive experience in naval security.

According to Pascale Mariani and Roméo Langlois writing in *Le Figaro*,[92] this company helped private military companies operating in Iraq employ "over a thousand Colombian combat-trained ex-soldiers and policemen." Some of these men were "trained by the US Navy and the DEA to conduct anti-drug and anti-terrorist operations in the jungles of Colombia" and "ready to work for $2,500 to 5,000 a month," said Jeffrey Shippy. He promised "considerable savings for a high quality product" to his clients.

When police looked for the aggressive Shippy, they found his luxury home abandoned. They did discover however, that he previously worked for DynCorp, a private US company that illegally sprayed Colombian coca farms.

Another American recruiting company, Hostile Control Tactics LLC of Fairfax Virginia (www.hctactics.com), offered to "provide in-depth training to individuals willing to acquire the necessary skills to do the job." It promises salaries of "$500.00 per day—up to $1,000.00 per day." In addition, they offer "Bonus pay raises" based on peer review system.

Such campaigns to use private mercenaries from Latin America and other parts of the world in lieu of US troops, has led to the rise of a parallel army. More than 20,000 non-US mercenaries supplement the regular troops in Iraq.

Diego Martinez served in the Colombian Navy and then went to Iraq "for a British military company, alongside about thirty other Colombians. I'm not "a lawless, faithless mercenary," he told *Le Figaro*. He boasted about his time in Baghdad escorting "important people between the airport and the Green Zone.

Like his fellow Colombian mercenaries, he has grown up with constant violence. For this reason, he thought Colombians were superior in security work.

On January 17, 2005, *El Tiempo* reported that Halliburton had "recruited 25 retired Colombian police and army officers to provide security for oil infrastructure in Iraq." The officers met in Bogota, in early December, "with a Colombian colonel working on behalf of Halliburton Latin America, who offered them monthly salaries of $7,000 to provide security for oil workers and facilities in several Iraqi cities."[93]

Imagine the power such pay holds in a poverty-stricken country!

Formerly headed by US Vice President Dick Cheney, Halliburton is the recipient of largest amount of government money for Iraq construction and along with its subsidiary, Brown and Root, has been accused of overcharging and accounting discrepancies.[94] A Colombian government source confirmed the story, *El Tiempo* reported. Halliburton officials denied it.

Blackwater, another US company that trains mercenaries, sent its pros into a Colombian military school in Bogotá, with permission from the authorities. Previously, Blackwater had recruited and trained Chilean military personnel, from the Pinochet days, to Iraq. No one knows the exact number of Latin American mercenaries now serving in Iraq. But they may be almost as numerous as US troops.

In early October 2005, my friend in the cafeteria asked me: "If they have so many private troops from Latin America in Iraq, why do they need my son?" She smiled sadly. "I hope Carlito, he's the older one, comes home for Christmas. But he doesn't know yet. He's in a place called Tikrit now and says the locals don't seem to like us all that much. What can I do? I pray."

Fernando Suarez does more than ask God for help. "Señor Bush," he shouted to a California student group in the Fall of 2004. "How many sons of ours does he need to fill his gasoline tank? How many dead American sons does he need to stop this war full of lies? I do not want any more dead sons of fathers, husbands. Stop this now!!! Señor Bush, I hope that God forgives you, because I can't."

Breaking the Constitution

"If somebody from al-Qaeda is calling you, we'd like to know why. In the meantime, this program is conscious of people's civil liberties, as am I. This is a limited program designed to prevent attacks on the United States ... limited to calls from outside the United States to calls within the United States. But, they are of known numbers of known al-Qaeda members or affiliates...We're at war with a bunch of cold-blooded killers who will kill on a moment's notice. And I have a responsibility, obviously, to act within the law, which I am doing. It's a program that has been reviewed... a program to which the Congress has been briefed, and a program that is necessary to win this war and to protect the American people."—George W. Bush, Brooke Army Medical Center, San Antonio, January 1, 2006

BUSH'S STATEMENT TO WOUNDED TROOPS CONTAINS SEVERAL lies and distortions that do not coincide with published facts. His eavesdropping program did not protect civil liberties; nor did he design it to prevent attacks or limit it to "calls from outside the United States."

Wiretaps covered tens of thousands of people who had no contact with Al Qaeda and far removed from what the enemy is thinking—if such an entity has a brain. Bush acted outside the law. Congress had not been briefed. The few Members who knew anything about the program had misgivings. Several members denied receiving any briefing.

How does the United States win a war against "terrorism," a word connoting violence against civilians, which has been going on since the beginning of history? In the past, wars meant U.S. engagement with enemy nations, not concepts.

"I'm a wartime President," Bush said. Did I miss the headlines the day Congress declared war against the Republic of terrorism?

"Next thing you know," quipped Gore Vidal, "Bush will declare war against dandruff as well."

"And as commander in chief, I've got to use the resources at my disposal, within the law, to protect the American people," Bush explained as his reason for unauthorized wiretapping. How it fell under the aegis of the law we have yet to learn.

In addition, Homeland Security spooks open citizens' letters. In December 2005, retired University of Kansas history professor Grant Goodman told reporter Brock N. Meeks that he "received a letter from his friend in the Philippines that had been opened and resealed with a strip of dark green tape bearing the words 'by Border Protection' and carrying the official Homeland Security seal."[95]

In 1974, I received some of my own correspondence in some 1,400 pages from the FBI and CIA in response to my Freedom of Information Act (FOIA) request. The CIA sent me letters I had sent to friends abroad. I was shocked not only from discovering my disgraceful efforts at prose.

Frivolity aside, the explanations, then and now, for contravening time honored rights, have little resonance with reality. During the Cold War, U.S. leaders referred to "internal subversion," magnified by an external threat of Soviet world domination. This supposed superpower collapsed in 1989 without the United States firing a shot at it.

Robert Scherrer, a former FBI Agent, laughed about the countless hours he spent in the 1960s interviewing "little old Jewish grandmas in the Bronx who had been members of the Communist Party. They were always polite and offered me tea and cookies."

FBI Chief J. Edgar Hoover never pursued the Mafia with the vigor he showed in his assault on the left. Mafiosos apparently used against him a photo of the director clad in a tutu while tripping the light fantastic in his living room—in a house he shared with another high FBI official (male). The Mob also practiced surveillance. Like government prying, Mafia snooping related to extending their power.

When I was a university freshman in the 1950s, the FBI opened a file on me for writing a letter to the student newspaper supporting free speech for communists. The documents I received from the Bureau under the FOIA contained dozens of pages of transcripts of my phone conversations in the 1960s and 70s. I read transcripts of conspiratorial phone conversations I'd had with my father about when I would arrive at his Santa Monica home with my wife and kids and how my mother was doing with her diabetes treatments.

I don't know if anyone actually listened or if the FBI simply recorded and then transcribed these calls. Nor do I know how much it cost the government to carry out wiretapping on thousands of people who did not even contemplate engaging in crime.

In 1956, top FBI leaders invented COINTELPRO, the acronym for Counter Intelligence Program, to target the left and even liberals. COINTELPRO was supposed to "expose, disrupt, misdirect, discredit, or otherwise neutralize" protest movements and their leaders. The Bureau kept this invasiveness going until 1971.

FBI Director J. Edgar Hoover and his cronies considered as "subversive" not only those few loonies who declared their intentions of overthrowing the government, but the Southern Christian Leadership Conference led by Rev. Martin Luther King Jr., whose goal was racial integration. Yes, the Bureau targeted the Ku Klux Klan and handful of Nazis as well.

In those days, the government used the "communist threat" to justify such measures. Today, as in the past, blanket surveillance has no relationship to security. It does, however, produce insecurity. Indeed, it forms part and parcel of the power package that the Bush gang has employed to govern. Bush speechwriters use "protecting" as a metaphor for taking away citizens' rights.

Ironically, no Administration in my lifetime has proved so incompetent at protecting its people, and responding to emergency needs, even natural disasters when they arose. Asleep at the switch before 9/11, the ears of the NSA became super active. Does this electronic listening target Bush political enemies? Or does NSA listen indiscriminately and bug peoples' e-mail as well? And for what end?

The Bushies did not predict the Iraqi insurgency, nor did they impede the various acts of terrorism carried out by Al Qaeda fanatics in Madrid, London, Indonesia etc…

Homeland Security officials under Bush seem very adept at opening retired professors' personal mail, but as Frank Rich reported, a Christmas week independent audit by the Transportation Safety Administration's inspector general "found everything from FEMA to border control in some form of disarray."[96]

Yet, Rich continued, the President assures the nation regularly that his aim is to protect them—as he appoints incompetent "cronies into top jobs in immigration enforcement and state and local preparedness with recess appointments that by passed Congressional approval."

I find it strange that millions of Americans continue to believe anything Bush says. He now assures the public that those who exposed unauthorized wiretapping "put our citizens at risk." Did he think terrorists would not suspect that the U.S. government listened to their calls? Did he not know that for decades the FBI concerned itself with transcribing conversations about the family matters of tens of thousands of liberals and lefties rather than analyze messages about those planning to sabotage the country?

Dick Cheney went so far as to tell the public that had NSA carried out such non-authorized surveillance before 9/11, the attacks might have been prevented.

Did he forget that FBI agents and CIA officials had recorded material indicating something foul afoot, that then National Security Adviser Condi Rice did nothing with that data?

Bush is commander in chief of the most incompetent administration in U.S. history. It has one objective: the exercise of naked power. Its "anti-terrorist" rhetoric to justify overstepping laws and limits should appear as a clumsy façade to the citizens.

Unfortunately, knowledgeable members of Congress seem reluctant to shout: "The emperor has no clothes." And the media, as Marshall McLuhan said, are the message: keep the pubic confused and distracted so they can shop and vacation. As if to emphasize this, on October 5, 2001, less than a month after 9/11, Bush advised citizens to "Get down to Disney World in Florida. Take your families and enjoy life, the way we want it to be enjoyed."

My question is: can freedom to shop coexist with the growing infringements on other freedoms?

Jarhead: From Sparta to Iraq

"Human kindness has never weakened the stamina or softened the fiber of a free people. A nation does not have to be cruel to be tough."—Franklin D. Roosevelt

The film, "JARHEAD," DERIVED FROM ANTHONY SWOFFORD'S 2003 BOOK, portrays an important aspect of contemporary U.S. culture, one that has evolved from ancient Sparta. Indeed, the U.S. Marine Corps has helped recreate that legendary homo-erotic military relationship. Who would have thought of marines as engaged in barracks marriage?

A Jarhead, a marine's close cut hair and exposed skull, symbolizes that empty space that allows the Corps to transform a human being into a beast by filling his head with a primitive urge to kill. The ritual known as basic training turns youthful testosterone flow into savage and gleeful slaughter of enemy creatures. Conversely, a marine will sacrifice his own safety to save his close marine buddy—*semper fi.*

"People fight better when they know each other," Major General James Mattis explained to Pamela Hess in Iraq.⁹⁷

U.S. military re-conditioning of normal people begins later than the model the Spartans developed. Elder Spartan warriors and the older boys would initiate the younger ones to endure pain and hardship on the path to becoming a Spartan soldier and citizen.

In Gulf War I, as marines waited for months to invade Iraq, officers forced recruits to jog for miles at high noon at a fast pace with their M-16 rifles on their backs. The temperature: 115 plus degrees. But the officers decided the men needed "exercise."

These eighteen year old marines, however, had it better than their Spartan counterparts who were dragged out of the home and into the soldiers' barracks at age seven. Older, already conditioned boys picked fights to toughen the neophytes.

The Spartan boy did not scream when whipped or buggered. He received minimal food, which encouraged him to steal more of it. If caught, the elders would beat him. Proud and fierce Spartans dressed in uniforms. They shouted at their superior officer when he spoke to them. "Sir, yes sir." They also chanted when they marched—perhaps an equivalent of "Jodie was there when you left."

"You're right," the Spartan youth might have retorted.

Like pre-pubescent summer campers, the marines engage in thinly disguised sexual banter and physical play—to build up that esprit d'corps. The male-female role playing—in the form of a practical joke—becomes part and parcel of the molding process by which young adult men regress emotionally to the level of inadequate children, who cannot easily escape their conditioning—especially after having signed enlistment papers. The making of a modern marine still requires an elder drill instructor, to strip away layers of human sensibility from younger men. The boys shape their own macho-feminine culture in the jism-filled barracks.

"Sir, yes sir." We've heard it before in Stanley Kubrick's Vietnam epic, "Full Metal Jacket." The drill sergeant forces the vulnerable recruit to scream answers to stupid questions. This act of obedience to ridiculous orders or acquiescence to absurd statements becomes part of the shit-eating ritual because "that's the way the marines do it." The officers teach the youngsters to love this limited view of existence.

Those who cannot bear the loss of their sensibilities desert their unit, or commit suicide. In Iraq in 2004, the First Marine Division proudly announced that only two in the entire expeditionary force of marines had killed themselves.

"We just do not understand what happened. He was doing good." General Mattis explained. "There are hunters and there are victims. By your discipline, cunning, obedience and alertness, you will decide if you are a hunter or a victim. ... It's really a hell of a lot of fun. You're gonna have a blast out here. I feel sorry for every son of a bitch that doesn't get to serve with you."[98]

The rehearsal for Mattis' 2004 fun fest began in the fall of 1990, during Gulf War I. Jake Gyllenhaal, playing Swofford, arrives with shaven, glistening head to the Saudi Arabian sun. His unit of similarly hairless snipers begins the waiting ritual as coalition forces slowly accumulate. Indeed, they waited for half a year to strike.

To make cinema out of waiting time, director Sam Mendes ("American Beauty") interlaces desert shots and marines pissing, drinking and jerking off, so as to simulate boredom without boring the audience. The snipers bond as they play their boys' games and then we see Jake using his girl friend's photo to simulate love in the privacy of a desert latrine.

The tans, browns and golds of the Gulf nation (actually filmed in Mexico) seep onto the screen and finally, as comradeship replaces male-female relationships, the orders arrive. North to Iraq.

By this time, the audience realizes that the men in the unit cannot trust the women they left behind. One marine's wife sends him a cassette of "Deer Hunter," but instead of Robert DeNiro in Vietnam, the men see a porn scene—a woman bent over as a man enters her.

"That's my wife," screams a marine. The others whoop and holler. The woman says sadistically into camera: "Now who's cheating asshole!"

The corps proves far more trustworthy as family than those fickle women. While Swofford masturbates to his girl friend's photo, her letters indicate that she has already dropped him for someone here and now. He remains in denial, but his jealousy grows ugly and makes it easier for him to become comfortable in his new killer role, inside of a social ambience of murder and brotherly love.

A sublimating Spartan warrior emerges, projecting his need for female affection into an unquenchable desires to kill the "other." But Gulf War I meant endless waiting as President Bush (41) allowed coalition forces to build to a large size to insure overwhelming and rapid victory—in a war that would end at the Kuwait-Iraq border.

Finally, the troops deploy. U.S. fighters zoom above them. A missile sizzles and the marines witness "friendly fire" killing some of their own. During their trek, the sniper unit discovers Hell, first in the form of a car and truck graveyard, littered with charred bodies and pieces of them. The desert road to perdition includes scenes after Saddam's forces set fire to the Kuwaiti oil wells. Orange flames lick the night sky. Black rain drops down on the men's faces and uniforms. Then, a white horse emerges from the darkness, dripping oil and sweat, the symbol of inhuman destruction.

War or a Francis Bacon painting?

Swofford's sexual frustration, his anger and jealousy, his new conditioning have now combined to produce a burning desire for battle. His rifle has become the instrument of self-realization.

For Americans who feel confused, not sure about college, unhappy at the job, looking for some identification, the Marines loom as an acceptable fraternity, from which people don't ever quite reintegrate into society.

The marines trained Swofford to enjoy shooting people. Finally, he gets his chance, aims his sniper rifle at an Iraqi officer—only to have his first kill frustrated by the "fly boys" who demolished the entire building complex to kill one man.

The war ended before he could murder—thanks to some General's decision to use high-tech aircraft. Will the urge to kill push Swofford one day to climb a tower and start shooting people as veteran Charles Whitman did in Austin, Texas in 1966?

Troy (Peter Sarsgaard, "Kinsey"), an ex-con, scout and Swofford's partner, felt even more frustrated by the interruption of the lethal act for which they had received so much training. He leaves the Corps and dies. Since he lied about a previous criminal conviction, the Marines would not let him re-enlist. Once conditioned to become a Marine, the Corps become the logical social unit—war or no war.

Staff Sergeant Sykes Jamie Foxx ("Ray") exemplifies his love of the Corps. He tells Swofford that he could have worked for his brother-in-law and made a nice six figure income. Instead, he is in this inferno 10 thousand miles from home and family. "But I thank God for every day He's given me in the Corps." Indeed, he cannot envision life outside this narrow framework. Marines have become desensitized to all but their Corps life.

A decade later, U.S. forces occupy Iraq. Should we act surprised when the UN, Human Rights Watch and Amnesty International report that U.S. troops routinely kill and torture civilians?

The Marines symbolize a destructive force in U.S. culture. Kill others without questioning, act tough when sensitivity is called for, exhibit stoicism when pain should make you scream; empty honor, the old and stupid military values evolved to the high tech world. They will remain as a model of manhood—at least until the empire disintegrates.

Istanbul Poem

Two tired looking men
Playing twangy stringed instruments
Singing in late twilight
Violet skies of Istanbul
White birds flew patterns
Young men and women
Flitted near the platform
For image and angles
To capture the unique
Moment on digital technology

The harmony of men
Their thin gray hair
Blowing with gentle breezes
Their comfortable bellies supporting
Instruments to accompany melodic
Poems somehow demanded reproduction
Time and space had
No claim Originality surrendered
To the eminence gris
Inside tiny cameras that
Directed operators to shoot

Did the men sing
To recall the past?
The fall of Byzantium?
The collapse of Ottomans?
Did they name emperors

A Bush & Botox World

Who brought disgrace to
The Turkish people's reputation?
Or did their words
Capture the surreptitious movement
Of a woman gently
Sliding her delicate hand
Onto her lover's leg

Ancient battles flashed in
Notes and riffs in
Positions of the moon
The gruff voices recited
Lessons from times of
Dervishes and delights metaphors
Of possibilities and demise
They bowed to applause
Camera flashes popped paparazzi
Darted for positions to
Capture essences in virtual
Time as one paunchy musician
Picked a crumb from his
Hanging mustache and
With helping hands descended
From the platform to
A familiar chair below

The lights of importance
Dimmed amidst a rising
Black Sea moon a
Muezzin's electrified crackling voice
Demands attention from the
Departing crowd the musicians
Placing their strings in
Leather do not heed

The message the lovers
Hold hands the cameras
Hang by straps indicating
That the event has
Passed and warnings to
Praise God fall on
Deaf ears in Istanbul

*As empires pursue their quest for control of other peoples' countries,
they also destroy life and property and alter the destiny of entire
regions.*

Mission Accomplished: Iraq is Broken

S INCE THE EARLY 1950S, U.S. PRESIDENTS HAVE USED TROOPS
and the CIA to break other countries, not fix them. In
1953, the CIA shattered Iran's integrity by overthrowing the elected Mossadegh government. Twenty-six years later,
Iranians overthrew the U.S.-backed Shah. In 1979, Iranians
showed the depth of their rage by also seizing scores of U.S.
officials as hostages. The Ayatollah's regime labeled the United
States "the Great Satan"—for screwing their country.

In 1954, the CIA smashed Guatemala by overthrowing a democratically elected government and replacing it with a military
gang that killed and looted for forty years. Embraced by the
Pentagon, these gangsters in uniform slaughtered as many as
200,000 Guatemalans (mostly indigenous peasants) and stole
their land. The country has not yet recovered.

On September 11, 1973, Richard Nixon helped rupture Chile
by "destabilizing" its elected government.[99] For seventeen subsequent years, Washington supported a bloody military dictatorship led by General Augusto Pinochet,[100] a specialist in assassinating, disappearing and torturing his opponents at home
and abroad. In 1991, the civilian government's National Truth
and Reconciliation Commission listed Pinochet's crimes: 3,197
people assassinated or disappeared, tens of thousands tortured,
hundreds of thousands forced into exile.

In the 1980s, Ronald Reagan and George Bush waged covert
war against the Sandinista government of Nicaragua. In 2005, the
gains in health and education made by the Sandinistas have long
vanished. Nicaragua is the second poorest country in the hemi-

sphere, and its government ranks with the most corrupt. It was broken. (In November 2006, Sandinista Daniel Ortega won the presidency, despite Washington's dire warnings to Nicaraguan's voters.)

Washington backed ruthless military thugs in El Salvador with a thin façade of "democratic government" overlay. They murdered over 70,000 of their own people, including the Archbishop Oscar Romero and scores of priests and nuns. El Salvador, like Guatemala and Nicaragua, today suffers from high levels of daily crime and violence and serious poverty as well. But according to the State Department, all three of these crippled nations are "democratic."

In March 2003, George W. Bush ordered the U.S. military to break Iraq under the guise of democratizing it. The U.S. arsenal quickly destroyed the electricity and water supply, damaged sewage treatment and other vital sanitary facilities and pulverized bridges, other public places and thousands of homes. Nothing got fixed.

The U.S.-led Coalition still has not restored what it demolished in Iraq, nor reestablished services to the level of Saddam Hussein's regime. But they have killed and imprisoned tens of thousands of Iraqis, subjecting many of those to systematic torture.

Former prisoner Ali Abbas told journalist Dahr Jamail that to break the will of Iraqi prisoners, U.S. guards at Abu Ghraib "used electricity on us" while millions of homes lacked electricity for hours each day. "They also shit on us, used dogs against us...and starved us." As Abbas told Jamail, "the Americans delivered electricity to my ass before they brought it to my house."[101] Estimates of Iraqis in prison range as high as eighty thousand, most of whom have not been charged.

In 1991, during the first Gulf War, the breaking of Iraq began. U.S. planes and artillery delivered more than 300 tons of uranium tipped bombs and shells to targets in southern Iraq alone. Residue from these weapons turned into particles that people, including U.S. troops, inhaled.

To "punish" Saddam, the US and Great Britain pushed the UN to authorize sanctions following the war. Saddam did not miss a meal. The Iraqi people, whom this measure was supposed to help, suffered serious deprivation. Iraqi doctors and scientists thought that the outbreaks of infectious diseases, like typhoid and cholera, weakened the immune systems of Iraqi children and made them more vulnerable to cancer. In 2003, U.S. bombers and artillery dropped more depleted uranium tipped shells into the Iraqi environment.

In September 2002, I saw dying kids in the Baghdad Children's Hospital. Several Iraqi doctors had already surmised that only the presence of depleted uranium could have caused such a profound spike in the cancer rates among children.

In June 2005, Dr. Thomas Fasy of the Mt. Sinai School of Medicine concluded that data from Iraqi hospitals indicated that depleted uranium's effect had shown up dramatically in a more than 400% rise in children's cancer in just over a decade. Uranium ions bond with DNA and this, he said, has also caused a notable leap in children's leukemia rates along with sharply elevated incidences of congenital birth defects. The United States literally released cancer-causing material into Iraqi air, soil and water.

This toxic metal had performed the coup de grace to the Iraqi health system, already devastated by US bombing and embargo, Fasy said. The cost of such breakage: human life.[102]

On the economic front, Washington broke Iraq as well—of its socialist habit. U.S. colonial administrator J. Paul Bremer forced a constitution down Iraqi throats to subvert their statist economic system. He planned to privatize some 200 state-owned enterprises. Management of port facilities at Umm Qasr went to Stevedoring Services of America, a U.S. company. "Bremer studiously ignored the rapidly rising unemployment and social disorder that arose from the destruction of a social order." "If privatization isn't halted," wrote Naomi Klein, 'free Iraq' will be the most sold country on earth."[103]

But Iraqis resist. They continually sabotage the oil pipeline. Indeed, such tactics have caused major oil companies to lose enthusiasm for owning Iraqi oil. Besides, they do well under the current OPEC arrangement ($60 a barrel) and have no wish to change it.

Iraqi workers also have not welcomed the selling of state-owned factories to foreigners. Some work forces have even threatened to assassinate prospective buyers. This does not make investors feel as if modern Iraq provides a welcome climate.[104]

The chaos that engulfs Iraq does not improve from the presence of U.S. troops. Iraqis who testified in the Istanbul World Tribunal on Iraq told about intense hatred of their people for the occupiers. The Iraqis feel abused by far more than the publicized incidents at Abu Ghraib. On routine U.S. patrols and raids, trigger-happy young soldiers gun down innocent Iraqis. Pilots drop bombs on coordinates where people live.

The 2004 documentary "Gunner Palace" resembles scenes from the TV show *Cops*. GIs bash down doors, charge into homes with fingers on rifle triggers shouting "on the floor mother-fucker," while women scream and children cry. The humiliated and handcuffed men go to prison. The soldiers then return to their posh living quarters and count the days remaining before they can go home. Like the GIs in Vietnam three plus decades ago, those in Iraq sacrifice lives, limbs and psyches. But as the film makes clear, most don't know the purpose of their military mission.

Indeed, Iraqis recall well how U.S. troops watched passively while massive looting took place of their national, historic treasure (How does one fix a broken Babylon?). A crime wave swept the country and armed Americans shrugged. Women can no longer walk the streets in safety as they once did. The U.S.

occupation has also pitted Sunnis against Shiites, Kurds against Turkmen. Since 2003, some 700,000 Iraqis have fled to Syria. Until 2006, Bush had ignored the violence and chaos that define daily Iraqi life. US personnel avidly train young Iraqis into constabulary form—those that survive the regular suicide bombings and other attacks aimed at the police and military.

This scenario—reality—has not penetrated the heads of key Democrats who continue to talk about "our obligation" to fix Iraq. Instead of picking up on the withdrawal demand, before more breakage occurs, foolish Senators like Joseph Biden (DE) and Hillary Clinton (NY) called for "staying the course" and even sending more troops to Iraq. Don't they understand that American soldiers break, not fix? Soldiers don't go to Iraq with hammers, saws and screw drivers; their tools are guns, bombs, tanks and artillery. The more U.S. soldiers in Iraq, the more damage they will do and the more enemies they will make. To limit damage, to act morally and responsibly, remove the cause of violence and chaos in Iraq: the U.S. military presence. Words don't fix broken lives or property. Commitment to democracy calls for more than the United States appointing an Iraqi government and calling it democratic or forcing an Iraqi election in which millions bravely voted, But for what never got reported.

The media, White House and key Democrats ignored the startling fact that in 2005 the majority of Iraqis voted against the U.S.-chosen Iyad Allawi and for the United Iraqi Alliance, which demanded "a timetable for the withdrawal of the multinational forces from Iraq."[105]

Bush ironically appeared as more moderate than his blustering Democratic opponents as he appealed for patriotic unity in the form of flying the flag on July 4.

What must Iraqis feel at the sight of that flag on July 4? In its name, the U.S. military has destroyed their cities, tortured their people, shot many of them for no reason at checkpoints or wherever the troops happened to be patrolling. Iraqis have scarce electricity, food and water and no secure jobs. Yet, Bush keeps repeating that he "liberated Iraq."

On June 28, 2005, addressing the Special Forces at Fort Bragg, Bush asked, implying that "our" people had given up a lot to wage his war: "Is the sacrifice worth it?" He quickly answered his own question. "It is worth it…"

The Iraq war has cost him a few hours of missed video golf. "We have more work to do," he stated. Yes, Bush stands as a national model of sacrifice (none) and hard work (most vacations of any president)! And Iraqis must think that those Democrats who ask for more troops are either crazy or stark opportunists. It will take them that much longer to restore some integrity to their broken society.

The author testified before the World Tribunal on Iraq, June 24-27, 2005, Istanbul

III. Bad Terrorists and Zealous Patriots

"The opportunists watched with expectation
When airplanes collided with towers
They could declare war amidst fear and trepidation
And exercise true naked powers."—Irving Q. Gribenes

Without admitting it, the high officials of the Administration
created double standards. The Bad terrorists opposed US policies,
even though some of them didn't practice or even advocate violence.
"Zealous patriots" described those who used terrorist tactics against
US opponents. Even democratically elected presidents who had not
undertaken or advocated violence against the United States became
painted with the pejorative brush used by the Bushies to color the
public's mind about Saddam Hussein—before the invasion of Iraq.

"He's supporting terrorism," said the White House of Venezuelan
President Hugo Chavez, without offering evidence to support the
charges. On February 2, 2006, Defense Secretary Rumsfeld took
the word "war" one step further by comparing Chavez to Hitler. The
media didn't ask him why.

Terrorism Then and Now

Officeal Washington has changed its criteria for evaluating terrorism. In October 1976, an era before most suspected terrorists had Arab names and received indeterminate sentences without charges, lawyers or trials at the Guantanamo Gulag, Luis Posada Carriles and Orlando Bosch hired agents to plant a bomb on a Cuban commercial airliner flying over Barbados. Three weeks earlier, on September 21, the Iowa-born Michael Townley, working with anti-Castro Cubans for Chile's secret police, attached a bomb to the underside of Orlando Letelier's car in Washington, D.C.

In the early and mid 1970s and throughout the 1980s (except during Jimmy Carter's years 1977-81), the United States installed and backed murderous—terrorist—regimes throughout the third world. Indeed, National Security Adviser and Secretary of State Henry Kissinger under Nixon and Ford preferred "authoritarian regimes," the euphemism Reagan's UN Ambassador Jeanne Kirkpatrick used in a notorious article that argued for pro-U.S. military dictatorships, because they caused fewer problems than elected governments.[106]

Kissinger and Nixon had encouraged the 1973 coup in Chile, led by General Augusto Pinochet, against the elected government of Socialist President Salvador Allende. With U.S. approval, Pinochet established DINA, a secret police-intelligence apparatus that epitomized his 17 years of rule (ending in 1990); more than 3,190 assassinated and disappeared people, and tens of thousands more tortured. In addition, Pinochet initiated Operation Condor in 1975, a network of intelligence-secret police agencies throughout Latin America, so that he and fellow military dictators could both monitor and assassinate their "enemies" abroad.

DINA recruited home-grown Chilean brutes to torture and murder as well as foreign "specialists" like Townley, a man who hadn't fulfilled his business executive-father's expectations. Townley did, however, teach himself (via manuals) electronics and explosives.

I first saw this handsome, light-skinned middle westerner in 1979, as he testified in Washington's Federal Court, against his fellow conspirators. Townley coolly admitted to taping a bomb of his own making to the I-beam of a Chevrolet belonging to Orlando Letelier, Allende's defense minister. He had equipped the "device" with a two-stage remote control detonator that two anti-Castro Cubans activated on September 21, 1976, as Letelier's car entered Washington's Sheridan Circle.

The Embassy Row blast, less than a mile from the White House, severed Letelier's legs and sent lethal shrapnel into 25-year-old Ronni Moffitt's throat. She had been sitting next to Letelier. They had both worked together at the Institute for

Policy Studies. Her husband, Michael, miraculously escaped with minor injuries.

Townley confessed that his superiors in DINA had ordered him to kill Letelier, and that he had recruited five anti-Castro Cuban exiles to help him with the task. Townley reached a plea bargain with the federal prosecutors and ratted out his fellow conspirators. The bargain included a clause requiring Townley to testify truthfully about other crimes in which he had taken part.

So, in February 2005, Chilean judge Alejandro Solis deposed Michael Townley—still protected of course by his plea bargain—and asked if he had assassinated another Pinochet enemy.

Townley readily admitted that he had assassinated the exiled Chilean General Carlos Prats and his wife in Buenos Aires, but of course he was only "following orders" of his DINA bosses.

Townley's words should nevertheless send chills down the spine of sensitive people. This terrorist, living under the witness protection program in the United States for many of the last 20 years, described in cold and precise language how he made, then "installed and detonated, the bomb in General Prats' car using two radios and pieces of a walkie talkie."[107]

"I made a call from one transmitter to the other and the electronic impulse activated the explosion," he explained. Ironically, fanatic Muslim killers used cell phones rather than more primitive electronics to set off their March 11, 2004 explosions in Madrid.

Twenty five years earlier, Townley's monotone voice mesmerized a Washington DC courtroom as he told a jury about the problems he encountered and overcame in making and planting the Letelier car bomb. He had to crawl under Letelier's car at 3 a.m. on a quiet residential street in Bethesda, Maryland, and tape the bomb to the car. At one point, a patrol car drove down the street and sweat dripped from his face. His heart pounded with fear that the cop would see him.

On Sunday night, some 20 hours after Townley had installed the device, Letelier and I rested our elbows on the car's hood, parked safely in his driveway. We finished a conversation we had started inside of his house. A day and a half later, as he drove into Sheridan Circle on his way to work, Townley's Castro-hating Cuban collaborators detonated the bomb. Letelier's car had carried the bomb for two days.

Similarly, Townley told Judge Solis of his vicissitudes in getting a bomb on Prats' car. "One day I found Prats' garage door open and went in, but I had to hide at a lower parking level for several hours because the concierge was really on the job. When I could finally go up to the level where he parked his car, I went under it and attached the bomb with a cord to a cross piece underneath the car's engine." Townley also had to wait anxiously for the opportunity to leave the garage unseen.

Prior to that, he had "spent several days trying to find the General until finally I caught up with him on the night of September 30, 1974. I saw him near the entrance to his garage. The detonator I inserted into the C-4 and TNT explosive had remained armed. So, I detonated it. I didn't notice anyone else in the general's car." Did he not see Prats' wife, Sofia Cuthbert, sitting next to him?

So poof! Parts of the Prats sailed as high as nine floors. Townley later told the FBI how he had subsequently perfected both his bomb making and detonating skills. In the ensuing two years between killing Prats and Letelier, he learned how to shape the charge to blow straight up. Letelier's legs were severed, but parts of his body did not land on the White House lawn. Yes, a lot cleaner!

In 1975, Townley also confessed to the FBI—with immunity from prosecution—that under DINA orders he had arranged the assassination of Bernardo Leighton, a Christian Democratic leader exiled in Rome. Townley contracted with Italian fascists to shoot Leighton and his wife in their heads. They both survived, but were effectively "neutralized."

Townley also told of DINA plans to kill other exiled Chilean political leaders in Europe and Mexico. These lethal plots included using his then wife Mariana as part of the hit team. Fortunately, these plans went awry.

Now in his mid 60s and using a new name, but no longer in the Witness Protection Program, Townley told Judge Solis what he had already reported previously to FBI agents more than 25 years earlier. At a "friendly dinner," his DINA bosses explained why Prats needed killing—for "national security" purposes, naturally. These two words magically converted cold-blooded murder into a patriotic act. Has Washington changed its own criteria in the ensuing years? Does anyone in the White House distinguish patriotic state-sponsored homicide from non-state sponsored terrorism?

Geezers Make GAS

Our cause is just, it's just to slay
Fidelista Cubans on any given day
If cops ever catch us, we could care less
Proud members of GAS will never confess

We are GAS
You bet your ass
We got class

We kill for cause and cause is a killer
Posada's his name, he's our Godzilla
We whack Commy dragons, they go straight to hell
The Commy of Commys his name is Fidel

We are GAS
We kick your ass
We are nass—ty

—Lyrics from the GASeous hymn

GAS, or Geezers Assassination Society, my Miami source claims, refers to a secret club formed by four pardoned anti-Castro terrorists, all in their twilight years. The group offered honorary membership—women can only become honorary members—to outgoing Panamanian president Mireya Moscoso, who on August 26, 2004, released the convicted men. A Panamanian court had sentenced them and two others to 7 and 8-year terms for threatening public security and falsifying documents. The prosecutor presented a large cache of plastic explosives, TNT and related gear with the defendants' fingerprints on them. Witnesses avowed that the men planned to use this material in 2000 to bomb Cuban President Fidel Castro—not engage in playful fireworks as the defendants claimed—during a scheduled speech at a Panamanian university.

The convicted men had claimed "frame up," but the secret GAS membership knew better. All GAS aspirants swear in blood rituals to dedicate the remainder of their lives—when not seeing prostate specialists—to plotting to assassinate Castro. GAS stole its credo *(Viva la Muerte!)* from Nazi pilots during the Spanish Civil War (1936-9).

The newly pardoned admirers of those Nazi aces caught a waiting airplane that carried them out of Panama. The plane stopped in Honduras to allow the padrino of Latin American terrorism, Luis Posada Carriles (78), to disembark. Guillermo Novo (67), Pedro Remon (62) and Gaspar Jimenez (70), other august GAS founders, all with impressive criminal records, continued on to Miami, where perspective GASers and groupies greeted them.

Out-going President Moscoso apparently contravened Panamanian law by issuing the pardons before the appeals process had ended. Moscoso immediately phoned U.S. Ambassador Simon Ferro, saying she had complied with Washington's request to release the men. Their arrival in Miami coincided with President Bush's campaign stop there. Bush had declared himself a mortal enemy of those who harbor terrorists. Apparently, he made a nuanced—and understated—exception for anti-Castro terrorists: "zealous patriots."

Some Panamanians suspected that the $4 million Moscoso deposited in a Swiss bank prior to issuing the pardons would offset the hurt feelings she suffered from the worldwide criticism of her actions. I empathized with Moscoso. The poor woman had become addicted to the lavish lifestyle she developed in her five years as President. But she spent only $23 million of public money on her personal needs and only $3 million on trips abroad. Her critics charged her with disguising personal tourism as state missions since her overseas junkets accomplished nothing for Panama. I say: "No one's perfect."

Unkind Panamanians called her a kleptomaniac. More generous compatriots considered this a slight exaggeration. But, her defenders pointed out, she resisted pressure to pardon the anti-Castroites until their advocates offered a sufficient sum of money.

The liberated but still grumpy seniors had also shared prior membership in various organizations like Omega 7 and the Cuban Nationalist Movement and had received support from some Cuban American National Foundation (CANF) members for their ongoing but unsuccessful efforts to whack Cuba's leader. They had, however, dispatched other, lesser Cuban officials and destroyed Cuban property in New York, Argentina, Mexico, Barbados and elsewhere.

Indeed, part of GAS' pledge week activities require aspirants to memorize Posada's decades of failed assassination attempts, just as religious Christians return to the film, "The Passion of Christ," to internalize the pain of Jesus, the Prince of Peace, en route to his crucifixion.

The Prince of terrorists, Posada Carriles, achieved world status in 1976 by directing the sabotage of a Cuban commercial airliner over Barbados. Shortly after taking off from Barbados International Airport, the bomb on board exploded, the plane plunged into the sea and all 73 passengers and crew members died. Posada denied involvement, but police nabbed two of the perps who identified Posada as the man who hired them to place the bomb on the plane before they disembarked in Barbados.

Posada's wife told a Venezuelan journalist of her mate's emotions. "When he started with the Barbados affair, I knew he would be successful because the 'poor guy' had dedicated so much effort, with so much passion."[108]

Born Luis Clemente Faustino Posada Carriles, he became known as Bambi to his terrorist pals—how sweet. He served on dictator Fulgencio Batista's repressive forces until the January 1959 revolutionary takeover. Posada then swore vengeance.

In 1963, the CIA trained Posada at Fort Benning, Georgia, on the fine points of spying, using explosives and other lethal devices. In 1971, he partnered with Antonio Veciana, founder of Alpha 66, another anti-Castro terrorist group, to plan a movie script type plot to assassinate Castro.

In 1996, Veciana told me how he and Posada had recruited a couple of Venezuelan hit men, disguised them as a TV news crew and sent them to Santiago, Chile, before Castro arrived on a visit. Meanwhile, the assassins "blended in" with the rest of the media. CIA technicians had outfitted one of their news cameras with a gun that would fire when they activated the camera. Fortunately, for Fidel, the assassins chickened out. Posada became enraged over their cowardice, Veciana continued, and recruited other assassins to use the same camera on Castro when he stopped in Caracas for a press conference on his return to Cuba. But those whackers also had second thoughts.

The plot failed again. Killing Castro continued as the driving force in Posada's life. Veciana quit the assassination business in 1973 after an unknown gunman shot him in the head.

Perhaps, Posada's frustration over the failed 1971 hits abated after the "success" of his 1976 Barbados air sabotage. But, alas, Venezuelan authorities charged him with that crime and threw him in prison, where he remained until August 1985, when leaders of a prestigious Cuban Miami organization bribed prison authorities to help Posada "escape."

Lt. Col. Oliver North then engaged him in the late 1980s to re-supply the CIA-backed Contras from El Salvador. In 1990, in Guatemala, a gunman shot Posada in the face. Down, but not out, the man who was determined to kill Castro hatched a plot to bomb Cuban hotels to deter the tourist trade. In one hotel bombing, an Italian tourist died. Cuban police nabbed a

Salvadoran man who fingered Posada as his recruiter. The attacks did reduce tourism for a brief time.

In a July 12, 1998 *New York Times* interview with Anne Bardach and Larry Rohter, Posada described "the Italian tourist's death as a freak accident." But "I sleep like a baby," he said. "That Italian was sitting in the wrong place at the wrong time." Posada told the *Times* that he "still intends to try to kill Castro, and he believes violence is the best method for ending Communism in Cuba."

Inevitably, the violence-prone Posada linked his fading professional destiny with another pit bull-like GAS co-founder and would be assassin of Castro, Guillermo Novo.

When the newly freed Novo landed in Miami in late August he passed quickly through U.S. Immigration. Luckily for him, his name wasn't Ted Kennedy,[109] or the authorities would have questioned him about terrorist connections. "We beat you," Novo crowed to Fidel. There were no reports that Castro had conceded or even acknowledged Novo's existence.

For Novo, like Posada, eligible to collect social security, terrorism has been the animating force in his life since 1964, when he fired a bazooka at the UN building in New York while Che Guevara addressed the General Assembly.

In 1979, a Washington D.C. jury convicted him of conspiring to assassinate former Chilean Chancellor Orlando Letelier. Novo appealed and got acquitted at a second trial, but was convicted of perjury for lying about his knowledge of the assassination conspiracy. But he had already served his time, the judge ruled. Novo rejoiced in the courthouse hall. Since then, he's had little to laugh about.

When Novo and Posada smile, it's not because they've succeeded in whacking Fidel. Remember, young babies also evince smiles when GAS enters their system.

Luis Posada and Bush's Drinking

HOW DID A JUDGE'S DECISION NOT TO DEPORT THE TERRORIST Luis Posada Carriles to Venezuela connect to the report that George W. Bush has again hit the bottle?

Bush never entered a recovery program for his alcohol and drug addiction, which he supposedly gave up at age 40 while jogging. God talked to him, or was it Jesus? This born again phenomenon apparently substituted for AA—along with exercise and praying.

W had ongoing problems, of course, in Iraq and Afghanistan. At home, his poll ratings fell to 40% or less by September 2005. Yet, Bush continued on Karl Rove's path, derived from Napoleon, Frederick the Great and the Nazi Party model of politics: forget about facts, truth, integrity, ethics; rely on audacity and aggression. This formula won him two elections, placed the gutless Democrats on the defense and secured the "stupid male vote," the dumbos who adore Dr. Laura and Rush Limbaugh and vote against their own interests.

The impregnable success model, however, eroded quickly and, according to *The National Enquirer*,[110] Laura Bush caught George throwing down a drink at his Crawford ranch. Drinking began after aides informed him of the Hurricane Katrina disaster and FEMA's failure to deal with the aftermath.

Laughing about the source? Before the "respectable" press got wind of it, *The Enquirer* revealed Rush Limbaugh's oxycontin habit.[111]

Jennifer Luce and Don Gentile reported that "Family sources have told how the 59-year-old president was caught by First Lady

Laura downing a shot of booze at their family ranch in Crawford, Texas.

"When the levees broke in New Orleans, it apparently made him reach for a shot," said one 'insider.' "He poured himself a Texas-sized shot of straight whiskey and tossed it back. The First Lady was shocked and shouted: 'Stop, George!'" She recalled in September 12 exchange with a journalist.

"Did they misinform you when you said that no one anticipated the breach of the levees?"

"No," Bush responded. "...When that storm came by, a lot of people said we dodged a bullet. When that storm came through at first, people said, whew. There was a sense of relaxation, and that's what I was referring to. And I, myself, thought we had dodged a bullet. You know why? Because I was listening to people, probably over the airways, say the bullet has been dodged...Of course, there were plans in case the levee had been breached. There was a sense of relaxation in the moment, a critical moment. And thank you for giving me a chance to clarify that."[112]

This mangled attempt at oral clarity hardly compensated for his non-handling of Katrina's aftermath. That, combined with bloodshed in Iraq dominated daily headlines. Popularity ratings went south. Gas prices went north. W went boozing.

"The sad fact is that he has been sneaking drinks for weeks now. Laura may have only just caught him—but the word is his drinking has been going on for a while in the capital," said an *Enquirer* source. "The war in Iraq, the loss of American lives, has deeply affected him... The result is he's taking drinks here and there, likely in private, to cope."

The nation has endured drunken Presidents, like Ulysses Grant and Warren Harding. But a "dry drunk?" Dr. Katherine Van Wormer, co-author of *Addiction Treatment: A Strengths Perspective*, applied this term to Bush, meaning he stopped drinking but still thinks constantly about relieving his anxiety with alcohol.[113]

On September 20, he returned to "N'Oleans" which he remembered fondly from his drinking days. Bush promised to "get the debris removed, get the water up and running and get the bridges rebuilt. But what you need to do is develop a blueprint for your own future. We look forward to hearing your vision so we can more better do our job."

"More better?" More disturbed, thought Laura. The following day, W unleashed another missile. "If you want to grow something, you shouldn't tax it. If you want to encourage small business growth, we ought to incent it to grow in that part of the world. Somebody said the other day, well, that's a tax break. That region is going to have zero income anyway."

"That region" conjured up images of poor people suffering. If he stayed for photo ops, he would have to shake dirty hands and hug smelly bodies. So, he remained "on vacation," watching TV golf, not images of floating bodies and desperate people.

The dry drunk got wetter. Van Wormer listed other traits of this addictive condition: "A rigid, judgmental outlook, impatience, childish behavior, irresponsible behavior, irrational rationalization, projection and overreaction." Dr. Van Wormer thinks Bush exhibits these traits and "some indications of paranoia."

She selected as an example Bush's declaration: "We must be prepared to stop rogue states and their terrorist clients before they are able to threaten or use weapons of mass destruction against the United States and our allies and friends." Such a statement indicated "projection is evidenced here as well, projection of the fact that we are ready to attack onto another nation which may not be so inclined."

He also displays his "judgmental outlook" in a statement on Israel. To fight evil, Bush turns Biblical. "Look my job isn't to try to nuance. I think moral clarity is important... this is evil versus good."[114]

Such pronouncements of an uncompromising terrorism fighter evaporated on September 27, 2005 and provided W more reason to drink. On that day, a U.S. immigration judge denied Venezuela's request to extradite Luis Posada Carriles. The U.S. government lawyer offered no opposition to the judge's ruling, although it carried heavy implications.

Posada, who Hugo Chavez's government labeled "the Osama bin Laden of Latin America," grinned. So did Osama bin Laden when he heard Bush's October 6 remarks.

"The United States makes no distinction between those who commit acts of terror and those who support and harbor them, because they're equally as guilty of murder. Any government that chooses to be an ally of terror has also chosen to be an enemy of civilization. And the civilized world must hold those regimes to account."[115]

How do these remarks coincide with Bush not deporting a terrorist? "God should have known that those anti-Castro Cubans, whom I owe for two elections, would not let me deport Posada. They call him a 'zealous patriot'."

Since Posada escaped trial for his lead role in the October 1976 bombing of a Cuban commercial airliner over Barbados in which all 73 people aboard died, Bernardo Alvarez, Venezuela's Ambassador to Washington, accused Bush's administration of using a "double standard" on terrorism.

At his Texas trial, the White House and Homeland Security collaborated with Posada by failing to counter his lawyer's unsupported claim that Venezuela would torture him. Indeed, the State department's most recent report exempted Venezuela from the list of states that practice torture.

Ironically, U.S. officials have routinely torture prisoners at Abu Ghraib and Guantanamo. One State Department official spoke anonymously, "Here we have someone who we know is a terrorist, and it's clear that we're actively protecting him from facing justice. We have zero credibility."[116]

Posada's case weakened W's terrorist reputation. A Texas prosecutor further weakened Bush's power by charging House

Majority leader Tom DeLay with multiple felony charges.[117] "The Hammer," as frightened legislators called DeLay, had rammed through Bush's tax cuts for the richest people in the country.

In addition, Bush's presence was further diminished when the SEC began to probe Senate Majority Leader Bill Frist's sale of stock in Hospital Corporation of America from his blind trust, just days before poor earnings sent HCA shares sharply down. Frist had also loyally obeyed White House dictates.

"Billy" claimed he sold the shares to avoid "conflict of interest" should he decide to run for president. But his kin also sold their HCA shares on that day. None of them aspired to public office. Frist denied that he saw clearly into his blind trust. Few believed him.

Then, the press chastised W for naming Julie Myers to head Immigration and Customs Enforcement. She was General Richard Myers' niece, who married Homeland Security head Mike Chertoff's chief of staff. So what that the agency was part of Homeland Security! Neopotism?

With his approval dropping, Social Security reform entombed and facing increasing voter dissatisfaction with the war in Iraq, Bush also took heat for rising gas prices.

Dr. Justin Frank[118] thought "that Bush is drinking again. Alcoholics who are not in any program, like the President, have a hard time when stress gets to be great."[119]

Posada grinned.[120] Bin Laden guffawed. Bush drank. The drama of our time: two terrorists and a lush?

Che: Man and Movie,
Terrorist or Saint?

Fidel asks the Cabinet: "Any of you guys an economist?"

Che raises his hand. Fidel, surprised, says "OK, Che, you're the new bank chief."

Afterwards, Fidel approaches Che: "You're an economist?"

"Economist?" says Che. "I thought you said communist."

At the 2:30 a.m. meeting, in July 1960, the new bank prez took his feet off his office desk at his president's office in Cuba's National Bank and admitted that he knew little about economics. Revolution inspired him, he told the visiting American students. "Politics," he emphasized, "not economics, should drive revolutionary policy."

THE DANGEROUSLY HANDSOME, BEARDED PHYSICIAN TALKED about his travels through Latin America, etched on the screen in director Walter Salles' "The Motorcycle Diaries" (2004). "The imperialists have sucked blood from the indigenous people of the Andes. Centuries of abuse have exhausted the land and the people," he lectured. "And U.S. imperialism continues to exploit."

He described poverty and underdevelopment in Argentina, where this son of an architect grew up. The conditions at Chile's Chuqicamata copper mines "are beyond belief," he said, accusing Guggenheim-Rockefeller family interests of exploiting the mine labor, and persecuting those who tried to unionize, especially the communists. "Imperialism," he snapped "has also wreaked havoc on the Amazon region shared by several countries."

He spewed facts. Less than 2% of the population owned 65% of the land; 72% of the rural people owned less than 4%. He cited dramatic data on malnutrition, income gaps and foreign owner-ship, as if Doctor Guevara was presenting his case for radical surgery to a hospital Board. UN data, he said, confirmed his own observations that he had recorded in notebooks from his early 1950s motorcycle journey. Only a continental revolution could bring justice to the poor majority and Fidel's guerrilla model had lit the path for such a movement.

"What would you like the United States to do during this revolution?" the student asked.

"Disappear," snapped Che, without cracking a smile.

Che stared at the student, who visibly gulped. The room was quiet. "I'm yanking your chain," said Che, now smiling.

Che emphasized to the students that revolution offers the best, if not the only, way to make one's historical mark on the side of justice and freedom. He radiated this contagious notion with perilous magnetism. At 3:30 a.m., he rose, shook hands and explained he still had work to complete before getting his four hours of sleep.

Forty-four years later, I stared into the face of Gael Garcia Bernal, playing the youthful fourth year medical student bounc-ing on a motorcycle, with his Jack Kerouac-like partner, (Rodrigo de la Serna) in the pit of Patagonia, the snowy Andes of Chile and on the Amazon. In "The Motorcycle Diaries," the asthmatic hero, struggling for breath, swims the un-swimmable river to the other side to spend his birthday with the lepers: determination, audacity, recklessness.

Five years later, now doctor for the guerrilla army of the Sierra Maestre in eastern Cuba, the real Che raced into no-man's land in the midst of a firefight to rescue a wounded comrade.

Che was "temerario," (Presumptuously or recklessly daring) Fidel told me in July 1974, one of the few criticisms he had of his most brilliant lieutenant. "I once tackled him [during the 1956-8 guerrilla war against Fulgencio Batista] when he stood up during a battle. 'You're too important to lose,' I told him."

In the film, Che's recklessness manifests itself not only by his daring physical feats, but in the scene of him coveting a mechanic's wife at a town dance while her husband drinks. Then he must flee to escape the wrath of angry townspeople. Young Che also jumps into a freezing lake to retrieve a duck for dinner. "Fearless," Fidel agreed.

"But he shouldn't have allowed his columns to lose contact," Fidel said bitterly, referring to the split of Che's guerrilla group in Bolivia. "And his relaxed attitude on security cost him," he remarked. Che had permitted Regis Debray, the French intellectual (author of the text on guerrilla strategy, *Revolution in the Revolution?*), to learn the guerrilla's whereabouts. Debray was subsequently captured. We now know, however, that CIA agents had tracked the guerrillas.

But in early July 1968, having just written the introduction to Che's *Bolivia Diary*, Fidel still anguished over the death of his comrade and the defeat of the Bolivian guerrilla expedition. He still clung to the *foco guerrillero* notion which, if properly applied, would serve as a model for third world revolution. A mobile guerrilla troupe backed by organized clandestine urban rebels posed a two-front dilemma for unpopular third world governments and their inept repressive forces.

In 1959, it had worked in Cuba, when Fidel's guerillas and their urban allies overthrew Batista and his 50,000 man army. So, in 1964, with Fidel's full support, Che organized a similar battle plan in the Congo. In his Congo diary (*Che in Africa: Che Guevara's Congo Diary*, by William Galvez), Che the scientist records his observations about reality in the Congo, as he did in Latin America.

His assessment: the Congo mission failed. One factor that contributed to the defeat of the effort, he observed, was lack of knowledge. The supposed Congolese revolutionary soldiers were "saturated with fetishistic concept about death and the enemy and have no organized political education." But Che the poet also took this personally.

Like a character from a Conrad novel, he concludes that "During those last hours in the Congo, I had felt more alone than ever..."

Just hours after writing these words, Che addressed his soon-to-depart comrades. Imagine the internal adrenalin it required to force these optimistic words into his mouth! "This struggle that we have waged has been a great experience. In spite of all the difficulties we've had, I hope that if some day Fidel proposes another mission of this kind, some of you will volunteer."

Che returned in disguise to Cuba, then led an elite group of veteran guerrilla warriors to join a Bolivian cadre to liberate the landlocked country. The *"foco"* method assumed support from the Bolivian Communist Party whom, despite protests from Moscow, Fidel had "convinced" to back the operation. But the Bolivian Communists, following Soviet orders "betrayed Che," Fidel charged.

Without the vital underground, the guerrilla foco floundered. In early October 1967, after months of unproductive struggle, Che and most of tattered guerrilla band fell into a trap. A sick and wounded Guevara then faced a Bolivian soldier, with CIA agents hovering nearby, who finally worked up enough courage to murder the guerrilla hero. This drama occurred in La Higuera, near the place where Jose Antonio de Sucre, Bolivar's lieutenant, fought the Spaniards more than a century earlier.

Che's death became and has remained an international event. Now, the movie offers insights into Che's character. Garcia Bernal conveys the young medical student whose addiction to princi-ples propelled him to action and injected him with the kind of courage that arises almost preternaturally from the wellspring of feeling and thought inside him; the qualities that made him charismatic. Thirty-seven years after his murder, his icon still entices noble souls around the world to try to "be like Che."

The slogan "Viva Che" appear on apartment walls in Damascus and Baghdad; his heroically drawn face on millions of T-shirts throughout the world. Yes, along with revolutionary sanctification, Che's image has been commercialized to sell products— even beer.[121] But those who understand what he meant will make their history in his way.

"*Seremos como el Che,*" appears on Cuban billboards and posters. Some students cynically reply, "Sure, we'll also become asthmatics." One student, however, insists that Che epitomizes revolution. She plans to spend her life working for the poor:

She cites sentences from Che's Congo diary. "You are only a revolutionary when you are willing to leave all your comforts to go to another country to fight." Che internalized the principle of "the recognition of necessity as the guide to freedom." The poet, doctor, warrior, revolutionary continues to inspire from his grave. "Once again," he wrote his parents as he prepared to embark for Africa in 1964, "I feel beneath my heels the ribs of Rocinante [Don Quixote's 'horse']." He describes "a willpower that I have polished with an artist's delight that will sustain some shaky legs and some weary legs. I will do it."

In the film, Garcia Bernal portrays Che with effortless changes of facial expressions and body language. Garcia Bernal's Che shows how an immature medical student transforms his middle class guilt into revolutionary will. He offers qualities of wit, intelligence and determination that the real Che manifested as he made history.

In the contemporary globalized world, guerrilla focos no longer respond realistically to systemic injustice. But understanding the nature of exploitation, as the movie "Che" confronts exploitation of workers and indigenous people, means one must act—in Seattle, Washington, D.C., and other venues where the WTO will meet. Viva Che!

"Paradise Now"—Movie or Life?

"I was depressed," said the comic. "I didn't have the energy to commit suicide. So, I started dating."

LIKE MOST GOOD JOKES, THIS ONE HIDES A TRAGIC INSIGHT. IF only Said and Khaled had caught her act! Unfortunately, for these Palestinians, outrage fed depression and turned it into righteous destructiveness—the ultimate in therapy, posing as politics.

Each day, Israeli occupiers prove to residents of the West Bank that they live in the opposite of Paradise; indeed, even a momentous distance from a contiguous and liberated Palestinian state. The beautiful future exists only in the fantasy of the two young male protagonists, and presumably those who have programmed them to take the violent route to Heaven.

The "Resistance" leaders weave their religious-infused thread of struggle through the thin surface layers of daily maintenance and sustenance. The 2005 film shows Palestinians at work, with family eating food, together smoking and playing. In the dusty refugee camp in urban Nablus, the "Resistance" also selects best friends, Khaled (Ali Suliman) and Said (Kais Nashef), whose futures look bleak, to the honored role of martyrdom.

Having established anger and pessimism in their lives, director Hany Abu-Assad ("Rana's Wedding") then takes the audience through a political and psychological discourse that goes beyond cinematic drama and gives "Paradise Now" an educative function for moviegoers of the world. Indeed, 90 minutes of pictures and sounds from a well-acted, character-driven film, prove more insightful than the millions of words analysts have exhausted on the volatile Israeli-Palestinian conflict.

The protagonists live inside limits imposed by Israeli policies, the evolution of their lives caged by the history of occupation, that grinding process that erodes optimism and molds rancor into their psyches.

The United Nations Conference on Trade and Development's annual report stated that the Palestinian economy "shrank 1% in 2004, one in three Palestinian workers was jobless at the end of last year and 61% of households had income below the poverty line of $350 per month."[122]

Concurrently, "Between September 2000 and through September 2004, more than 24,000 Palestinians living in the Gaza Strip have been made homeless by Israeli house demolitions," according to the 2004 Arab Human Development Report. Since 2000, over "12,000 homes have been either demolished or damaged in the West Bank."[123]

In case people feel shock over this fact, or attribute it to necessary steps to protect Israel, pay attention to an Israeli bulldozer operator, who told the *Yediot Ahronot* newspaper (May 31, 2002) after the IDF's 2002 incursion into the Jenin refugee camp: "I wanted to destroy everything. I begged the officers...to let me knock it all down: from top to bottom...For three days, I just destroyed and destroyed...I found joy with every house that came down...If I am sorry for anything, it is for not tearing the whole camp down..."[124]

The Nablus refugee camp inhabitants understand the bulldozer operator's mentality. He could be a typical Israeli soldier staring death daggers at Palestinians at checkpoints, the fanatic settler randomly shooting a Palestinian. Jewish settlers persecute Palestinians mercilessly.

"Across from Hadassah House is a school for Arab girls, called Córdoba, after the once-Muslim Spanish city," wrote Jeffrey Goldberg.[125] "On one of its doors someone had drawn a blue Star of David. On another door a yellowing bumper sticker read, 'Dr. Goldstein Cures the Ills of Israel.' The reference is to Baruch Goldstein, a physician from Brooklyn, who, in 1994, killed twenty-nine Muslims when they were praying in the Tomb of the Patriarchs, just down the road. Across the closed door of a Palestinian shop someone had written, in English, "Arabs Are Sand Niggers."

A group of Yeshiva students see "two Arab girls, their heads covered by scarves, books clutched to their chests.

'Cunts!' one of the boys yelled, in Arabic. 'Do you let your brothers fuck you?' another one yelled." Such routine behavior by the settlers makes Palestinians bitter, incensed or weakens their will.

Said's father grew depressed, lost his will and the "Resistance" executed him as a collaborator, a traumatic blow for a young child. He doesn't blame his father, he says. Instead, Said understands how living in Nablus, a human "prison," had eroded his father's strength.

The media doesn't show Palestinians' living conditions, so the opening scenes of "Paradise Now" may shock US audiences. Israeli soldiers at check points aim guns at each Palestinian entering or leaving his territory. They treat them with disdain, suspicion and hatred. The film relies on that opening scene to evoke "oppression," since we don't see further images of the daily harassment and human rights violations imposed by the occupiers. Indeed, the director assumes that filmgoers already know about the humiliating body searches, the bulldozing of Palestinian homes as collective punishment, the Israeli soldiers shooting kids throwing rocks.

He assumes the public will appreciate the symbolic and real meaning of the Israeli wall (452 miles long when completed) that cuts into Palestinian land. Indeed, in a July 9, 2004 advisory opinion, the International Court of Justice called it "contrary to international law."

Law, however, has become an ambiguous word in the occupied territories. In 1968, after Israel seized the West Bank in the Six-Day War, Rabbi Levinger rented rooms in an Arab hotel, in order to hold a Passover Seder. Then he refused to leave. He struck a deal with the Israeli government, and moved his family and his followers to a hill just northeast of Hebron, where, with the state's cooperation, they built the settlement called "Kiryat Arba" of over seven thousand settlers.

"In 1988, Levinger killed a Palestinian shoe-store owner in Hebron. Levinger told the police that he was defending himself from a group of stone throwers." He served less than three weeks in jail.[126]

Such humiliation administered by Israeli occupiers, however, does not explain suicide bombing. Palestinian fury does not have to mean martyrdom. Indeed, "Paradise Now" vibrates with the possibility of an alternative, one that negates suicide as viable politics. It suggests that this tactic poses as a crucial element in the political struggle, but really has no role in a larger strategy.

Suha (Lubna Azabal), the film's third main character, a European-educated middle class daughter of a martyr, feels the passion in Said, the soulfulness in his sad eyes. But she cannot reason politically with a man whose psychic despair drives him to avenge his father's death, punish the Israelis and cleanse the family name and thus his own soul as well.

Later in the film, however, she does persuade Khaled that suicide will not only deprive the resistance of a valuable actor, but that its violence against an enemy with far superior armament represents the ultimate in futility. In truth, suicide bombing—in the name of struggle—helps unify a potentially divided enemy.

Suha also snaps Khaled out of his religious fervor, his parrot like repetition of the hereafter dogma fed to him by Jamal (Amer Hlehel), a member of an unnamed Palestinian group who guides the friends on their deadly mission. Two angels will transport them to Heaven and the "Resistance" will protect and look after their families, Jamal assures them. Yet, he doesn't explain how the fatal deed will help Said's mother recover from the loss of her son.

We watch the elaborate purification ritual of the would be martyrs, culminating in their physical transformation from shaggy, rugged auto mechanics to clean cut human bombs sporting identical "belts" underneath their new black suits.

Khaled, initially more spirited about their endeavor, experiences the first glimmers of cold reality when the video camera recording his impassioned pre-mortem statement malfunctions. Like an actor, he must do another take, in front of the crew more interested in devouring their pita sandwiches and ready to call it a wrap, than in the profundity of his final remarks.

The video, we learn, will find its way to the shelves of a small West Bank version of Blockbuster Video. In that video shop that sells collaborators' taped confessions along with the last speeches of martyrs, the store owner claims people would pay more for the collaborators' tapes, a statement that underlines the callous foundations of Palestinian life produced both by the occupation and the hitherto frustrating results of resistance.

The occupiers themselves, who we have seen only at checkpoints, take on greater dimension as the two erstwhile exploders take their last ride. For the first time they, alongside the film's audience, can compare Tel Aviv's prosperity and glistening sky-rise buildings overlooking the sparkling blue sea coast, to the reality of Nablus, the latter filmed in mostly grayish hues to evoke the stifling feel of the decaying city.

The bomb-loaded young men, the only objects in distinctly black and white, stand as symbols of the oppressed in their death uniforms. Abu-Assad's astute direction doesn't allow the audience to assume that facile one-dimensional storyline by preaching good versus evil, right versus wrong. Rather, his account about suicide bombers dramatizes the complexity of human response to contemporary oppression.

Instead of mounting spectacularly choreographed Hollywood fireworks, "Paradise Now" relies on subtle, ironic moments to explore an explosive subject. After the first aborted suicide mission, Said screams in pain when his handlers remove the adhesive tape that secured the bombing device to his body. Such a believable reaction from a man who moments before had committed himself to incineration raises questions about both characters and presents the immediate reality of human anatomy: it hurts to have the tape ripped off.

It also raises the issue of whether Said really has the will to continue the mission. By the middle of the film, Suha's luminous presence, her growing affection and compassion for Said, should provide—at least ideally—a counter lure for his mission of death. Could she represent the means by which Said can transcend his desire to avenge his father's death and offer him a loving way out of his misery?

In their last screen time together, the camera captures a sensitively acted exchange of longing looks and one light but very tender kiss: a statement of love or a sad goodbye?

If nothing else, before potential suicide bombers commit to martyrdom, they should confront Palestinian poet Mahmoud Darwish's lines:

> "We have on this earth what makes life worth living:
> April's hesitation, the aroma of bread at dawn,
> a woman's point of view about men,
> the works of Aeschylus,
> the beginning of love,
> grass on a stone,
> mothers living on a flute's sigh and the invaders' fear of memories...
> We have on this earth...the Lady of Earth, mother of all beginnings and ends...
> She was called Palestine. Her name later became Palestine.
> My Lady, because you are my Lady, I deserve life."[127]

(with Farrah Hassen)

Munich and the Hamas Electoral Victory

HOW DOES STEVEN SPIELBERG'S MUNICH (2005) RELATE TO Hamas' January 2006 electoral victory?[128] Israel presents this organization as the epitome of Palestinian terrorism. This caricature could lead Washington to deny aid to the Palestinian people

Munich starts with the recreation of the kidnapping and slaughter of Israeli athletes during the 1972 Munich Olympic Games. The Palestinian Black September group, frustrated by not getting support or even attention for their cause, seized Israeli athletes at the Olympic dormitories. The Israelis, stunned by the Munich events, began to support a Palestinian religious movement—that later turned into Hamas. Israeli leaders also secretly devised a strategy of assassination, which Spielberg portrays in a vivid scene.

In grainy footage the audience sees armed Palestinians grabbing Israeli athletes, negotiating to fly them out of Germany and then the foolish German attempt to trick the kidnappers at the airport, resulting in the death of kidnappers and athletes.

In another Spielberg film "inspired by real events," a non-Jew bribes cynical concentration camp officers during World War II to let Jews live and even gives them their rationale for corruption: the Jews will produce for the Nazi war effort. Like *Schindler's List*, *Munich* also uses money as the means to its end.

This time, the Mossad offers very high bribes to a family of French cynics to find the location of certain Palestinian targets, so that the film's hero and his helpers can assassinate, not save them. Since the Israeli government—not barbaric Arabs—has fashioned a calculated plan to eliminate people, we instinctively root for the killers and hope they can overcome the obstacles placed in their murderous paths. What worthier cause for murder than Israel? As the Mossad agents kill, they also find themselves hunted and assassinated—by the PLO or the CIA or Soviet Union? The hero discovers that every time he murders a Palestinian, it costs Israel (or the US taxpayer) more than $1 million. Money again!

After witnessing the killing of the athletes, Hollywood film grammar alone would demand violent vengeance. So, we are not surprised to see the highest Israeli officials authorizing international assassination as state policy. Ironically, Spielberg presents two Israeli representatives that cause one to wonder about the very nature of this Jewish obsession. Ephraim, the Mossad case officer, played by Geoffrey Rush, runs squads of assassins. This cynical, middle aged spook, bereft of human compassion, represents the needs of the Israeli state and its compassionate, motherly Prime Minister, Golda Meir.

We also meet the other contender for the most obnoxious Israeli character of the decade. Spielberg portrays the mother of the attractive Avner (Eric Bana), the head of the assassination squad, as a self righteous, racist nationalist who thinks exclusively of herself. Gila Almagor pretends to love Avner and Israel, but her flawless acting shows a self infatuated woman projecting narcissism onto some mythical Israel.

Spielberg's brilliant portrayals of some characters combine with predictable Hollywood grammar in the story and plot. Sex, murder, internal conflict among the assassins, and growing doubt as plot ingredients end up with predictable liberal moralizing.

Israelis and Palestinians both have compelling arguments for their causes, but violence is a dead end. If only the two sides could overcome their obduracy. Spielberg makes no mention of the World Court decision that Israeli occupation of Palestinian land is illegal, or the overwhelming UN votes that affirm Palestinian ownership of those occupied territories.

Yet, Spielberg also transcends the cliché about Israel being inherently virtuous and helps shatter the myth of Israeli innocence. The film's release, just preceding Hamas' electoral triumph, also challenges the consistency of Israeli democracy. The Palestinians elected a party that both speaks the Israeli force language and has accepted Parliamentary protocol.

Spielberg, who has focused on violence in *Saving Private Ryan* and *Schindler's List*, uses graphic assassination scenes both to captivate and repel the audience. After Black September's bloody Munich fiasco, Israeli policy makers decide to get tough. Avner, a policeman, leaves his pregnant wife. How can he refuse an assignment in the name of Israeli state security? He must also be careful to leave no traces to Israel while he exacts revenge. The Israeli decision makers supposedly wish to teach a lesson to those who perpetrated the slaughter of the athletes and any who might think of repeating such an act. But their conspiratorial bent transcends the instinctual thirst for revenge and lesson teaching.

Avner and company learn gradually that knocking off the eleven supposed Palestinian authors of the Munich kidnapping in different countries derives from more devious motives. Serving Israel, Avner assumes, is a righteous cause, but assassinating becomes his way of life, not just a means to accomplish a political end. Murder transforms him and his team and begins to reshape their characters. And the victims may not have been involved in the Munich affair.

Assassins, as Avner learns, never enjoy emotional peace. He also discovers that by carrying out cold-blooded murder, even in the name of justice and Israeli security, good men will descend quickly into layers of purgatory.

Their new roles vitiate their intelligence and sensitivity. These representatives of democratic Israel become killing machines.

Yet, like the "terrorists," they have histories, families, interesting hobbies and vulnerabilities. One team member gets horny and meets his fate at the hands of a pretty woman hired by an opposing intelligence service.

The Mossad killers buy at a very high price the name of the woman assassin from their French source and proceed to assassinate her. Ironically, she is just like them, a professional killer who would just as easily have worked for the Mossad as any other service.

By focusing the film on Israeli assassins, Spielberg turns the black and white, right and wrong worlds of the Israel-Palestine dispute into ugly shades of gray. Even with his concessions to old Hollywood grammar (close up sex and violence), and even with the most attractive assassins, *Munich* presents an Israel stripped of innocence and virtue. For some Arab groups, this was not sufficient. They claim that Spielberg presented caricatures of Palestinians—men whose only identity and overriding passion is with their ancestors' olive trees. In an unexplained plot twist, Avner meets a Palestinian hit squad and they share an apartment. He asks Ali if he really misses his father's olive trees.

"Well, of course," Robert Fisk writes. "Ali does rather miss his father's olive trees. Ask any Palestinian in the shithouse slums of the ...refugee camps in Lebanon and you'll get the same reply."[129]

Pro-Israelis have also skewered Spielberg for betraying Israel by showing Israeli agents not only as assassins, but people who come to doubt the methods of their State to the point of reconsidering the "Israeli cause."

When Avner finally quits, reunites with his wife in New York and begins to get it on with her, he cannot stop thinking of the naked Dutch woman that he and his team have assassinated to avenge the killing of one of his team.

Spielberg gets a bit crude when he presents the image of this young woman in her last seconds of life, naked with two bullet holes in her throat and chest, juxtaposed with Avner astride and penetrating his wife.

Avner knows he has murdered innocent people, certainly people who had nothing to do with the Munich plot. The Geoffery Rush character, who represents the Israeli state, would murder anyone if the policy makers ordered it.

Whatever the defects, Spielberg displayed the courage to question Israel's supposed morality. The film's hero and his supporting heroes learn the harshest of lessons, unlike real Mossad agents who keep assassinating. In 2004, Israeli assassins murdered the blind quadriplegic Sheikh Ahmed Yassin. A month later, they killed Hamas leader Abdel Aziz Rantisi. As American forces have discovered in Iraq, the "eye for an eye" strategy results in re-producing zealots faster than you kill them.

Avner burns out on killing. So, his handler, Ephraim, travels to New York. Come home to Israel, he tells Avner. Now skeptical, Avner asks for assurance that those he murdered really did plot Munich. He also invites Ephraim to dinner at his home. But Ephraim rejects the dinner offer and refuses to assuage Avner's guilt. Avner becomes paranoid, thinking Mossad might kill him as well.

After all, Israel has used violence—alongside democracy—since its inception. At one point, to undermine the PLO, Israel even supported a nascent Hamas, thinking that religion would distract Palestinians from their desire for statehood and independence. Hamas turned out to bite one of the hands that initially fed it, the Israeli government.

Hamas won an election democratically because they and not their secular rivals showed they could deal with Israel both from a tough and clean—unlike the organization Arafat wielded—position. Calling Hamas "terrorists" misses the point. Hamas is a symbolic child of Munich—with both Palestinian and Israeli ancestors. Now, the world must decide what to do about it. The

Spielberg movie will not offer much guidance. But it does raise important, myth-shattering questions.

IV. A Sexy Environment in a Botox World

A Happy Family in a Bush and Botox World

PRESIDENT BUSH AND HIS ENTOURAGE UNDERTOOK THUS FAR unsuccessful nation-building projects in Afghanistan and Iraq. Some of the most zealous foreign policy activists in the Administration want to do more: kick out all the undemocratic, old fashioned, non-market oriented, Islamic zealots and substitute the happiness and harmony that our middle classes enjoy. I found a typical example that Bush spinners might want to employ to export this 21st Century model of family bliss and psychic stability.

My daughter's friend's mother looks almost as young as her seventeen year old; well, like her slightly older sister. She produces soap and shampoo commercials. Her husband is a VP for a marketing firm, which orders its executives to vote Republican and to contribute generously to that Party as well. But the couple appreciated good Democrats like Bill Clinton, who except for that silliness with Monica, "really knew how to govern." Clinton "reformed" welfare and committed the country to free trade, they say, and "created an atmosphere of freedom and creativity in the corporate world." Clinton's tax cuts made more sense than the extreme measures of Bush, they opine. If you push the poor too much, they might rebel and that's disturbing to stability; bad for business. On the other hand, Bush's tax cuts meant a few thousand more to spend each year.

They bought a split level home in suburban Los Angeles for less than a million. It's worth more now. They still pay less than $2,000 a year in real estate taxes. Modern barbecue technology in the manicured yard works well for their frequent parties.

"My husband keeps his staff and the other VPs happy," his wife boasts. "We spend thousands on booze and steaks, but it pays off. You know how the corporate world is."

The elder daughter is a senior at the suburban high school, and the younger son a freshman at a private, faith-based school. He left public school after being caught with a bag of marijuana. President Bush would approve of the youngster's new school. The father hoped the kid would find redemption through God. Neither he—although he doesn't admit it to the kids—nor his son have yet found that sense of Christian certainty that Bush exudes.

Both kids spend significant parts of their $400 a month (each) allowance on clothes. The older girl drives a 2003 SUV, a birthday present and a reward for achieving a B average. Her father does not know, or pretends not to, that she smokes weed with the other kids, drinks at weekend parties and does more than heavy petting with boys. If he knew, he would take the SUV away and ground her.

Based on overheard conversations (arguments), she speculates that dad fools around. But, that's how families behave on HBO movies. Does mom reciprocate? Why does she work so hard to look so young? Just to please dad?

On Sundays, the family attends a fundamentalist church, but doesn't follow the orthodox dictates of the preacher. "He's a good counselor," mother said after he recommended that they remove the boy from the public school and place him in a "faith-based" environment. The preacher eschews drinking, but the father wouldn't even consider this prohibition. His fellow fun-loving executives would goad him mercilessly if he showed such puritanical behavior.

The family has learned to live with contradictions. Indeed, they rarely talk about morality. Shopping, however, absorbs endless hours for mother and daughter. Often, they venture together to sales and spend the better part of a Saturday or Sunday afternoon at up-scale stores at the nearby malls.

On Saturday morning Dad golfs from eight to noon. Even though he has improved his game (low 90s) he doesn't love golf like some office mates. But he finds it pleasant, outdoors on the green. He felt a mild resentment against some group of environmentalists who waved placards at his windshield last month, complaining of something related to the amount of water used to maintain the golf course. Occasionally, a global warming headline disturbs him. But he long ago stopped reading the newspaper. He gets some news from Fox. But even that generates feelings of unpleasantness that" divert his thoughts from his marketing job and from his aspirations to become CEO and accumulate his fortune.

At home, he eats weight conscious lunches (usually salad) and on Sundays, from September through January, after church, he sits in his $1,500 leather recliner and watches professional football on his $2,000 plasma screen TV. He sips beer, even martinis if his business buddies join him. He consciously limits his alcohol and food intake. He knows that exceeding limits could affect his career—and possibly his health.

He enjoys seeing the expressions on the faces of football players after they get hit with bone crushing tackles. "Tough guys," he mutters. "The Super Bowl," he philosophizes, "represents one of the greatest occasions, the day when the strongest and the most athletic compete in the most scientific and interesting game."

His son watches with him. Often neighbors also drop in to see the spectacle on his high density TV. They hold lengthy discussion before and during the 2005 Super Bowl during commercials about the relative virtues of the Carolina Panthers and the favored New England Patriots. All noted that Patriot quarterback Tom Brady attended President Bush's State of the Union address.

Once in a while, a neighbor will say something about Iraq or other current issues. "Saddam was one SOB," a real estate accountant offered. The others assented. "Good that we got him," another remarks. Heads nod in agreement. The war has made dad uncomfortable; not the actual bombing and invasion, but the daily killing and wounding of Coalition forces. "I thought this would be cleaner," he confided to one neighbor.

"We should get out of there. We did what we had to do. Now let someone else clean up," another said. All agreed with that as well. None showed interest in the failure of investigators to find weapons of mass destruction in Iraq or links to Al Qaeda terrorists.

During the game, mom and her friends conversed for hours about their skin, figures and diets. They compared Botox doctors and liposuction clinics. "I can't help gaining weight," one neighbor confided, "and my husband complains that my boobs and butt are too big. But it doesn't stop him," she laughed.

In such a large group no one dares mention the hot gossip item. One of the neighboring soccer moms supposedly underwent vagina tightening and labia trimming at a Hollywood cosmetic surgery clinic. Apparently, her husband complained about the quality of her post-partum privates.

Mom shudders over such a thought, but nevertheless plans to continue with liposuction treatments if needed and will keep getting regular Botox injections for wrinkles. But she hasn't told her friends—or her husband, who doesn't seem to notice. She leaves the room and puts on another CD of what she calls "cool jazz." Her daughter calls it "elevator music."

The women discussed "kid" problems, especially dangers related to drugs, alcohol, sex and cars—the four perils of adolescence in suburbia. "I hardly remember the early 1980s," says a perky blond with three teenagers. She doesn't work, but her husband sells houses in the Rancho Cucamonga area. "I smoked a little pot and I sure did drink. Hey, all of us did things we shouldn't have done in the car." She giggled. The others smiled nervously, worrying about their kids and perhaps regretting stupidities of their own adolescence.

The football game ended and the women went home to "fix" dinner. The men continued their Super Bowl conversation as the murmuring sounds of "60 Minutes" mixed with background music. "New England had offense and defense...." One of the neighbors had drunk too much.

The family ate greasy, take-in Chinese food. The daughter retired to her room "to do homework." She looked in the mirror, made a face and said a prayer: "Please God, don't let me be pregnant, or worse." She regretted that she had allowed herself to get talked into unprotected sex in the back of her own SUV, no less. "Too much booze," she explained to herself.

The brother played his new hip hop CD, locked his door and pulled the new *Playboy* from between the pages of his algebra text.

The mother applied creams and moisturizers in her bathroom. She stared at her youthful face and her model's figure. "What will happen to me when I start to look my age?" she asked herself, trying to subdue the rushing waves of panic that she felt every day.

The father checked his agenda before slipping into his silk pajamas. He had not yet figured out how to cover up his recent mistakes at the office or how to shift blame onto his subordinates. He reran a few plays from the Super Bowl in his mind. "There are always different options," he said silently. He fantasized about manipulating the foxy, new buyer into an after-work drink; maybe a roll in the motel bed. He switched on the bedroom plasma screen to HBO channels, flipped past Bill Maher's "Real Time" and Larry David's "Curb Your Enthusiasm" and settled on "Real Sex," something that might direct his thoughts toward his wife. The overweight woman on the screen explained the therapeutic effects of orgies. He locked the bedroom door. He didn't want his son walking in and seeing his father watching such smut.

He said a quick prayer. "Please, God don't punish me for bad thoughts." He felt better immediately. The desire for his wife had dissipated. He relaxed, assuring himself he would sleep peacefully.

Iraqis and Afghanis might one day enjoy the spiritual depth of the American way of life practiced by a family that thought of itself as very typical.

Sex and the Country

"Religion is the sigh of the oppressed creature, the heart of a heartless world and the soul of soulless conditions. It is the opium of the people."—Karl Marx, Critique of Hegel's Philosophy of Right

EXTRAPOLATING FROM NOVEMBER 2004'S VOTING RESULTS, I conclude that at least half the country disapprove of "Sex in the City," "Six Feet Under" or the other HBO programs whose scripts include sex as routinely as they do eating or, in the case of "The Sopranos," killing.

Programs that entertain millions also violate taboos held by millions of Christian, Jewish and Moslem fundamentalists. Do diametrically opposite morality tracks run through the country? Do both of the tracks scream: "follow the money?" TV makes fortunes from sex shows. But the sexual sentries also cash in. Those who personify modern Puritanism, people H. L. Mencken described as possessed by "the haunting fear that someone somewhere may be happy," collect far more from their TV appeals than they do from the parishioners in actual church buildings. And the advocates of "No Sex in the Media or for the Non Married" get federal money.

The Bush Administration allocated $168 million for 2005 to fund abstinence-only programs. Bush himself told a pious audience of no sex before marriage proselytizers that "through your educational programs, you reach out to countless young people to give them the support they need to make that responsible choice."

Do as I say, the president in effect told the pious, not as I did for decades when I gallivanted with women and used intoxicating substances. When California Democratic Rep. Henry Waxman evaluated the abstinence-only curriculum that circulates in some public and many religious schools, he found that some adolescents learn that pregnancy can result from just touching genitals, and you can catch the HIV virus through sweat and tears. Waxman's report concluded that 80% of the "factual" information in the abstinence-only programs about reproductive health was false, misleading, or distorted.[130]

As we learned from the lead up to the invasion of Iraq, Administration ideologues don't think facts matter when they fashion policy. So, an ignorant public serves them well. Indeed, these neo-Puritans distract a section of the public from even thinking about Bush's plans to privatize social security. The "p" word means that working Americans would have their carefully overseen pension funds transferred to private brokers who would then invest it for them—after slicing 15% off the top.

Like Bush, orthodox preachers also favor the private sector—except in war, where Bush still must rely on the US military to do God's work. In December 2005, as the number of U.S. soldiers killed in Iraq neared 2000, and the Iraqi casualty soared beyond 100,000, tens of millions of Americans maintained their focus on abstinence. Apparently less concerned by bloodshed in Iraq and Afghanistan than about teenagers "getting it on," members of Concerned Women for America joined their counterparts in the Abstinence Clearinghouse and Focus on the Family to preach not safe sex, but no sex—until marriage, and even then in a very limited way.

These modern guardians of chastity want the government to teach sex education—abstinence. The Administration discovered that funding such programs under the heading of faith-based initiatives does not seriously reduce teen pregnancy and STDs, but the programs do depoliticize the population. And therefore make them more pious?

By targeting sexual freedom—not massive destruction in wars—as the most offensive element in U.S. culture, fundamentalist preachers successfully divert their flocks from thinking about terrestrial reality. The 17th Century Puritans understood the religious uses of fear and repression of sex. It would help bring about redemption, they promised

Today, those twin engines of distraction obfuscate mass murder in the name of virtue. Indeed, some TV preachers, golden cufflinks, diamond-studded ties and Rolexes shining in the klieg lights, beseech their flock to love the unborn and pray for those fighting the Lord's fight overseas.

Satan placed homosexuals and other "perverts" on earth, they warn. These demons wait to pounce on innocent youth and win their hearts and bodies. All Muslims, some preachers imply, fit these satanic categories as well. The Rev. Jerry Falwell even said, "Mohammed was a terrorist."

Contemporary fear-mongering rhetoric rings hollow in the context of 17th Century Puritans. They had posited their mission as building a "Zion in the Wilderness," a moral society fit for redemption and thus Christ's return. The new fundamentalists have diluted— polluted—this theology. Their Kingdom of the Apocalypse, followed by Rapture for the chosen people, will occur only after the Armageddon War brings the world to an end. They have reduced 17th Century hairsplitting Puritan theology to slogans like "God bless America." You can guess what He should do to the rest of the world!

Puritan theologians who landed in Massachusetts Bay in 1624 drafted rules of permissible behavior—morality. They understood that these restrictions ran directly counter to actual human instinct, i.e., temptation to sin. But the Puritans came to the new world precisely because the old one had grown too corrupt for salvation. They foreswore drinking, dancing, sexual experimentation and even poetry that might suggest the above. Their dogmatic, repressive and also complex theology died in the 1690s, shortly after they burned several "witches" (devil's agents). But their legacy filtered down into today's simplistic political-sexual guidebook.

Contemporary bible thumpers, hardly scholars of Jonathan Edwards' discipline, maintain the old taboos but incorporate modern empire, and especially the Middle East, into their pseudo Godly mission. Pat Robertson even claimed that God talks directly to him—a statement that would cause Cotton Mather to frown.

Like their mission-bound ancestors, the 20th Century hard edged preachers defined smoking, drinking, dancing and sex as the Devil's activities. Teenagers in the Bible Belt—even those about to go to war—still share the inherited wisdom: "Don't do it standing up lest you be accused of dancing."

Some teenagers hide folded copies of *Playboy* and *Hustler* photos inside inspirational novels by Tim La Haye. But the Sodom and Gomorrah signs of cultural decay (widespread masturbation, homosexuality and non-married sex—or thoughts of the above) have acquired neo-satanic tinges.

In case the non-ultra world tries to avoid dealing with the contemporary Puritans, movies like Bill Condon's "Kinsey" bring out the contemporary sex haters. One Jewish extremist, Judith Reisman, attributed to Kinsey the basic moral decline that she associates with sexual promiscuity and cultural degeneracy. This ex-communist, Jewish woman, allied with the evangelical prudes who have even tried to limit the screening of the new movie, sees herself as a protector of morals. Her book, *Kinsey: Crimes and Consequences*, compares Kinsey to Nazi scientists and insinuates that his teenage involvement in the Boy Scouts was equivalent to membership in the Hitler Youth. Reisman called Dr. Alfred Kinsey a high priest of perversion, who opened the door for the Age of Pornography.[131]

Fifty-six years after the Harvard educated Indiana University professor published his *Sexual Behavior in the Human Male*, the "Uptights" continue to fight their "moral war" against the sexual facts. Indeed, in 2004, they won a presidential election over largely sexual issues, disguised, of course, as moral values (gay marriage and abortion).

Kinsey, a zoologist who observed insects' mating behavior, also noted how his colleagues failed to scrutinize human practices. Indeed, he heard fellow professors offer their students biblical passages passing as sex education. So, he decided to find out about human sexual behavior. Having studied wasps, Kinsey knew he had to go beyond observation to categorize American sexual mores. His team asked questions. The sample of those who confided in Kinsey interviewers revealed that a substantial sector used their genitals in "taboo" ways.

For example, more than half of the rural Indiana males that Kinsey interviewed confessed to "doing it" with animals; not just sheep and cows, but pigs as well. At least they weren't dropping their seed on a barren rock, a biblical taboo.

Kinsey also discovered that men—and later women as well—practiced a vast range of sexual behavior. Indeed, Americans behaved pretty much the way the rest of the world did from time immemorial.

But these facts did not deter the carriers of diluted Puritanism, who still maintain that pleasure from sex is inherently wicked and that knowledge of it should remain restricted. Indeed, those shocked by sexual pleasure coincidentally got money for advocating such "moral" positions.

Reisman, for example, lobbied the Senate for legislation that would force them to hold hearings about whether Kinsey and his team during their interviews sexually molested children. Federal funds would, of course, finance such "research." Her previous research has served the straitlaced set—and financially served her.

The Abstinence Clearinghouse already receives substantial federal money to promote its "don't have sex" programs in public schools. The Department of Health and Human Services funds a variety of faith-based abstinence-only movements who spread their blather through public school curricula.

Reisman holds Kinsey, and Masters and Johnson who followed him as sex studiers, responsible for destroying traditional morality. Reisman referred to these "scholars" as homosexual proselytizers. This line played well before former Rep. Steve Stockman and Kansas Republican Senator Sam Brownback, who continue to try to slip funding for Resiman into legislation.

What a divided nation! Over sex? HBO viewers must have shaken their collective heads in disgust over the flap around Janet Jackson's exposed breast during the 2004 Super Bowl. But the prudes successfully mobilized around that mammary issue and the FCC fined the offending network—and put a chilling effect on all the media.

To counter the pleasure haters who benefit financially from their odium, philosopher Woody Allen offers a guiding lesson. "Is sex dirty? Only if it's done right," he said.

Fidel Promotes Sex Tourism?
JFK Rolls Over in his Grave

N A JULY 16, 2004 SPEECH IN TAMPA, GEORGE W. BUSH LEVELED his human rights gun—mouth—at Cuba for promoting sex tourism. "The regime in Havana, already one of the worst violators of human rights in the world, is adding to its crimes. The dictator welcomes sex tourism," Bush said at the National Training Conference on Combating Human Trafficking forced labor, sex and military service.

On July 16, *Associated Press'* Scott Lindlaw appropriately placed Bush's remark in the "pandering for votes" column. "By combining the human-trafficking issue with his hard-line rhetoric against Castro," Bush hoped to win more "Cuban-Americans in the state that decided the 2000 election. Friday's trip was Bush's 23rd as president to Florida."

The once boozing-drug taking but now fastidiously moral Bush told the Tampa audience that "We have taken action to stop American tourists from participating in the sexual abuse of children in Cuba or anywhere else in the world...But we cannot put them out of business until and unless we deal with the problem of demand. And so that's why we are going after the unscrupulous adults who prey on the young and the innocent."

I shook my head in disbelief. If Bush was serious, police would make thousands of arrests at both the Republican and Democratic Conventions. In 2000, police estimated that several thousand prostitutes serviced delegates of both parties at their conventions. Police did not check IDs to determine whether the "fancy ladies" were 18, but some looked decidedly underage to me.

I imagine that Fidel will guffaw over the idea that he or any other Cuban in his right mind would welcome sex tourism. The people who made the revolution in the late 1950s remember well types like Bush—before his cleansing Christian conversion, of course. John F. Kennedy, in his own pre-presidential playboy days, routinely used the U.S. Ambassador's mansion in Havana to romp with uninhibited "professional" Cuban women. The Massachusetts senator epitomized the high side of sex tourism: wealthy foreigners take advantage of young (often underage) native women or men because they can afford to pay them.

Kennedy, like the current President, attended an Ivy League school. Both Harvard and Yale, we should recall, originated as divinity schools. Over time, as recent Ivy League presidential graduates (Kennedy, Clinton and both Bushes) demonstrated, the divine has more than mixed with the earthly—if not down-right carnal.

The current president may have his feet firmly planted on the golf course and treadmill, but his brain seems unable to translate into words a critical sensibility, that characteristic allowing a person to apply his own standards beyond their immediate target of political convenience. Bush, for example, seized on Castro's description of Cuban hookers as "the cleanest and most educated prostitutes in the world," as if Castro intended these words to lure respectable Christian Americans to Cuba and away from Las Vegas.

Bush said Castro has turned Cuba into a major destination for sex tourism, which is "a vital source of hard currency to keep his corrupt government afloat." I immediately imagined a newspaper headline: "Decline in Sex Tourism Brings Collapse of Castro Government." I wondered if Bush would address the issue of Las Vegas luring foreign and domestic sex tourism! Indeed, Nevada's notorious Mustang Ranch, i.e. whorehouse, has become world famous and advertises itself as such at home and abroad, even though the US government is not yet desperate for seedy sources of hard currency.

Before the 1959 revolution in Cuba, Meyer Lansky occupied a suite at Havana's Hotel Nacional, from whence he ran gambling and other criminal enterprises linked with tourism and sex. Indeed, Havana and Las Vegas had become twin cash cows for the Mafia

Now, Nevada—a red state—maintains the same relationship toward sex and gambling that Cuba used to have before the revolution. Indeed, Bush took Castro's quote out of context. In 1992, Castro explained to Cuba's Parliament that prostitution, outlawed several years after the revolutionaries took power, had reappeared in force as a result of the economic downswing in the post-Soviet era. Castro was trying to look on the bright and light side of a serious issue; Bush issued a serious and hot accusation—albeit light on documentation.

Indeed, as visitors to Cuba since the late 1980s can ascertain, women of the night have become ubiquitous in the tourist areas. Indeed, around the hotel areas of Havana one might have counted almost 20% of the number of such professionals as one would find in much smaller areas in Las Vegas.

In Vegas, young Mexican men on the busy streets hand out flyers advertising with explicit photos the many possibilities for kinky fun before one loses one's money in the casinos. Some of the casino and lap dance club owners belong not only to the Republican Party, but to the high donors section of that elite configuration. Somehow, their participation in moral turpitude did not receive the scolding from Bush's bully pulpit that the chief executive used to taunt Castro. Nor will Bush punish the Vegas sin sellers for perpetuating—and advertising—their lucrative business vices.

Imagine opening the morning paper and seeing the headlines "Bush cuts off all federal aid to Vegas." "All commercial flights banned from Vegas Airports." Think of the Post Office automatically inspecting all mail for illegal checks sent by family members to needier kinfolk in Nevada's sin city.

The association of pimps, motel, hotel and casino owners would hardly tolerate such actions after all the money they contributed to Bush's campaign!

Bush tried to provide context for his sex tourism charges by swearing that "My administration is working toward a comprehensive solution to this problem: the rapid, peaceful transition to democracy in Cuba." Translation: "I am seriously pandering for votes and hope that no one in this audience thinks about how little the Justice Department has done to stop sexual commerce in the United States—including with kids."

Indeed, the very report Bush cited in his anti-Castro fusillade[1] stated that traffickers bring up to 17,500 people into the United States every year, to make profits on them for performing sexual acts as part of their servitude. Some are called domestic workers. In other words, the United States suffers far more from sex-trafficking than Cuba.

The day after Bush linked Castro and sex tourism, the *Sydney Morning Herald* reported that Bush's then appointed Prime Minister in Iraq summarily executed six suspected insurgents in a Baghdad police station. Paul McGeough wrote that Iyad Allawi, just before he took his Prime Minister post, dispatched the alleged "terrorists" by shooting them in the head while they were blindfolded and handcuffed. About a dozen Iraqi policemen and four Americans from Allawi's personal security team "watched in stunned silence."[132] Allawi's office denied the allegations.

The breaking story from Iraq should have helped people understand Bush's latest vituperations toward the intellectually superior Castro. Sex even used as an accusation against a politi-

---

1   Johns Hopkins University School of Advanced International Studies' report from its legal human rights focused Protection Project

cal enemy diverts the public from the overwhelming human rights issue of our time: the US occupation of Iraq.

Indeed, Bush sought to use sex in Cuba as one means of misdirecting public attention from the all encompassing issues of war and peace.

Castro might have responded to Bush's charges of promoting sex tourism by imitating Vice President Dick Cheney's Senate behavior. On June 24, 2004, Cheney told Senator Patrick Leahy (D-VT) to "go f... himself." Indeed, Fidel could tell Bush to take his sex trafficking charges and stick them where he applies his Preparation H. Or, book Bush for a speech in Vegas to peddle his "sex tourism sermon!"

(Castro underwent surgery in early August and by the end of 2006 he had not made a public appearance. In mid December 2006, top US spy chief John Negroponte declared with certainty that Fidel had cancer and only weeks to live. Top Cuban officials categorically denied he had cancer and said he was recooperating.)

Geriatric Apprehensions

I fear I have
Forgotten how to fall
Asleep the spelling of
Words once dissected in
Triumph at spelling bees
Impressionism obscures detail misplaces
Objccts in time people
In spaces they did
Not occupy a woman
On a train becomes
A burden on my
Overloaded brain filled with
Traces of overlapping dialogue
Indistinct images of parents
Teaching me to fall
Asleep with words from
Animals of happy valley

I fear I will
Forget to wipe my
Ass say goodbye thanks
Lose track of memory
Taste tactile sensations numbers
Birthdays of children addresses
Schemes to calculate tips
Words to say at
Ever frequent funerals
Names of dear friends

A Bush & Botox World

Lovers and even jokes
Fear of dying replaced
With temporal frost panic
Over past sins un-confessed
Eroding the lines of
Virtue that define fact
Sanity serenity and sleep

Imperial Portrait: For Hearst Enough Was Never Enough

AFTER SPENDING $40 FOR TWO 75 MINUTE GUIDED WALKS through some of the 165 rooms and guest houses of La Cuesta Encantada (The Enchanted Mountain), I learned what Gore Vidal already knew about tasteless millionaires: "The more money an American accumulates, the less interesting he becomes."

In the first decade of the 20th Century, after forging a new style of sensationalist journalism in the 1890s, William Randolph Hearst (1863-1951) served two terms in the House, and then aspired unsuccessfully to govern New York City, then New York State and finally the United States. Failing to win electoral backing, Hearst built his own, more formal kingdom by accumulating vast media holdings and castles.

Hearst hired Julia Morgan, a stylish architect, to arrange imported cathedral ceilings and Roman columns. Morgan added taste and talent to Hearst's crude accumulation habit. His hotel-sized kitchen and royally-proportioned dining room gave me hunger pangs, the kind Hearst must have experienced whenever he saw a valuable object that belonged to someone else.

The Castle at San Simeon, located on 240,000 acres about midway on the coast between Los Angeles and San Francisco, now belongs to the State of California. His father, mining mogul George Hearst, had inhaled vast California landscapes and seascapes for less than $1 an acre. When Hearst died, his family learned how expensive maintenance would be and they ceded the gloomy and ornate mansion to the State.

As the bus driver carefully navigated the sharp curves on the winding, narrow road away from the coastal highway, I tried to conceive what might have motivated this eccentric man to erect the palace looming above us, like a set from a Dracula movie. At age ten, the precocious Hearst started collecting expensive art. A decade later, Harvard expelled him for bringing a mule into the Dean's office with a pejorative reference attached to it. As he used the newspaper business to build on his father's already impressive fortune, Hearst's pranks turned downright vicious: like trying to start a war.

In 1895, Hearst bought the *New York Morning Journal and* spent lavishly to win a circulation war with the *New York World*, owned by Joseph Pulitzer. He lowered the paper's price to a penny, increased the number of pages, added more comic strips and, ironically, out-sensationalized Pulitzer, who had invented the "appeal to the base instincts" style journalism. By 1898, Hearst's front page featured headlines like "Spaniards Rape American Women in Cuba," (not true) to paint Spain as the blackest of hats in its war to prevent independence in Cuba. Hearst wanted the United States to go to war and used his newspaper shamelessly and successfully to manipulate public opinion for intervention.

He liked big events, like wars, and big buildings to live in. He also liked to invite adoring guests. Hearst instructed Julia Morgan to join each bedroom with a private bathroom so that Jean Harlow would not have to share a commode with Harpo Marx.

In the 1930s, Cary Grant, the tour guide informed us, made thirty-four visits to the Castle. The Castle "was a great place to spend the Depression," quipped Cary.

In those economically bad times, while millions lived without indoor plumbing and waited on bread lines, Mary Pickford cheerfully played tennis with Charlie Chaplin at Hearst's private courts. Gary Cooper swam laps in the Castle's tiled pool of dreams and

Harpo practiced acrobatics in the Castle library. Why not, since Hearst's vast collection of books looked unread!

The guide showed us the movie theater where guests watched first run films after dinner. Alas, we missed the bowling alley—that would have been Tour #3. The State dismantled Hearst's private zoo, a place for the magnate to retreat when looking at famous people got boring.

The Castle tours left me with an overwhelming desire to consume. Had Hearst's ghost infected me? Instead of grazing at the greasy hamburger/hot dog/French fry stands that the State offers to tourists at the bus station below the Castle, I ate pumpkin fudge that the State also markets to those who realize that the cure for looking at overindulgence is indulging.

As I ate more disgustingly sweet fudge, I concluded that the Castle tour had taught me to think like Hearst, who clearly rejected the adage that "enough is enough." Indeed, the first sugar aftershock stirred my brain maliciously.

Hearst lived much of his life in this bizarre and incongruous place with his mistress, actress Marion Davies, until he died. His children, from his wife, Millicent, whom he never divorced, and his grandchildren, also enjoyed spending time staring at the infinite number of imported gewgaws, ornate engravings and tiles in almost every room.

Did his granddaughter Patricia's Castle experience link to her 1974 kidnapping and then supposed capitulation to the "Stockholm syndrome," and thus her membership in the Symbionese Liberation Army (SLA)?

This group of so-called revolutionaries supposedly brainwashed Patty and then transformed her from spoiled rich kid to bank robber. The non-descript heiress became Tania (named after the woman warrior who died with Che Guevara in Bolivia in 1967), a bisexual, gun-toting revolutionary spewing condemnation of the vile capitalist class.

After serving 21 months of a seven-year prison sentence for bank robbery, Patty regained her ruling class senses. To save her wealthy ass, she ratted out her Symbionese comrades, those she briefly loved, and went on to star un-brilliantly in several films. In 1998, Bill Clinton gave her a presidential pardon.

When the SLA kidnapped Patty, her father, who inherited the *San Francisco Examiner*, might have wondered if his old man had somehow offended the Republic of Symbia. Did Patty's participation in proletarian armed struggle offer a poetic epitaph for her conscienceless grandpa?

Or maybe, Patty's flirtation with guns related to grandpa's obsession with power—no matter how misused. After entertaining Mussolini's mistress at his Castle, Hearst checked out the Nazis.

"I flew up to Berlin and had a long talk with Hitler yesterday," he wrote in 1934. "Hitler certainly is an extraordinary man. We estimate him too lightly in America. He has enormous enthusiasm, a marvelous faculty for dramatic oratory, and great organizing ability. Of course all these qualities can be misdirected. I only hope that he and the Germans may have sense enough to keep out of another war."[133]

Journalist George Seldes attributed Hearst's pro-Nazi stance to Hitler's manipulation of the easily flattered—by power—media baron. Seldes reported that U.S. Ambassador to Germany, William E. Dodd, said that "[When] Hearst came to take the waters at Bad Nauheim [Germany] in September 1934...Hitler sent two of his most trusted Nazi propagandists...to ask Hearst how Nazism could present a better image in the U.S. When Hearst went to Berlin later in the month, he was taken to see Hitler."[134]

Seldes also said that Joseph Goebbels, the Nazi propaganda minister, cut a $400,000 a year deal with Hearst, after which he "completely changed the editorial policy of his nineteen daily newspapers the same month he got the money."

Hearst sued over such claims, but Dan Gillmor, publisher of the magazine *Friday*, told the court that "Promptly after this visit with Adolph Hitler and the making of said arrangements... plaintiff, William Randolph Hearst, instructed all Hearst press correspondents in Germany, including those of INS (Hearst's International News Service) to report happenings in Germany only in a friendly manner. All of correspondents reporting happenings in Germany accurately and without friendliness, sympathy and bias for the actions of the German government, were transferred elsewhere, discharged, or forced to resign."[135]

Whether Hearst actually took Nazi money in return for good U.S. press remains in the realm of cloudy biography. The extremely wealthy have ways to turn megalomania into eerie designs. Hearst's accumulation addiction led him to overextend his own fortune. He had to sell part of his art collection and halt construction on the Castle.

When he died, Hearst still had enough money to hold on to his news empire. The film, "Citizen Kane," showed Hearst as a victim of childhood trauma. In his adult life, he compensated for childhood slights by abusing his power to punish "enemies."

Hearst's life exemplifies the sickness of empire—personal or national. Vast amounts of wealth warp sensibilities. Those who inherit, steal or even make fortunes tend to think they can export their grandiose notions and magically solve the maladies of others. They call it democracy, of course, or the American way of life.

After two and a half hours of seeing the results of avarice, I grew weary of Hearst's limitless appetites for power, women, and possessions. During the height of the 1930s depression, Hearst deposited $50 thousand a day from the largest publishing empire in history and into his personal account to maintain the Castle. His spending habits on the Castle outstripped even his gargantuan income. He had to sell some accumulated treasures and stop expanding the mansion.

Might this teach a lesson to those who run the U.S. empire today?

A Ritual in Ashes Tossed from the Mesa

A little kid walks
Too close to the edge
You try hiding hysteria
A billion ants gobble
Your sexy naked ankle
Dry dusty wind slices
Into your tiny pores
Sucks moisture from lips
Ignores grandma's teary cheeks
The big boss of
The mesa blows its
Merry way slivers through
Suffering sagebrush slips into
Trouser pockets ear lobes
And suitcases locked in
Trunks of parked cars

The kid picks wildflowers
Near the edge again
The snake suns itself
Still life in dust
I contain my panic
A casual drifting eagle
Dipping rising with drafts
Examines the parched ground
A mouse a mole
Must have seen him

A Bush & Botox World

Before he saw them
An animal eternity passes
We toss her remains
Into swirling petulant wind
Ashes blow back symbolically
Into your grieving face

Elegy to the Salton Sea

N 19TH CENTURY ENGLAND, WILLIAM WORDSWORTH STROLLED through his garden. "I am at one with Nature," he declared. Hemingway's 20th Century hero Nick paddled with his father in the canoe in the unspoiled Minnesota lakes. He put his hand into the ice cold water, "It was good." Why don't I, like those great writers, feel some organic relationship with Nature?

Could I aspire to become a 21st Century Nick in the North Woods, as I looked at the unruffled picture post card water, with a background of pristine landscape reflected by the desert sun? The tamarisk trees cast flimsy shadows on the lake's surface. Southern California's largest body of water, the Salton Sea, exudes calm and natural beauty—as long as you have a clothes pin on your nose.

Pull it off and the stench ramrods its way through your sinuses. This invasive redolence combines red algae bloom with residues from agricultural runoff (pesticide and chemical fertilizer), sewage from surrounding desert cities (Palm Springs, Coachella and Indio) and even some toxic waste from maquiladoras that float in from nearby Mexicali, across the border.

The lake itself measures 35 miles in length, up to 15 miles in width and has about 115 miles of shoreline. On the western edge, tens of thousands of carcasses of dead and festering birds and fish belie its tranquil image and add to the pernicious odor.

In 1996, government agencies affirmed that 1,200 endangered brown pelicans died of avian botulism. In addition, 19,000 waterfowl and shore birds from 63 species perished. In 1997, 10,000 plus birds from 51 species died. From January through April, 1998, 17,000 birds from 70 species caught Newcastle's disease and avian cholera. The immune systems of thousands of eared grebes became weak, probably from ingesting selenium, and they succumbed to avian infirmities. Their carcasses decompose on the shore alongside the other skeletons. Some biologists predict that all the fish will soon die as salt levels increase.

In the early 1960s, one of several floods occurred. Surrounding agribusiness owners had irrigated their overly-chemical drenched soil with a larger than usual amount of water. They did not consider—or they didn't care—the impact of their action on the Salton Sea. Residents had to abandon modest retirement homes and vacation cottages. The celebrities abandoned their less modest lakeshore estates and along with empty motels, a yacht club and restaurants, these vacant family edifices loom like graveside monuments to a lake-side community that after World War II had mushroomed on the edge of the Salton Sea.

The origins of the current predicament date back to 1905, when a dam in the Colorado River broke and water raced through mineral heavy canals for two years to collect in a pre-historic dried-up lake bed. The new body of water contained a high salinity level. This new physical culture proved ideal for certain salt-water fish, as well as a place where birds and ducks and geese could migrate and breed. Indeed, scientists have observed more than 400 species of birds at the sea. During the 1950s, experts estimated that in winter some four million birds used this artificial water body. For flying non-insects, it became the most utilized sea in the nation. New flora also grew on the shore: desert scrub, creosote bush, saltbush, and tamarisk.

Developers and speculators built tourist facilities that serviced some 200,000 visitors a year, including campsites, trails, playgrounds and boat ramps. The lake became a virtual speedway for boat racers who took advantage of the high salt content that gave their craft more buoyancy. Water and jet skiers roared past annoyed fisherman. By 1958, the North Shore of the lake sported a yacht club, with one of the largest marinas in Southern

California. In the 1950s, Jerry Lewis docked his boat there. Desi Arnaz and Johnny Weissmuller played on the 18-hole golf course and hung around Salton Bay Yacht Club sipping cock tails. Bulldozers paved the streets.

These forsaken structures have shed their paint. Motels and yacht clubs, places from which water skiers once took off, have also lost their essence: the neon has leaked out of their signs.

Like other ghost towns that once vibrated with life and crackled with festivity, some of the Salton Sea communities now symbolize ecological disaster: conditions that arise when hustlers attempt to manipulate Nature for profit without acknowledging that the future may involve very high costs. Like Melville's white whale, the Salton Sea today threatens to become a metaphor for Biblical punishment. "You have gone too far," the great voice in the sky might have roared. "You are playing with my creation!"

"Hey, that's the nature of capitalism," the developers might well have replied.

To regain their profitable relationship with people and Nature on the Salton Sea, the "men of progress" call upon "science," the ubiquitous magician, to solve environmental messes.

"Fix it," they metaphorically order the men in white lab coats. "And get the government (taxpayers, not corporations) to pick up the tab."

So, the Environmental Protection Agency, Department of the Interior, Bureau of Land Management and various California agencies contacted scientists who dutifully began to study this putrid body of water more than three decades ago. They differ about how to apply their magic to sections of the lake, in some areas fifty feet deep, covered with thick layers of viscous silt. Some marine biologists wonder if anyone can clean up this peanut butter-like deposit of chemical slurp that looms as a major ecological calamity.

Nature seemed to rebel in the form of an ecological chain reaction. Altering the flow of Colorado River water to create the Salton Sea also led to the diversion of river water to irrigate the Imperial Valley. The ensuing runoff flowed naturally into the unnatural Salton Sea. When farmers poured their "excess" water into the Sea, the Sea rose—having no outlet for the excess water—and flooded the shoreline residents, including those on land belonging to the Torres-Martinez Reservation.

Geologists call the Salton Sea a "terminal" water body, one that receives water flow, but has no outlet. So, it had no place to send the agricultural run off, post irrigation water that contains chemical fertilizers, pesticides, selenium and other minerals and salts—other than onto the shore, with its people and edifices.

The levels of poisonous materials have risen steadily. The Sea diminishes only through evaporation. Allowing it to dry up would mean that poisonous selenium dust would infect all living things in the area. In 2004, scientists estimated that the Salton Sea contained 25% more salinity than the ocean. Even most saltwater fish cannot survive in it. Today, the Sea's ecosystem suffers from significant stress. Several million fish and birds have already died from disease and depressed levels of dissolved oxygen.

Not all the nearby residents have fled, however. In the eastern shore communities of Bombay Beach and the Slab City trailer community, some people live on meager social security checks. "I like it better here than in rural Alabama," says a man with confederate flag sewn on his trucker's cap.

The bar flies at Bombay Beach's Ski Inn drink, smoke and gossip about daily life. They have become accustomed to living in an environmentally challenged area. From the bar, they drive in Mad Max vehicles to their trailers or small homes. The disgusting odor that pervades the western bank occasionally infiltrates their community as well. It seems worse in the summer when the thermometer rises above 110 degrees.

Some fishermen still drop their line in the lake and duck hunters hide in the blinds on the lake shore. "I sure hope they don't eat what they catch or shoot," says a man who has watched the Sea deteriorate over the decades.

The residents wait for the conflicting interests, like urban water authorities, conservationists, agribusiness, and native peoples, to figure out a "cure" for their ecologically diseased Sea.

One interested party, the Torres-Martinez tribe, had to change their life in 1905 when the Colorado River water overflowed their reservation. Like the fauna, flora and people in the area, these Native Americans adapted to the new environment and abandoned their traditional hunting and gathering culture for fishing and modest farming, as they debated whether to build a casino. In the 1960s, more flooding and increasing salinity and pollution of the Sea further threatened their future.

The Salton Sea, like the Aral Sea in Central Asia, which is 400 times its size and shrinking fast, symbolizes ecological catastrophe. Soviet industrial "planners" had treated Nature just as the California capitalist developers did: they employed "productive" technology without calculating—or even thinking about—consequences. Nearby resident animals and plants suffered horrendous consequences.

But humans learn slowly. They know that reproduction of the species requires a healthy environment—clean air and water and uncontaminated soil. Some of the smartest engineers, however, can lose sight of that truism when offered the chance to manipulate Nature for short-term profits.

Indeed, these "forward looking" individuals view Nature as something to dominate, not nurture. Will it take the rule of romantic poets to teach that tornadoes, hurricanes, El Niños scream metaphoric messages? "Hey, there's something more powerful than all of you!"

Environmental nightmares like the Salton Sea have not humbled those who exude "progress" but lack the sensitivity to understand that serious lessons follow the modification of the

Earth's ecology. In 2005, developers sold hundreds of low cost houses to those who could not afford housing in more convenient locations. "They get used to the smell," said one real estate salesman. "And it's a low crime area." The casino construction began in 2006.

I think of Wordsworth's Nature: "The language of the sense,/ The anchor of my purest thoughts, the nurse,/ The guide, the guardian of my heart, and soul/ Of all my moral being."[136]

Mercury in U.S. Lakes; Cyanide in India—Trust the CEOs!

"Capitalism is the astounding belief that the most wickedest of men will do the most wickedest of things for the greatest good of everyone."—Sir John Maynard Keynes

O N AUGUST 24, 2005 THE ENVIRONMENTAL PROTECTION Agency (EPA) declared that more than "one-third of the nation's lakes and nearly one-fourth of its rivers contain fish that may be contaminated with mercury, dioxin, PCB and pesticide pollution."

"It's about trout, not tuna. It's about what you catch on the shore, not what you buy on the shelf," said EPA administrator Mike Leavitt. "I want to make clear that this agency views mercury as a toxin," he said. "This is about the health of pregnant mothers and small children, that's the primary focus of our concern."

Though Leavitt claimed that mercury emissions "from human activities" had dropped over the last decade, EPA nevertheless posted mercury advisories for fish in 44 states. In addition, Montana and Washington (major fishing states) warned their citizens of possible widespread contamination of river and lake fish. Fly fishermen, in other words, can catch as many bass and trout as they want, but the Food and Drug Administration (FDA) alerted people not to eat more than one six ounce portion a week of fish in U.S. sweet waters.

By blaming "human activities," Leavitt employed a euphemism that evokes guilt from citizens without any connection to poisoning the streams. Why not just say: "CEOs of specific industries knowingly dump poison into lakes and rivers." After all, these CEOs understand that mercury and chlorine emissions from their coal-fired power plants will alter the chemistry of the waters. Corporate executives know that mercury and PCBs seep out in the processes of burning hazardous and medical waste and that they end up in rivers and lakes.

Unlike some toxic elements, which lose potency over time, mercury's ability to damage the nervous system endures. So, concluded, Leavitt, "man-made emissions need to be reduced and regulated."

Leavitt sounded serious about the pollution issue. But his boss, George W. Bush, remains less than zealous in regulating the polluters. Bush has warm feelings toward CEOs—especially those who contribute to his campaign coffers. He respects and trusts these virtuous and very religious company bosses; ergo, they should regulate themselves.

The fact that CEOs of major energy and waste disposal companies have continued to dump toxic materials in the public water for decades has not affected Bush's judgment. He is bullish on corporate morality and bearish on public health. He's also pushing to open up protected federal lands, wildlife and other preserves for more drilling and energy exploration—processes that would worsen the already critical condition of the lakes and rivers.

The President's optimism appears in his "Utility Mercury Reductions" plan, a characteristically misnamed project that actually increases the possibilities for polluters and frees them from the responsibility of cleaning up the mercury they engendered. According to the Sierra Club's January 30, 2004 Watch, the White House plan would permit three times more mercury to get dumped over the next decades.

So, what's a citizen to think? On the one hand, the FDA warns—especially pregnant women—not to eat mercury-laden fish. On the other, EPA, following the Bush guidelines, relies on the good faith of CEOs to voluntarily diminish dumping more mercury poison from its production facilities.

Under Bush's premise, the corporate executives represent the highest levels of public morality and therefore should police their own environmental behavior. Willie Sutton (the 20th Century's most colorful bank robber) should be named trustworthy enough to guard the bank at night.

Bush adheres to the corporate publicity apparatus' dogma: government is bad and the private sector good. This blatantly ridiculous tenet existed long before the Bush era. Indeed, even before the Reagan presidency—"trees cause pollution"—the mind manipulators had blitzed the public with a barrage of messages about the inherent virtues of the private sector. "Business class" became far more than an airplane seating reference. It signified efficiency, high level competence and practicality—the virtues of our age.

Leading business executives, however, routinely conspire to rip off the stockholders and the public. Their public relations teams simultaneously create halos over their heads. The 19th Century Robber Barons became "Industrial Statesmen" while the gonifs of Enron and Halliburton merited the highest level access to political power. Dick Cheney met with these larcenous executives to plan the nation's energy policy.

The Enron and WorldCom scandals and headlines about Halliburton overcharging the Pentagon should have at least made a dent in the façade of virtue that covers these global production and distribution giants. Yet, adding up the business hanky panky with the environmental destruction, one arrives at an obvious conclusion: corporate profits come before protecting the environment or people.

Bhopal, India provides a dramatic illustration of how corporate America responded to a 9/11 size catastrophe. On December 3, 1984, more than 3,000 residents of that Indian city died in hours when cyanide gas leaked from a U.S.-owned plant and found its way into the lungs and eyes of 3,000 people as they slept. Subsequently, 12,000 more succumbed to the impact of methyl isocyanate.

In addition, hundreds of thousands suffered from diseases related to the deadly chemical's effect on the human organism. Dr. Nalok Banerjee, of India's Center for Rehabilitation Studies, found levels of respiratory ailments, eye and gastronomical disorders at almost four times the levels in other Indian areas.

The perpetrators of this slaughter belong to Al-Carbide, not Al-Qaeda. The top executives of Union Carbide, now owned by Dow Chemical, did not "waste" their stockholders' money by investing in safety procedures that could have prevented the industrial mishap; nor did this company subsequently rush to pay compensation to the victims or their families or even contribute to cleaning up their deadly mess. They said, in effect, "to hell with those people. They had the misfortune of sucking cyanide into their lungs." That's how the cookie crumbles in the Third World.

Unlike the fiends who attacked the World Trade Center and Pentagon, the Indian managers of Union Carbide in Bhopal did not set out with malice to slaughter thousands of civilians.

Likewise, those CEOs that ordered toxic wastes dumped in rivers and lakes did not intend to make trout sick and uneatable or cause health problems in humans. The disasters came as by-products of routine corporate behavior.

The CEOs apparently didn't learn in church that people should not defecate in the plate they eat from. The pious Christians who occupy power in government and industry are hardly unaware that corporate fouling of the human nest occurs repeatedly throughout the United States and the Third World.

In 1989, the oil tanker Exxon Valdez struck a reef in Alaska, spilling more than 11 million gallons of crude oil, the largest in U.S. history. The spill killed birds and animals, and threatened the delicate food chain that supported the region's fishing industry.

A government commission identified "privatization, self regulation and neglect" as root causes of the tragedy. "The disaster could have been prevented by simple adherence to the original rules" but "concern for profits obliterated concern for safe operations."

In Nigeria, Shell, Mobil, Chevron and other major oil companies colluded with corrupt governments to stop protests in the Niger Delta where farmers claimed, with compelling evidence, that drilling operations have made them sick and ruined their land and water supply.

Similar oil company activities have brought devastation to indigenous people in Ecuador. Throughout the third world, CEOs have ordered actions that have led to death and environmental destruction. Have these and thousands of more examples not taught the Bushies the obvious lesson: regulate?

The quest for corporate profit invalidates concern for the environment, unless, of course, that concern means hastening the end of the world, so that the chosen few can enjoy the Rapture that accompanies it. The "non-chosen" should remain confused and ignorant about the imminence of the environmental decay. Better they should focus their fears on Al-Qaeda than Al-Carbide.

This indifferent attitude on environment has led the Administration to coddle Al-Carbide (Dow Chemical) rather than insist it compensates the victims of Bhopal and cleans up its cyanide mess. The media, by not reporting follow ups on the Bhopal disaster, toed the White House line.

Thanks to grass roots groups in India, other third world countries and the United States, environmental concerns find their way to public attention. Perhaps, Bush can advise fishermen to ignore FDA warnings. "Eat as many fish as you want. Mercury is good for you."

As far as the 15,000 dead Indians—well, in the world of global production, cyanides happen!

Derision in Digital

A Trinity Poem

Imagine losing face
By allowing access
To data base
Collections of olio
Stored in computers
A digital portfolio
Compartmentalized you see
Not very romantic
Computer and me
Alone with passwords
On secret webs
Just the nerds
Digitally literate crowds
Living very compressed
Inside electronic shrouds

The Mass Media, Symbols and Ownership

How to understand torture by a free society with a free press!

OVER THE LAST TWO YEARS, OVERWHELMING EVIDENCE FORCED the media to report that U.S. military personnel had tortured Muslim prisoners. In September 2005, an honorable Captain of the 82nd Airborne told Senator John Warner that his troops had routinely tortured Iraqi prisoners—for sport and intelligence. In May, 2005, *Newsweek* had broken a story about a prison guard who had flushed a copy of the Koran down a toilet.[137]

Apparently, millions of Muslims took this insult to the Koran more seriously than they had taken the killing and torture of thousands of Muslims. Riots broke out in several cities.

Ironically, the Bush Administration chastised the messenger. Bush made *Newsweek* a target of his wrath—for inaccurate reporting. The rest of the media piled on. They accepted White House spin and simply ignored reliable sources—including FBI agents who had already documented Koran desecration by U.S. military and CIA personnel. Instead of deepening the torture stories, leading news organs sent their reporters to examine whether the actual "flushing down the toilet" incident had occurred.

The fact that this incident, not any of thousands, ignited the riots did not seem to provide incentive for probing deeper into the torture stories. Rather, the media made *Newsweek* the issue: "did they or didn't they have sufficient proof to run the story?"

Newsweek retracted the story several days later. The rest of the media not only failed to support the news magazine, but failed to see the disproportionate response. The headlines trumpeted *Newsweek*'s error, and offered minute space to the story of Koran and human desecration by US officials.

During the Vietnam War, some self-designated patriots thought flag burners merited the death penalty for desecrating a piece of cloth. Symbols inflame zealous publics: a "holy" book hitting a toilet can mean more than torturing live people. (No one asked what it did to the toilet)

The Pentagon released its report on the affair late on Friday afternoon, June 3, 2005, a typical ploy to minimize readership. The report cited "two other cases of desecration." One involved "a two-word obscenity written in English inside a prisoner's Koran." In another episode, "one soldier deliberately kicked the Muslim holy book, other guards hit it with water balloons and a soldier's urine was splashed on a prisoner and his Koran."[138]

The *New York Times* reported that "the guard urinated near an air vent and the wind blew his urine into a detainee's cell."[139] The *Times* did not ask if the guard's urine went astray because the Guantanamo base lacks latrines. Was the guard pissing on the prisoner who happened to have his Koran in hand when the pee hit the cell?

Previously, newspapers and TV news programs carried photos of U.S. personnel using sex and animal torture. Reports from the Red Cross, the FBI and other first hand observers added sleep deprivation, incessant noise and other forms of torture outlawed by the Geneva Conventions and the UN Convention Against Torture.

The attack on *Newsweek* and its subsequent retraction for having printed a basically accurate story marks the second occasion in the past year that the U.S. public has witnessed righteous anger aimed successfully at true stories. In 2004, CBS also pulled back publicly from an accurate story because the ultra right and the Bush Administration aggressively accused them of bad reporting. And the rest of the media piled on.

Dan Rather's "60 Minutes" Wednesday story aired on September 8, 2004. Bushies screamed that CBS had used forged documents and timed the story to coincide with the presidential race. A chorus of right wing AM radio talk show hosts chimed in. "Liberal bias," they screamed, had motivated CBS' broadcast of a show that impugned Bush's military record.

"60 Minutes" offered four written documents. Rather said Lt. Col. Jerry Killian, now dead, wrote them. Killian was Bush's Texas Air National Guard commander in the early 1970s. The documents showed that Bush disobeyed orders to report for a physical exam, and that Bush family buddies intervened to "sugar coat" his Guard service. The memos showed Bush as a shirker who used family influence to stay out of Vietnam and then reduce the time he agreed to serve in the Guard. Killian's then secretary backed up the thrust of the documents in her appearance on the show.

Bush supporters immediately challenged the documents' validity, but even if the actual papers were forged, CBS had accumulated sufficient material to support the gist of their story. The forgery complaints obscured the focus of the reporting and shifted the issue to one of "integrity in journalism." CBS retracted the story. Instead of the media focusing on how Bush got out of service while his rival Kerry served in dangerous combat, the media helped the Bushies turn the story into its opposite.

The liberal media was out to get Bush. Meanwhile the "Swift Boat" vets began a defamation campaign against Kerry, implying that he didn't deserve the medals he got for his combat.

On January 10, 2005, CBS continued its capitulation ritual by firing three executives for their role in preparing and reporting the Bush-National Guard service story. CBS Chairman Leslie Moonves deeply regretted "the disservice this flawed "60 Minutes Wednesday" report did to the American public, which has a right to count on CBS News for fairness and accuracy."

Senior producer Mary Mapes accused Moonves of making her a "scapegoat." She said, correctly, that he acted out of "corporate and political considerations—ratings rather than journalism."

Viacom, a multinational corporation, owns CBS. The other networks belong to similar transnational titans who have a basic interest in staying on the good side of the U.S. government. Multinational corporate owners don't want their media outlets to de-legitimize government. Indeed, instead of attacking corruption, they often turn their guns on the "investigative journalist" who God forbid made a tiny factual error in reporting a big and otherwise true story about government criminality. (Warning: journalists, check your facts carefully!)

In the early 1970s, *Washington Post* reporters got encouragement to report on the White House connections to the Watergate break. *Post* owners, who also owned *Newsweek*, kvelled over the role their reporters played in forcing Richard Nixon to resign. What a difference three decades make. In 2006, revelations of government and corporate misdeeds vitiate corporate interests.

For decades, the old "60 Minutes" show had exposed government and corporate corruption. But in 1995, the relationship of the CBS Corporation and an exposé of the tobacco industry forced the show's producers to compromise.

In 1995, CBS decided not to air a "60 Minutes" report produced by Lowell Bergman on Jeffrey Wigand, a former vice president of Brown & Williamson, the tobacco company. Wigand said that the tobacco executives purposely "hid the truth about tobacco's addictive and harmful properties from the American public. CBS and the key producers and reporters all had interest in tobacco stock and softened the attack against the giant tobacco producers."[140] A CBS lawyer told Bergman that "the corporation will not risk its assets on the story."

Ironically, the ultra right still rant endlessly about the liberal media. In fact, as the retractions by *Newsweek* and CBS show, the supposedly liberal networks cannot even report the news accurately because they must legitimate both their own corporate interests and that of the government, which protects and abets them in their international pursuits of greater wealth. Thus, an editor, who explicitly or implicitly understands these facts of corporate power, will not eagerly assign reporters or commit resources to stories that might conflict with basic corporate interests—despite the fact that the public needs to know about them.

The major media adores celebrity news—marriage, pregnancy, divorce, drugs— which obscures stories about unaccountable corporate and government power. It is rare to find equally complete coverage on issues like the adverse health effects of depleted uranium, the 2002 Downing street memo that showed Bush and Blair colluding to go to war against Iraq and the billions apparently skimmed by Administration-friendly companies in Iraq.

Those who represent multinational corporate interests—network and newspaper executives—understand that their media must reproduce and prosper by validating the corrupt system that spawned them. Such a reproductive process requires government power. The law doesn't restrict the U.S. press, but the owners obviously do. For the time being, search the internet and non-U.S. sources for accurate news and proper context for the events that define our history. With proper information and analysis, citizens can participate in the process of their own history.

Aggression Dominates the Airwaves

EORGE W. BUSH HAS INSPIRED NOT ONLY POLITICAL EXTREMISM in action, but in words as well—especially on the radio. Cruel and mean words proliferate on prime time AM radio. The "John and Ken Show," an afternoon talk program in Los Angeles, targets "illegal immigrants" and praises vigilantes who hunt them down. The co-hosts of the show manifested their serious intellect and level of humanity by stopping just short of calling for the immediate castration of Michael Jackson during his 2004 pre-trial and trial days. They also think that life imprisonment rather than lethal injection is sufficient punishment for illegal aliens who return to California after being deported.

Mean spiritedness of the radio mouth, however, pales before some really vicious deeds. For centuries, sectors of peaceful and kind Americans have cohabited with another group whose pent-up aggression has awaited only a tiny provocation for release. Contemporary ire first emerged in its full ugliness during the late 17th Century witch trials in Salem.

Although the Puritan elders ultimately failed in their theocratic attempt to build a sin-free world in the Massachusetts Bay Colony and then spread their mission to the rest of the continent, they did leave a lasting legacy. Religion, repression, empire and violence have fit well together ever since as leitmotifs in U.S. history.

For two plus centuries, millions of slaves experienced the cruelty of masters and field supervisors who routinely beat and raped their work forces and separated families—all justified, the men of God explained, by the Bible. After slavery, the new apartheid rulers routinely lynched black men, raped their women and effectively segregated much of the country—deeds again condoned by sections of the politicized clergy who now interpreted segregation as God-given.

Under the guise of "settling the West" with civilized people, malice took center stage in the personae of the military. The "civilizers" prevailed in two centuries of Indian wars, imperial battles with "enemies" who possessed inferior military technology. U.S. officials had learned their lesson in the 1812 war to annex Canada from England: pick your enemies carefully and don't fight tough foes with advanced armaments.

Under commands from the War Department, U.S. troops massacred tribes and stole their land. The U.S. invasion and occupation of Indian lands stands as a cruel and aggressive imperial model. (Indeed, both President Bushes criticized Saddam Hussein for doing similar deeds in Kuwait in 1990)

U.S. soldiers carried out mass murder when they occupied the Philippines (1898-1932). U.S. occupation armies in Haiti, Cuba and Nicaragua during this same period also provoked less than loving reactions from those they invaded.

What could have been crueler than the World War II dropping of nuclear bombs on two Japanese cities, the fire bombing of civilian populations in Germany and Japan? And the ugly side of the non-military—or ex-military—American face showed in the 1990s bombings of the Oklahoma Federal Building and countless abortion clinics, not by fanatic Muslims, but by home grown, U.S.-army-trained young men.

Cruel deeds also find their reflection on the airwaves. Behind the angry and moralistic bluster, however, often lies a malevolent transgressor. The nasty talking Rush Limbaugh, for example, confessed to an Oxycontin addiction. The very man who wanted to jail other addicts and give the death sentence to dealers admitted to taking up to 100 pills a day of this "rural heroine." (Oxy is similar to heroine, which is hard to get in non-urban counties) Listen, but only once, please, to the homicidal ranting of Michael

Savage and his lust to slaughter Muslims, and the Puritanical orthodoxy of Dr. Laura, who posed naked for the camera while living in sin—a situation she deplores for other women. But these political potty mouths pale before the folksy wit of perennial radio talker Paul Harvey.

At 86 and fresh from signing a ten-year $100 million contract with Disney-ABC, this perennial radio personality apparently decided that the time had finally come for him to articulate a point of view that he felt certain his listeners would share.

On June 23, 2005, he said on his daily ABC radio show: "I've been choking on something for weeks. Let's get it up and get it out, for what it's worth. After the attack on Pearl Harbor, Winston Churchill said that the American people and this is a direct quote: 'We didn't come this far because we are made of sugar candy.' That was his response to the attack on Pearl Harbor. And that reminder was taken seriously and we proceeded to develop and deliver the bomb even though roughly 150,000 men, women and children perished in Hiroshima and Nagasaki. With a single blow, World War II was over."

Did he get your attention? Now for the application of history to the present, Harvey labeled "New York's September 11 Pearl Harbor. Winston Churchill was not here to remind us that we didn't come this far because we are made of sugar candy. So following the New York disaster we mustered our humanity, we gave old pals a pass even though men and money from Saudi Arabia were largely responsible for the devastation of New York and Pennsylvania and our Pentagon. We called Saudi Arabia our partners against terrorism and we sent men with rifles into Afghanistan and Iraq and we kept our best weapons in their silos. Even now, we're standing there dying, daring to do nothing decisive because we've declared ourselves to be better than our terrorist enemies, more moral, more civilized. Our image is at stake, we insist."

Harvey did not pause for "page 2," his traditional transition to a commercial. He continued: "We didn't come this far because we are made of sugar candy. Once upon a time we elbowed our way onto and into this continent by giving smallpox infected blankets to Native Americans. Yes, that was biological warfare. And we used every other weapon we could get our hands on to grab this land from whomever and we grew prosperous. And yes, we greased the skids with the sweat of slaves."

A lightning course on how the United States became a great nation! "And so it goes with most great nation-states, which feeling guilty about their savage pasts, eventually civilize themselves out of business and wind up invaded and ultimately dominated by the lean, hungry, up and coming who are not made of sugar candy. Paul Harvey—Good Day."

Harvey made a case for slavery, genocide and nuclear and biological warfare as legitimate methods with which to build "our" great nation. The stations syndicate Harvey to over 1,000 radio stations with an estimated audience of 18 million! Disney-ABC did not inform his listeners that Paul Harvey served in the U.S. Army Air Corps from 1942-44 and was discharged via Section 8—mental illness.

What a transformation Disney has undergone, from Mickey, Minnie, Donald and Daisy to a defender of monstrous acts! Walt Disney and his staff drew these family-friendly animals without genitals—to make them unthreatening, or protect children from the knowledge that even animals have them? He even drew white gloves over their paws—for purity or to cover up the fact that paws are not exactly hands?

In 2004, Michael Moore tried to distribute his film "Fahrenheit 9/11" through Disney's subsidiary Miramax, which was also the principal investor in the film. The May 5, 2004 *New York Times* reported that a Disney executive said since "Disney caters to families of all political stripes and believes Mr. Moore's film...

could alienate many," it would not allow Miramax to distribute the movie.

The Disney executives have thus far not seemed concerned about Paul Harvey's endorsement of a variety of what several treaties define as crimes against humanity and war crimes— slavery and targeting civilian populations with nuclear and bio weapons. Nor do Disney executives fear that censuring Harvey might offend millions of those mean spirited people who listen to his folksy and reactionary platitudes.

Consider the 17 hours a week of prime time slots given to Limbaugh and Dr. Laura, not to mention angry right wing ranters and ravers like Michael Savage, Al Rantel, Larry Elder, G. Gordon Liddy and Oliver North. Indeed, these extremists almost monopolize the talk show time. On AM and FM religious stations, fundamentalist preachers dominate; their politics dovetail with the more secular mountebanks on non-religious radio. Ironically, the talk show hosts chime in as one loud chorus in their complaint about "liberal control of the media."

As liberals waxed eloquent in their condemnation of U.S. tortures of Iraqis at Abu Ghraib in 2004, Limbaugh suggested that the prison guards were "just having fun" and "blowing off some steam." Limbaugh's idea of "harmless fun" included sodomizing prisoners, attaching wires to the fingers, toes, and penis of another to simulate electric torture and raping children. Like fraternity and sorority parties at fun-loving campuses, the MPs at Abu Ghraib just played around as a male soldier raped a female prisoner.

Imperial aggression, from the Puritans' notion of spreading God's Word to George W. Bush's spreading God's liberty everywhere, coincides with cruel and illegal behavior. It also jibes with dangerous and close to the surface anger of millions of people in this country.

In the name of God and goodness, freedom and democracy, US soldiers, ordered by their political and military leaders, have done atrocious things around the world. The least articulate of American psychopaths can wait with assurance that they will hear justifying words from "authorities" like Paul Harvey and the more religious charlatans of AM air time to confirm that God validates their urges toward homicidal violence.

Missionaries Forever

To Allen Ginsberg

I have seen the best minds of my generation
Become obsessed with Viagra
Lust after the woman's market niche

Imagine, she's 70 plus and still looks 40
A Botox drip hidden in her lip?
Sex and image, skinny and rich

I want to howl at the out-of-date Allen
A shocker in his time
War continues, life's still a bitch

THE AMERICAN MISSION BEGAN WITH THE 17TH CENTURY Puritans who failed to build their Zion in the Wilderness in New England. Cotton Mather sermons extolled the residents of Massachusetts Bay Colony to live up to their God-given task to remake the world, so that Christ could return and usher in the Kingdom of the Millennium. Imagine Mather opening his e-mail and receiving an offer to "say goodbye to cellulite," his wife looking over his shoulder at "Body Shape, the Alternative to Cosmetic Surgery." But instead of a middle-aged woman with flab everywhere, a young beauty in a bathing suit smiles provocatively.

Would Mather—if reborn—have dared to smile at the absurd notion of his once pressing vision? Perhaps he would try to explain to George W. Bush and the advertising community that they had not quite gotten the essence of His message.

Four centuries after the Puritans failed to extirpate the Devil from their midst, goofy missionaries continue to harangue the populace. Bush spreads freedom as if it would substitute for cream cheese to shmear on any Arab's sesame bagel and lox. I wonder if a "higher power" (rhetorically) has taken to political comedy script writing—for Her own amusement, of course.

But Bush, the missionary, has counterparts in the advertising world. "If you haven't tried Viagra, you don't know what you're missing. Heh, heh!" Freedom, Viagra, a new SUV, a cruise in the Caribbean—all will provide the missing ingredient in your life, whether you live in Podunk or Baghdad.

In fact, advertising has become a form of missionary activity. Instead of pushing Jesus on the natives, advertisers push soap, hair spray, and drugs that take U.S. consumers up, down and sideways—and promise to cure their impotence and acne. The missionary factor in American life extends even to alternative life styles.

Allen Ginsberg, the spiritual descendent of Walt Whitman, "saw his mother screaming psalms at demons." He appealed to the sensitive, the Hell's Angels to chant the Indian mantras, eschew heterosexual Judeo-Christian demons that refused to respond to his mother and assume pacifism as the only viable world view. The naïve and openly homosexual "beat poet" who died in 1997 did not spend time sitting at his computer, gazing at websites that pushed Republican sado-masochism.

In pursuit of American freedom, the White House manipulators might have rationalized, take advantage of any tactic that God makes available. Former House Majority Leader Tom DeLay, an expert in availing himself of money by any means to do God's legislative work, has taught this lesson well. Even after his indictment on felony charges, he insisted that all his actions followed from God's word.

Bob Dole, another Republican stalwart who ran for President on his party's ticket in 1996, has emerged as a new kind of missionary. He has taken up the cause of selling a drug company's remedy for what Archie Bunker in the sitcom "All in the Family" once called "conubibal problems."

Dole and other celebrities have become public sales pitchers for the product that pharmaceutical companies also push through daily e-mail spam. The message that accompanies the "You need Viagra, Cialis and other erectile dysfunction remedies" message suggests that without these drugs a horrible situation could arise: "What if a tender moment turns into the right moment and you're not ready?"

"You're always ready," Ginsberg would have said. He preached sexual freedom with peace, justice, tolerance, and openness, while the right wing Christian establishment branded Allen and his homoerotic pals as "kinky faggots." Orthodox Jews shuddered because by birth and thus forever, Allen was a member of the Tribe—who did not believe that Palestinians should be removed from their land and have their arms broken by Israeli soldiers.

All the prissy denominations excluded Allen, who celebrated his genitals, while establishment luminaries decried the sight of a bare breast on a statue. In 2002, then Attorney General John Ashcroft ordered that subordinates place a burkha over an exposed stone mammary in the Department of Justice.

Moralists became enraged—at least 150 million suffered acute trauma—at the 2004 Super Bowl halftime show when they saw the real thing exposed by Janet Jackson. Yet, for a nice fee the pillars of the establishment stand up for erections—TV promos for Viagra—without of course mentioning "those parts." (Pfizer Drug Company paid Dole and the other luminaries very well for promoting their instant boner product)

Televised sporting events like NASCAR racing, NFL, NBA and Major League Baseball regularly feature hunks, like baseball slugger and super steroid imbiber Rafael Palmeiro, promoting the libidinous potion. "What if 'a tender moment' turns into the right moment, but you're not ready?"

Bob Dole admitted that "it's a little embarrassing to talk about ED, but it's so important to millions of men and their partners that I decided to talk about it publicly."[141] Indeed, the Pfizer sales force must be drooling over the possibilities of promoting their product on TV in "Liberated Iraq" and Afghanistan as well.

Ironically, some of the very people who writhe in angst over a bare breast finally took official umbrage at the millions of daily ads that guarantee erections as if just discovering that these ads are about sex. What if the little ones are watching Viagra commercials and ask: "Mommy, does Daddy suffer from ED?"

Congressman Jim Moran doesn't want our innocent young people finding out about such monstrously disgusting subjects— at least not until after 10 p.m. The northern Virginia Democrat introduced a bill to ban advertisements for erectile-dysfunction drugs such as Viagra, Cialis and Levitra until the late-night hours. Presumably, the innocent are asleep after 10 p.m. "It bothers me, the saturation of these ads during viewing times when you're normally sitting around with the kids. I don't have any problem advertising these products after 10, the way we do with...hard liquor," Moran said.

"When Bob Dole was doing the ads, it didn't really bother me, but now there's just too much sexual innuendo," Moran told the *Associated Press*.[142] I think of Dan Quayle, who does not support Viagra, because he tried it for a week and nothing happened. "It's the worst suppository I've ever used."

I would do with Bush's freedom spreading ideas in the Middle East what Quayle allegedly did with his Viagra.

The Ascent of Fashionism,
the Decline of Consciousness

EARFUL FRIENDS WARN, "FASCISM HAS TAKEN HOLD," REFERRING to how Bush has used the Patriot Act[143] to whittle away liberties (like habeas corpus and protection from government eavesdropping) and increase the power of Homeland Security. They point to his increased use of the military in the post Hurricane era to "keep order."

"It's fashionism, not fascism," offers another friend, a more accurate way to describe contemporary American reality. "Each day, we receive thousands of unsolicited daily commercial messages, which lead us to lose focus on the world of citizens. For example, can we intellectually separate urgent ads to buy cut rate cell phones with news that experts have declared our military as seriously over-extended in Iraq and Afghanistan? Can we multi-task between buying at a 'pre-season sale' and assuaging anxiety when polls report that the rest of the world hates us because of our cruel, illegal and aggressive actions, especially in the Middle East?"

He's right. The purpose of newspaper, magazine, web, TV and radio ads is to tell us that we're the center of the universe and remind us of our individual inadequacies. They simultaneously also alert us to the fact that our environment is rapidly eroding. Indeed, some environmental ads imply that we citizens share the blame for allowing this environmental decay to develop because of the over-consuming life styles we chose.

One side of the newspaper page exhorts us to buy a new car, which will increase our prestige and enhance the satisfaction of our sex lives, while the parallel column offers us a news story about how car emissions cause global warming. Another page promotes sex lives of the stars; an adjacent ad preaches about how we too can—and should—become part of that "glamorous" world by erasing wrinkles.

For example, the July 15, 2005 *San Jose Mercury News* revealed that muscle magazines paid $5 million to consultant California Governor Arnold Schwarzenegger, who campaigned for his post on a platform that opposed special interests. Indeed, he pledged to take no salary as governor. The consultant money, however, derived from magazine sales which, in turn, came from ads placed by makers of "supplements." Coincidentally, the Governator vetoed a bill that would have prevented students from participating in high school sports if they used those "performance-enhancing" ingredients.

"News" of corruption alternately shotguns us with mixed message ammunition: Congressmen getting free trips or taking sordid money for re-election, gang and drug-related violence, stars marrying, divorcing or entering drug treatment programs. Where do we focus?

The commercial media operates without a guiding intellect, unable to direct its message toward the public good while presenting details of public malfeasance. The media presents history unfolding as a series of mostly catastrophic facts (plus ceremonies) without context or analysis, while commercials interrupt the stories to remind us to buy commodities that will help us on the road to individual perfection—as if everyone knew the world revolved around each one of our precious daily yens and itches. The ubiquitous presence of communication technology ensures that all but the hermits will hear and see the commercial assault on our senses.

When societies ingest new technology, they also add what Karl Marx referred to as a "force of production." Such "forces" also change habits—thanks to the always hidden hand inside the new inventions. This elusive commander then re-shapes daily patterns.

Think of how in one century the automobile has changed life! Consider TV's impact on culture and the family! How computers alter routines and the way we think of Time and Space! These instruments form the basis of the modern productive and distributive systems and they enter the public consumption sphere as well. Computer-based technology restructures entire labor forces. Computers "revolutionized" the task of taking inventory in large department stores or super markets!

Look at the impact of new gadgets like video games on the world of fashion and how they have modified aesthetics. Those pernicious and invisible dominators squirrel themselves inside of "technology" and attack even the toddler market.

According to an October 2003 report released by the Henry J. Kaiser Family Foundation,[144] millions of those who can barely walk have not only experienced TV and videos as babysitters for hours a day, but they also learn to use computers and play video games before they can read. Some barely learn to read even as they grow up.

"Children six and under spend an average of two hours a day using screen media (1:58), about the same amount of time they spend playing outside (2:01), and well over the amount they spend reading or being read to (39 minutes)."

Thanks to interactive digital media technology, 48% of children six and under have used a computer (31% of 0-3 year-olds and 70% of 4-6 year-olds). Just under a third (30%) play video games (14% of 0-3 year-olds and 50% of 4-6 year-olds). Even the youngest children—those under two—are widely exposed to electronic media. Forty-three percent of those under two watch TV every day, and 26% have a TV in their bedroom (the American Academy of Pediatrics "urges parents to avoid television for children under 2 years old"). In any given day, two-thirds (68%) of children under two will use a screen medium, for an average of just over two hours (2:05).

Vicky Rideout, vice president and director of the Kaiser Family Foundation's Program for the Study of Entertainment Media and Health, who led the team that issued the report, said that the "wiring" trend goes beyond adolescents and to "babies in diapers as well. So much new media is being targeted at infants and toddlers, it's critical that we learn more about the impact it's having on child development."

The study also shows that kids with a "TV in their bedroom or who live in 'heavy' TV households average 22 minutes more a day watching than other children, and less time reading or playing outside."

Those living in "heavy" TV households are more likely to watch every day (77% v. 56%), and to watch for 34 minutes more a day and are less likely to read. In fact, they are less likely than other children to be able to read at all. Only 34% of children ages 4-6 from "heavy" TV households can read, compared to 56% of other children that age.[145]

Millions of kids stay in their rooms, absorbed in virtual reality games that ooze from plasma screens. Speakers bark loud sound which, along with digital illusion, has also altered the modern aesthetic. Indeed, certain sounds and images automatically refer to violence.

Thanks to the digital revolution, "fashionism" has reached beyond new markets and into new depths as well. Entertainment business executives have used their hackers, animators, designers and programmers to elevate what was once known as special effects into a department of virtual defects. Those who write plots and dialogue now assume as axiomatic the needs for graphic displays of blood, bone and gore. Sound engineers rev up the slurps and thwacks, the subtle tones of explosions and gunshots. In the R and above rated films, the sound mixers imply those familiar bedroom spiritual flashes that all people having sex should feel but never, of course, do. These scenes, in turn, set the stage for massive e-mail campaigns for penis and breast enlargement, and for the pornography inundation that has afflicted web surfers as well.

So urgently does the profit bell ring in the ears of the Pavlovian dogs of entertainment CEOs that they use technology to thwart even the right wing religious censors who hover like birds of prey over anything that might give children—or themselves?—a hint of lusty sex.

Obedient to both the prurient sales team and the aggressive tastes of the active prudes, the profit side of Hollywood decides how to accommodate to both the pious and hedonistic aesthetics and thus produce and distribute appropriate products in movie theaters, airplanes, DVDs and anywhere else they can sell them.

To finesse these moral guardians, the makers of "Mr. and Mrs. Smith" and "Batman Begins," for examples, substituted violence for sex, and thus escaped the dreaded R rating. Thrill-seeking underage movie goers pour into the theaters to watch ferocious and bloody scenes—in the virtual sphere. With photo-shopped special effects, the standards set by the NRA and mighty fundamentalist reverends no longer stand as impediments. The moral monitors have deemed violence watching as healthier than looking at people doing "it"—those nasty things that millions of ordinary people have done for thousands of years.

Don't get confused. The Hollywood formula contains the same basic ingredients that the original Hollywood moguls distilled for bored and desperate audiences more than a century ago. A handsome—and often rich—hero saves the world from an evil fanatic. This usually accompanies a romance that brings him happiness for the rest of his life—until the sequel, anyhow.

Technology's infinite hidden hands can enhance violence, but will it be enough to lure the 12-25 year olds to theaters and away from DVDs? Or will movie theaters become as obsolete as typewriters.

By removing sex from movies so as to avoid parental permission provisions for theater entry, Hollywood marketing geniuses may drive those old enough to actually have sex at home, stimulated by watching violence on the smaller screen.

"Pow, crash, bang."

"Hey, this turns me on."

"Me too."

"I don't want to miss any of the action."

Those too young—Viagra has overcome age—to enjoy themselves can still enjoy themselves virtually with DVD copies rented by older siblings. Imagine, their parents leave them happily at their computers—with baby sitters supposedly doing homework— and go to an R rated movie.

Yes, cultural trivialization marches forward, alongside reports of daily Iraqi carnage, the spread of poverty, famine and AIDS in Africa and the ever spine chilling stories about the impact of global warming—more benignly referred to as "climate change." carnage. The new "fashions" in clothes, houses, games, computers and cell phones define contemporary American culture, the product that Bush offers to export to the rest of the world as "freedom." With it, presumably, he would finish "liberating" Iraq—or just finish Iraq. So, when Bush insists that Congress restore the Patriot Act intact, he doesn't mean fascism, but "fashionism."

V. A Third World Development Dilemma?

Vietnam Diary, March 2006

ARRIVED IN HANOI IN THE LATE MORNING. THE SUN FLITTED through the clouds, and I couldn't decide whether I needed my light wind-breaker. The temperature hovered in the mid 60s, with enough humidity to let some reality into my brain to share space with older graphic images—from a very different era. The January 1968 *Life* magazine cover showed Lee Lockwood's photo of a Hanoi street covered with man holes and covers, where people took shelter when the B-52s conducted their daily bombing of the city. Who in my generation could forget the image of the napalmed little girl running naked down the road or the South Vietnamese general shooting a prisoner in the head with a pistol?

Most Vietnamese I talked to either in English or through an interpreter see the war as ancient history. Thang, a hotel manager, insists that "most Vietnamese have no memories of it." Indeed, the majority of the country was born after 1975, when the war ended. In the early 1970s Vietnam had a population of about 40 million. That number has more than doubled: 82.7 million in 2004.

Unlike many of my students, who know only that the Vietnam War occurred sometime after the Greco-Roman era, several Vietnamese university students, one with an NBA T-shirt had learned the details of war—such as the facts that U.S. planes dropped 15 million tons of bombs on their country and sprayed huge areas of forest with Agent Orange in order to defoliate the countryside, which produced lasting health effects among the sprayed populations. I met an American expatriate who runs an

NGO to help rural children incapacitated by the effects of that chemical.

One student, at a cafe near Hanoi's Hoan Kiem Lake, sang a few bars of heavily accented hip hop. I laughed. Others joined her. They were disappointed that I didn't know about U.S. youth music. Nor were they impressed that I recalled the 1954 battle of Dien Bien Phu when General Vo Nguyen Giap surrounded twelve French battalions attempting to stop his armies' advance.

They had studied in school the famous siege, which included waves of assaults followed by artillery attacks. As the French military situation worsened, Secretary of State John Foster Dulles proposed dropping of an atomic bomb on the Viet Minh forces to relieve the French.

Ike refused, and after almost two months of siege, Giap's forces had captured or killed the entire French force (13,000) and won independence—or so it seemed. The students also knew about the subsequent conference in Geneva, when France, the United States and Ho Chi Minh's Vietnam agreed to a series of steps toward independence. The U.S. made sure, however, that the scheduled 1956 elections would not take place.

In his Memoirs, Dwight Eisenhower estimated that Ho would have won 80% of the vote. Instead, the United States created "South Vietnam" and imported a Catholic president, Ngo Dinh Diem, to run a non-Catholic country. Diem's regime was characterized by corruption and oppression of those who sided with national unification.

One student described how his history books taught that Ho Chi Minh had ordered armed resistance units (the National Liberation Front or Viet Cong) to attack Diem's forces. I told them I recalled how Eisenhower and Kennedy responded by sending in armed "advisers" and multiplying the size and technology of the newly created South Vietnamese armed forces. The

Vietnam War had begun even before Lyndon Johnson used the fabricated Gulf of Tonkin attack on a U.S. ship to ask Congress for authority to send in massive numbers of US troops. In 1975, after 58 thousand Americans died, hundreds of thousands were wounded and God knows how many went crazy, Congress cut off funds for the war. The U.S. cut and ran.

I asked them if it was true that 3 million Vietnamese died. They did not know the casualty figures. But one young woman, studying linguistics emphasized that "that period of our history is over. We like Americans."

Over the first four days in Hanoi, I sensed no anti-Americanism. Indeed, people assured me that the war is remembered in museums and history books.

The country has entered a new era. The nation that 1960s Defense analysts described as having no "industrial backbone," has begun a visible and dramatic development program.

Some of Hanoi's estimated 4 million people—many freshly arrived from the impoverished countryside—now work in industrial parks, clusters of factories owned or controlled by foreign multinationals. A giant Canon plant, built amidst rice paddies on the road from the airport to the city, shares the landscape with billboards advertising major companies, not consumer products. There are plenty of those signs—Coke, Samsung, Nokia—in the city.

Adidas and other sporting goods chains have assembly plants in Vietnam. A U.S. businessman who runs a company here told me that the Vietnamese resent the methods of Taiwanese and Korean managers. Young men and women fresh from the countryside earn sweatshop wages, but that pittance is more than they eked out on the farm.

The government contracted with foreign companies to build huge highway and bridge projects across the Red River—no sign of redness in it—on Hanoi's east. The modern construction machinery stands in sharp contrast to the house boats and shacks along the river's edge. A delegation of U.S. investors from major corporations arrived on March 10. They declared their intentions of building plants in Vietnam and supporting the country's bid to join the WTO. The government appears overly friendly with the United States. Indeed, last year, the United States was Communist Vietnam's largest trading partner.

Two U.S. expatriates and a retired Vietnamese diplomat chuckled when I asked if Vietnam was truly "socialist," as in Socialist Republic of Vietnam. "Socialists don't invite the most aggressive of the multinational corporate elite into their country to exploit their people," sneered one American who owns a small business in Hanoi.

"What socialism?" asked the retired diplomat. "The government should at least stop being hypocritical and make their politics coincide with their economic policies and allow for open parties and a free press as well." The businessman said that government leaders routinely promise development with environmental controls and social equality. All three complained of corruption, poor leadership and a deteriorating environment.

What development means in daily life is heavy air pollution in the capital city. A Vietnamese friend gave me a tour of Hanoi. I sat on the back of his motorbike and imagined myself starring in a remake of "Perils of Pauline" as he weaved the small motor bike through the densely populated streets. Perhaps, I thought, this constituted a population control measure. I assumed the mortality rate from traffic accidents and respiratory diseases should be impressive.

Hundreds of thousands of these Japanese, Korean and Chinese-made engines emit noxious, unfiltered gasoline exhaust. Until recently, bicycles prevailed, but these recently arrived machines have taken over the streets and the sidewalks.

The Vietnamese drive as if they had watched archival footage of OJ Simpson. Instead of eluding enemy tacklers on foot they navigate on wheels through fields of oncoming and competing bicycles, motorbikes, cars, SUVs and buses. They must also negotiate with fearless pedestrians. Miniature women with bamboo poles and loaded baskets of fruit hanging from each end stride into swarms of oncoming cars and miraculously get to the other side of the street.

Frying meats, fish oil and engine exhaust mix together with the scent of fresh roses, carried by women or sold from shops on the street. The vehicles, like fish of distinct shapes and species, head toward their own individual locations, motivated by impersonal but urgent need to get to someplace as quickly as possible.

We passed only one accident on the way. I closed my eyes as I imagined imminent death. Yet, no driver gets intimidated. Rather, each moves forward as if the only important thing is to continue the journey. Why did no one tell Lyndon Johnson that he could not intimidate the Vietnamese?

A day trip to a "snake village" just outside Hanoi looked like an extension of the city. The driver talked to the snake handler who reached into a tank with a forked stick and put a cobra in my face. A chill crept up my spine. I continued filming with my video camera as the snake's head formed a wide hood and hissed. Maybe I just imagined the sound and the angry look in the serpent's eyes as its slimy tongue swept from left to right. Would this cause my fatal heart attack? I didn't look in the tank to see how many more deadly vipers were inside; nor did I try to find another snake establishment. I declined lunch at the snake man's dining room—broiled cobra over rice.

Looking for a Cuban businessman

I read the March 15 *Vietnam News* (English language daily) at the modern Hanoi airport. VinaLand, I learn, has invested more than $200 million into Vietnamese real estate, a "hot sector," according to Merrill Lynch. The Wall Street giant calls Vietnam "one of the last emerging markets in the region." Merrill Lynch advised "investor attention over the next decade."

Sharing front page space with real estate, Venezuela's Assembly President and his Vietnamese counterpart extol their joint working relationship.

Can Vietnam cooperate with Venezuela's socialist goals while U.S. investors speculate in Vietnamese real estate? Can Vietnam enjoy the "fruits of foreign investment" and still have a viable socialism? Or do such questions reveal my short-term thinking, inappropriate in the face of Vietnam's conflictive past? As empires have successively conquered this nation, its people have become resilient. In the "American War," preceding the mid 1970s Liberation of Cambodia and subsequent border war with China, few families escaped death, injury or displacement.

Indeed, rubble remains from the ten years in which U.S. military technology showed its lethal capacity in cities like Hue. In the 1968 Tet Offensive, the Viet Cong captured Hue and hoisted their red flag from the citadel, the early 19th Century fortress that dominates the city's landscape. The VC, as the U.S. military called them, systematically dismantled the South Vietnamese government structure, eliminated its supporters and rebuffed South Vietnamese counterattacks.

Then, U.S. bombers and artillery pounded suspected Viet Cong positions. The Vietnamese revolutionaries fired mortars at advancing U.S. troops. Afterwards, thousands of dead soldiers and civilians covered the ground. The ancient citadel was reduced to debris.

Former Vietnam veterans now tour the rebuilt fortress with sad –perhaps nostalgic—looks on their faces, alongside tourists from Europe, Asia and other parts of Vietnam. Our Vietnamese guide, Do, in his late 20s and who learned English and Japanese at the university, explains that it will take some years before the government finishes reconstructing parts of the citadel destroyed during the 1968 battle. Tourists roam the walkways amidst workers who ignore them. Their job is to repave the corridors where bearers once carried the Queen Mother to see the Royal Theater perform. The Queen Mother was plump. She ate and got carried everywhere. I have seen few overweight Vietnamese.

Plump Western visitors, however, applaud the singing and dancing of the slender members of the Royal Theater Company (trained by the Communist government). No royalty or concubines attended the performance—at least not in costume.

Boats with painted dragons on their prow haul tourists down the Perfume River—named because of the wide variety of fragrant flowers along its banks—to visit ancient pagodas. On each boat, boat owners try to sell tourists handicrafts, art work and clothing along with the local Festival beer.

The economy of Hue depends on tourism. I asked Do what he thought about the past, when 3 million Vietnamese died in "the American War", and the present where he and others whose families suffered make their living by catering to U.S., European and Japanese tourists.

He smiled. "We have put that in the past and we have moved on. We do not feel hatred toward Americans," he said. Every Vietnamese we ask repeats this mantra. I have come to actually believe it. Do assured me that Iraqis, too, will forgive the

Americans for what they are currently doing to that country. I wonder if the Vietnamese had been Muslims. Didn't the "American War" teach the Pentagon not to fight enemies who fight back?

An ancient "garden house" on the outskirts of Hue reveals how green thumbs applied their magic over centuries. Elegant and natural looking floral arrangements dot the patio, without exhibiting any apparent effort. I want to bite into the mangoes, jack and dragon fruits and the plump green figs hanging from the branches. Do, noting my interest in development and socialism, explains that "the government says we are only at an early stage in developing communism and we must have patience." I smile. He smiles. "I'm not sure I believe we are ever going to experience that stage of perfect equality," he says with a twinkle in his eye.

On the walk to the hotel from the river, I note that almost every store offers tourist items, from sun tan oil and mosquito repellent to clothing, art, craft and booze. The DMZ Café resonates with the sound of American pop music. U.S. tourists drink beer inside.

Early next morning, video camera in hand, I film streams of bicyclists and motor bike riders crossing the Trang Tien Bridge over the Perfume River. I inhale nostril-searing fumes. On the riverfront, women try to sell me tickets for boat rides, men offer to drive me to my destination on the back of their motorbikes or on bicycle driven cabs to see the sights.

At the upscale Saigon Morin Hotel, a French tour guide tries to hurry his flock to board the tourist boat. France colonized Vietnam from 1860 until Ho Chi Minh's troops threw them out in 1954. A frustrated Japanese couple shouts heavily accented English at a taxi driver, presuming he will understand better if the volume goes up. Japan ruled Vietnam during World War II.

Ho's independence forces fought them until August 1945, when Japan left and Ho declared Vietnamese independence. For one month, under Ho, the sovereign Republic of Vietnam ruled the country. Then, the French troops returned and war began. Now Vietnamese get tips from tourists coming from the very empires that oppressed them.

On the bus to Hoi Anh, further south on the coast, two Australian high school teachers comment on the good food and reasonable prices. I also hear Danish, German, French and Japanese. Some travelers get off at Danang, once a U.S. military base and now an example of "development." High rises under construction dot the landscape. An army museum displays a U.S. jet bomber shot down during the war, alongside other captured military equipment in the "American war."

Hoi Anh, despite the ubiquitous presence of the motorbikes, leaving trails of rancid gas exhaust, has retained qualities of an ancient city. Hordes of tourists flood the old quarter to eat, drink and buy paintings, post cards, tailor-made clothing and mass-produced "marble" Buddha statues.

Tourist hotels and internet cafes dot the streets. Vietnamese teenagers play video games on the web; others sit in small open air café-cinemateques and watch DVDs of Kung Fu films on mid sized TVs.

"Life became so much better since the government opened the economy in 1986," says Le, a former English teacher who now works with an NGO that helps street kids. The people of Hoi Anh, like those of Hue, welcome the tourists. "It's preferable. From 1975 to 1986, the government gave everyone 4 meters of cloth per year and small amounts of food. People lined up for hours to buy bus tickets to Danang." He spoke about the abundant food now available on street markets. We still have a communist government, of course, but you can see people feel free. We can buy motor bikes. Before, we had only bicycles."

Ironically, his best friend died in a motor bike accident. Le blames the anarchy of Vietnamese traffic. "We have no rules."

I mention the penetrating blare of the motorbike horns. "Until 1986, Hoi Anh was a city of looms, much noisier and more polluting than motorbikes. When the government decided to promote tourism, the textile industry moved to areas outside the city."

At lunch, the 17-year-old waitress brings us a spicy, flavorful crab soup and lotus root salad. Then she goes outside the tiny restaurant. "Good food," she shouts, trying to steer two grouchy Germans inside.

I look at Le skeptically. "Before tourism, the young people left for larger cities to find jobs. Now, they're returning, along with overseas Vietnamese, the boat people who fled in the 1980s. Some have actually invested here. When they left the government called them traitors. Those same people are now called patriots," he laughs.

Vietnam had remained inside the Soviet economic model until 1986, when Gorbachev admitted that the model did not work. Vietnamese Communist leaders quickly began to integrate their nation's economy with the flow of the dominant world forces.

In twenty years, the economy has become transformed from a Soviet socialist to a visibly capitalist model. The March 18 *News* showed an unsmiling Fidel Castro gripping the hand of Nguyen Van An, Vietnam's Assembly Chair. An "admired Cuba's remarkable achievement in the difficult context of the current international situation." Earlier, An had addressed a joint Cuba-Vietnam Business Forum and emphasized that "Vietnam is now a favored environment for foreign investors, including Cuban businessmen."

On my next trip to Havana, I hope to meet one of these Cuban businessmen.

The New Road

Ho Chi Minh City (HCMC) swings, rocks and buzzes. Its teeming traffic dwarfs the worst of Hanoi's. In upscale hotels like the Rex, Caravelle, Sheraton, Hyatt and Continental, tourists mix easily with locals. Neon signs for U.S., European and Asian products litter the landscape and new and old buildings. Hustlers abound with offers to tourists for all kinds of services. No sign of that lack of urban energy, the absence of commercial activity that characterized many cities in the Soviet orbit in Vietnam's cities.

The broad boulevards in the hotel area, the magnificent opera house and city government palace—signs of French imperial architecture—make HCMC distinct from Hanoi. HCMC also has twice the population (about 8 million and 2 million motorbikes) of the northern capital, and the flavor of a modern, buzzing albeit clearly third world metropolis.

The smug, smarmy smile of the KFC colonel faces restaurants that serve delectable dishes. Fried chicken versus succulent dumplings dipped in nuc mam (pungent fish sauce), with lotus seed salad? "Hey," my wife reminds me, "some people like prison and hospital food."

A young Vietnamese woman in a KFC uniform smiles for a photo in the March 21 *Saigon Times* (English language business magazine). "U.S. products have gained a lot of prestige in Vietnam," although most Vietnamese can't afford them, the *Times* confirms. The telling statistic, however, shows that from

2002-2005, Vietnamese exports to the United States increased by 46%.

Vietnam's rising level of exports and imports, especially to and from the United States, and the growing foreign investment and tourism in the country will inevitably shape the country's political direction. Indeed, note how many articles of clothing sold in U.S. malls bear "Made in Vietnam" labels!

Ho Chi Minh City's growth also signals the future direction of Vietnam. A university official explains that the government maintained the hotels from 1975 to 1986, even though they "had a low occupancy level." In late March, rooms became scarce because of an Asian tourist industry convention. The lobbies of the Rex, the rebuilt Caravelle and the spanking new Hyatt and other expensive hotels have become meeting places. Vietnamese in suits and ties—or more casually dressed—meet their western counterparts and head off in air conditioned SUVs.

In the growing industrial park, south of the city, dozens of new factories produce a wide variety of goods, including high tech electronics. At 5:15 in the afternoon, the motorbikes lined up at the traffic light near the plants. I could not see the end of the line on the horizon. The green light flashed. A thunderous roar of two and four stroke engines blasted the atmosphere. In awe at the sheer size of this daily motorcade, I watched the mostly young—teens and twenties—pass by en route to their homes.

"Many share rented space," a biologist friend explains. "They earn about $40 a month, and send money home. They can't afford apartments. They need motorbikes to get to work." So, factory workers, like government employees, have access to credit and buy bikes, some for less than $500.

Nearby, newly built high rises, for sale or rent, house the burgeoning middle class. Those that have cashed in on Vietnam's "opening" buy spacious and well-designed homes—valued at $300,000 each. Korean, Taiwanese and Japanese plant managers, floor bosses and skilled technicians also share the new housing. Outside of a condo complex, a deli displays a sign in Korean and English: "Specializing in Korean and Japanese food." Next door, real estate offices have opened and upscale shops display Visa and MasterCard stickers.

Late afternoon traffic congestion reminds me of Mexico City—except without rules, other than might makes right. Motorbikes dart into the street, stop when larger vehicles threaten and give no quarter to pedestrians. I learn to walk between oncoming vehicles and trust God to pay attention. Each crossing becomes an exciting adventure, a virtual exercise in broken field running.

At the Saigon River, near Cholon's vibrant market (the city's Chinese section), the government relocated tens of thousands of slum dwellers, some from house boats, to more adequate housing. In their place, a riverfront highway will alleviate some traffic. In addition, the government plans to build a subway. What happens when motorbike owners trade up to cars?

Inside the massive market, women and men sit at stalls selling dried shrimp, spices, fruit, vegetables, plastic kitchen ware and fabrics for clothes, drapes and anything else one could imagine.

The new Vietnam reeks of capitalism, old and new, small and large. The State retains control of some key "productive forces." The new privatization schemes allow foreign capital a means of securely buying substantial interests in some of formerly nationalized industries, like the French owned Victoria Hotel chain that began as a joint venture and is evolving into a privatized hotel business.

On the social front, even the lowest wage workers and poorest farmers must pay small fees, which hurt the very poor and are unaffordable for the rural poor for health care and education. My biologist friend assured me that without paying people don't get decent treatment.

In two weeks of traveling (Hanoi, Hue, Hoi Anh, HCMC, Can Tho, Chau Duc), I have yet to meet a Vietnamese who wants to return to older models, although some worry about consequences of the new road.

Two academics, Party members, speak approvingly of the prosperity and growth. They also express concern about looming environmental nightmares that accompany fossil fuel burning models. China, after all, is next door.

They speak warmly of Cuba, "although they need help in development," and admiringly of the United States, "a country we need in order to develop our own country."

The War Museum is crowded with Western and Asian tourists. The modest structure stands in stark contrast to the buildings around the hotel area.

Silently, people move from photo to photo. Hanging on one wall is an anguished, frightened-looking GI, with a five day growth, cigarette hanging from tense lips. Nearby, hangs the Vietnamese girl running down the road photo. Her face, contorted with pain from the napalm, was burned into my memory decades ago. Below that black and white photo, another photo shows the girl as a woman thirty five years later, holding her own child. Burn scars cover her arms and shoulders. Several walls contain exhibits of children victimized by chemical warfare, too horrible to contemplate, yet undeniably real.

We read about U.S. troops carrying out massacres, journalists killed, villages destroyed. A smiling Lyndon Johnson stands with General Westmoreland. Next to that photo is one of General Giap and his North Vietnamese high command. Some viewers are Vietnam vets age. Their somber faces preclude conversation.

I asked a young blond woman with freckles how she felt. "Disgusted," she replied in an English accent. "And they never learn do they?" I signaled that I didn't understand.

"The politicians who make war in Iraq," she replied. "They're doing it all over again."

In one room, children's art adorns the walls, art of hope, brightly colored, but with some pictures showing bombers raining dioxin on the land. Why isn't every U.S. presidential candidate forced to spend two weeks locked in this museum?

The solemn crowd moves to the courtyard to see captured U.S. tanks and artillery pieces, and an unexploded bomb of massive proportions. The explanatory sign gives its weight in kilotons. Next to it, museum curators have placed a jet bomber felled by anti aircraft. Then groups explore the "gift shop," selling replicas of U.S. army gear along with post cards and cheap jewelry.

Near the Hotel Rex a legless man begs for money. He tells our Vietnamese friend he stepped on a landmine left over from the war. In the opulent hotel area, the crippled man serves as a grim reminder of "the American War." Do tourists or locals think about him as they join in choruses of "yum and um" over spicy fish-noodle soup, delicate steamed spring rolls and succulent green papaya salad? I try unsuccessfully with young University faculty members to engage in political discussion. Don't you take into account the past war with 3 million dead, dioxin, napalm, relocation?

"It's over, done," says Tuan, an economics student: "Time to move on." Yes to economic growth, control pollution and get more U.S. investment. No to the Iraq war. "I think America did not learn its lesson from 'the American war.'"

I mention socialism. "Between 1975 and 1986 we had lots of problems, not sufficient food and inefficient government services. Since the collapse of the Soviet Union, life in Vietnam has improved. Just look around," says Van, a science student. Unemployment and sub-employment remain problems, the students admit, but foreign investment will create jobs.

An environmental science professor says she is not naïve. "We know foreign companies want to take more out of Vietnam than they put it. But for now, this is the best, maybe the only road, we can choose."

A conversation stopper.

The Mekong Delta

Each morning, a floating market arrives at Can Tho, a city of 1.2 million on the banks of the Mekong River. Hundreds of small boat owners buy products from farmers up river and then drop anchor in the middle of the river near downtown so that retailers, hotels, restaurants and families can row or motor their own or hired boats to the water-based mall.

A man on the supply boat hands pumpkin after pumpkin to a buyer on a smaller boat. He repeats the process with melons. The buyer hands several dong notes to the man on the larger boat and receives change. On a nearby boat, a man reaches over to grab a sack of onions and pays the boat owner.

Tourists now visit the floating market and make small purchases, three dragon fruits or two mangosteens (plum-like fruits) at prices higher than locals pay. They also purchase Ho Chi Minh T-shirts, locally made jewelry and even books. We buy a pumpkin and a watermelon; twenty cents—without bargaining.

Our Vietnamese guide, a university student, says that the floating market is an old institution, but in the last twenty years has gained renewed vigor. I notice women on shore step down from their riverfront houses to wash their clothes and faces in the moving well of pollution that flows south from Tibet for some 2,000 miles. Women from the market that faces the river wash vegetables in the visibly filthy river water. The Vietnamese guide, studying to be an English teacher, shrugs her shoulders. "That's the way they've always done it," she smiles apologetically.

The people of Can Tho have not always hustled tourists, however. Leaving the hotel, I inure myself to the pleas of children selling anything from bottled water to Vietnamese phrase books to miniature Ho Chi Minh statues. Tourism in Southeast Asia means rich visitors travel to poor, developing third world countries to buy goods and services for bargain prices, or take a quick look at something exotic so they can tell stories when they return home. This sets up a confrontation between those seeking the unusual and poor people trying to survive. Rich tourists and poor locals—a scenario for degradation!

In early March, a Vietnamese court found former British rock star Gary Glitter, age 61, guilty of sexually abusing two preadolescent girls. Sex trafficking is well underway. In late March, police in HCMC busted a ring that had lured hundreds of women from the countryside under the guise of getting them guest worker jobs abroad. According to Vietnamese News Service, some were sold to Malaysia; others were forced to work as prostitutes in Vietnam as well. The government reported that "since 1998, 4,527 women and children have been traded." Almost 6,500 more are missing and "are believed to have been trafficked." Many more unemployed rural people seek jobs and the predators know it.

Most of the visible hard sell, however, takes the form of legitimate services like rides on the backs of motor bikes or in tiny carriages; or restaurants. A young woman smiles, blocks your path and invites you in to eat the "best food." But tourism comprises a small part of this country's growth leap.

We travel by car, from Ho Chi Minh City to Can Tho, and take a short ferry ride across the Mekong River from Vinh Long Province. Trucks, busses, cars, motorbikes and bicycles sped aboard. Ten minutes later, they race off. A Japanese company is building an enormous bridge to reduce crossing time.

Can Tho, like HCMC, is booming. New homes and apartment complexes dot the extending suburban area, which has invaded ancient rice fields. A growing industrial park and new hotels also adorn the landscape of this sweltering Mekong River city.

We hire a small speed boat to take us to Chau Duc, close to Cambodia. The captain ties up near a small warehouse at a jerry-built dock, where rice is stored in plastic sacks. Boats routinely stop and load the rice for market in Can Tho. Other boats carry farmed fish, vegetables and fruits that each farm produces. Manual labor and primitive machinery!

Rooted in the river mud by long bamboo poles, stands a weather-weary gray shed emitting smoke. My wife and I stop and film three men pouring material into a noisy, motor driven grinder that renders it into pellets. The processed rice leftovers and fish parts smell foul, but they provide food for the catfish being grown in pens of water adjacent to the rice field. Another man loads the straw baskets of ground fish pellets into an ancient wheelbarrow. He takes it to the fish ponds where another man tosses the pellets to the hungry swimmers below. Hundreds of fish leap from the shallow water to get their ration. In an adjacent pond, a man aerates the water, which allows thousands of fish to share a small space. They won't endure the crowded conditions for long.

"They grow in weeks from eggs to marketable size catfish and birdfish," says the captain, translating literally. He didn't know the English word. We tried one for lunch. Yum!

"I'm 78," the wiry, whiskered farmer tells me through the captain. "The secret of longevity," he confides with a chuckle, "means working every day in the rice field." Beats the South Beach diet, I think to myself. He returns to weeding the recently harvested rice field. He foresees good markets for his peas and sesame seeds. The farm also has papaya, banana and mango orchards, alongside chili plants and lemon grass.

"Lemon grass repels poisonous snakes," the boat captain explains. Snake catching and eating had become so popular that the rat population multiplied and chewed seriously at the rice crop. Snakes eat rats. So, the government outlawed commercial snake killing.

A young man missing his front teeth hauls a pesticide tank on his back, connected to a thin dispensing rod. He doesn't want his picture taken. "People in America have mechanized pesticide dispensers, not primitive things like this," motioning to the machine on his back and chuckling.

In the fish food factory, a woman sweeps away the remains, to leave no temptation for rats. Next to her, a two burner hotplate cooks fish and ice—lunch for the extended family. Two dogs sleep on the floor. A small boy runs around one of them. "Some dogs catch rats," the captain explains.

The little factory room also contains a TV set and an empty pack of Marlboros. Indeed, we have seen TV antennas on most of the plumbing-free small farm houses along the Mekong. In villages without electricity, people power TV sets with car batteries. This extended family lives in a new cement house with five bedrooms.

"Life has improved," the old man explains. "During the war," he says, answering my question, "I heard shells landing. But I was lucky. I didn't see it or join it."

Back on the river, the captain tells me his father worked as an interpreter for the U.S. forces and spent a year in a re-education camp after the war. "My father didn't have to fight. But now he receives no pension." Like most of the people we met, the captain has relatives in the United States, most of them in either Orange County or San Jose, California, or the Houston area.

Along the river, crane-operated dredgers haul mud from the bottom of the Mekong River onto barges. Mekong farmers buy this rich soil additive since their land has grown more salinated from the steady dumping of factory and lumber mill waste. China plans to build a large dam on the Mekong, another future headache for those down river.

As the boat nears Chau Duc, we see sugar cane, a nearby sugar refinery and rows of brick ovens with smoke pouring out. Teenage girls haul heavy loads of bricks on their backs to small waiting boats.

In Chau Duc, a city of about 60,000, we see our first mosque—under repair. I ask one of the workmen: "Muslim?" He grins. "Assalamu alaikum," I say.

"Wa'alaikum assalam," he replies.

"Imam?" I ask.

He says something in Vietnamese, which I interpret to mean the Imam is not there. Two other men near the mosque drive by on motorbikes wearing kufis, prayer caps. Children hover around us. Curiosity! We take the return ferry and find the motorbike hustlers eager to show us around town. The temperature feels 100 degrees with almost equal humidity. We decline and retire to the air conditioned upscale Victoria Hotel to sample the local fish and Pho, Vietnamese noodle and meat soup, served with mint, other greens, chilis and nuc mam (pungent fish sauce).

After two weeks traveling from Hanoi to Hue to Hoi Anh to Ho Chi Minh City to Can Tho and Chau Duc, we rate the food from superb to very edible.

In the morning, we take a boat to Pnom Penh.

Cambodia

French and British tourists discuss silk scarf purchases on the Mekong River boat ride from Chau Duc to Pnom Penh. The mighty Mekong makes the Mississippi look like a trickle. The river runs from the Tibet south through China, Myanmar, Thailand, Laos and Cambodia. It empties into the ocean at the southern tip of Vietnam.

Streams, estuaries and smaller rivers flow in and out of it. Alongside these water routes, endless trails and little roads wander off into the countryside. In 1969, the great intellectual National Security Adviser, Henry Kissinger, secretly ordered the bombing of Cambodia to stop arms supplies from North to South Vietnam. This genius thought that B 52 bombers could "interdict" the infinite streams and estuaries.

Hubris? Ignorance of history and geography?

I saw no signs of bombing, nor effects of dioxin, the poison contained in Agent Orange, dropped in massive quantities on Vietnam to defoliate it and reduce enemy hiding places. These toxins produced horrific diseases, deformities and birth defects—and still do. But tourists on a boat, however, saw only the bucolic river life and compared the "friendly quality of the Vietnamese," as one Sheffield resident phrased it "with the more surly Koreans."

Cambodian farms replace Vietnamese along the river and the level of agricultural energy noticeably drops. In place of the diversified Vietnamese farms, we began to see one-crop farming. Vietnam's agricultural and industrial economies are booming; Cambodia depends on tourism and agriculture. The Vietnamese boat guide explained that the better-off Cambodian farmers tend to do the minimum amount of upkeep on their land, while living in town or city homes. Children seeking relief from the heat dove into the river. Occasional small fishing boats, with men leaning over the side tending nets, rocked gently in the speed boat's wake.

As the boat nears Pnom Penh, smoke stacks from lumber mills emit steady streams of pollution. Hotels and restaurants for tourists adorn the avenue running above Pnom Penh's river bank. Following a *Lonely Planet Guide* suggestion, we lunched at the Foreign Correspondents' Club.

The waiter made a tent with his hands and bowed gracefully in greeting. The busboys and even the bartender smiled. We sampled Fish Amok, a curried white fish wrapped in banana leaf over rice, and pumpkin soup—three stars.

On the street, the level of commerce is clearly lighter than in the Vietnamese big cities. Pnom Penh lacks the energy of Ho Chi Min City and Hanoi. Locals move more slowly than in Vietnam—it's a little hotter—and appear peaceful and courteous. Less horns blow. How could such gentle people have engaged in wanton slaughter during the holocaust?

Before Pol Pot died in 1998, he told a journalist that he had "a clear conscience." Yet, between 1975 and 1979 he oversaw the executions, starvation or death by overwork of more than 1.5 million people who shared a common history, including one of the eight wonders of the world.

Some of the walls at the Angkor Wat temple, built between the 9th and 14th Centuries, still contain pock marks made by bullets, residues of Vietnamese and Cambodian "communists" fighting each other amidst the splendor of palaces built by grandiose kings.

Located outside the city of Siem Reap, 315 miles north of Pnom Penh, Angkor Wat now connects with the world. A daily flight links Seoul with Siem Reap. An Iceland Air plane and a Bangkok Air jet filled with Europeans landed just after our flight from Pnom Penh.

The surrounding archeological area contains 100 temples, now administered by a joint UN and Cambodian government commission. But they have not figured out how to recover the missing Buddha heads and other "archeology" pieces that thieves purloined.

Siem Reap's main street, however, has aspects of Las Vegas. Bright neon flashes from 102 hotels—more under construction— and one casino. The tourism rush has transformed this once sleepy village. Banks and travel agencies that provide guides, cars and cash for the thousands of Asians, Europeans, Americans and Australians share the real estate with expensive restaurants and clubs.

The super friendly, if not overly servile, hotel staff does not appear to be groveling for tips. Did any of their parents rat-out their grandparents to Pol Pot's goons for slaughter?

In 1949, Pol Pot received a government scholarship to study in Paris where he quickly became a communist. By 1953, just after France granted independence to Cambodia, he established the Khmer Rouge, the Communist Party. From 1960 to 1963, he led the Party from a jungle lair where he had fled to escape Prince Norodom Sihanouk's police. Can we blame his French education—France ruled Cambodia until 1953—for his murderous propensities?

By 1968, the Khmer Rouge emerged as an armed struggle movement, seemingly typical of the period: Cambodian guerrillas fighting government troops in the name of poor peasants. Maoism!

Between March 1969 and May 1970, Kissinger ordered some 3,600 B-52 bombing raids on Cambodia. Kissinger later lied to the Senate Foreign Relations Committee saying he had selected only "unpopulated" areas of Cambodia for bombing.

Somehow, between 600,000 to 800,000 civilians died in these "unpopulated areas. This carnage occurred before Pol Pot won power. Refugees from the bombing abounded; others left because of poisonous herbicides dropped by U.S. military aircraft. Neither Vietnamese nor Cambodians have recovered from this toxic side of the "the American War."

Kissinger's undeclared war against Cambodia also included overthrowing the government of Prince Norodom Sihanouk. A pro U.S. military coup produced an ineffective regime and subsequently led to the seizure of power by the Khmer Rouge. How little Kissinger "the realist" knew of reality! Or maybe he didn't care!

After a more obedient government let the U.S. do what it wished in Cambodia, the Prince allied himself with the Khmer Rouge to resist the coup.

At the time, Washington offered a domino theory—if Vietnam fell to the communists, then neighboring states would topple like dominoes. But such "theories" ignored bitter rivalries and hatred in the region. In 1960, the indissoluble Soviet-Chinese communist marriage, a U.S. axiom, ended in a rude divorce in 1960. Pol Pot lined up with Beijing; Vietnam depended on Moscow for arms and supplies.

In 1975, Congress cut the military operations budget in Southeast Asia. The United States cut and ran and North Vietnam quickly won the war. The Khmer Rouge grabbed power from the demoralized army, killed their own people and staged incursions into Vietnam.

Pol Pot launched an "agrarian communist revolution" backed by China and, as Vietnam's enemy, Washington also supported the Khmer Rouge government's "killing fields."

In 1978, Vietnam invaded Cambodia. Pol Pot's troops fled into the jungle. By 1993, the Khmer Rouge had grown sufficiently weak so that the Vietnamese could withdraw. Conflicting Cambodian parties signed a peace agreement. In the ensuing UN-supervised election, boycotted by the Khmer Rouge, the royal party triumphed, but somehow members of the KR managed to squeeze significant posts out of the new government.

By 1997, Ieng Sary, Pol Pot's brother-in-law, threw in the towel, along with some 10,000 other members of the guerrilla army. Pol Pot ordered subordinates to murder one of his defecting generals and his family. In June 1997, Pol Pot's own troops took him prisoner. He died a year later.

The attorney for a French hotel chain shook his head. "This country is still traumatized," he whispered. "Up to 2 million Cambodians died and then the new government granted amnesty to all warring sides." He laughed cynically. "It will take time."

Our Cambodian guide, Sam, short for a much longer name, repeatedly stressed Pol Pot's unspeakable horrors. "But it's over," he smiled, as he pointed to a seemingly endless mural etched into the Angkor Wat walls in sandstone depicting life in the 12th Century. Suryavarman II (1113-1150) initiated the temple construction, dedicated to Vishnu. In 1177, invading Chams sacked the Khmer temple, but King Jayavarman VII restored it and built Angkor Thom a few miles north. Art adorns the walls; the architecture makes me feel small. At sunset the temple reflects in the moat in front of it. Tourists gaze in awe.

"Cambodians will recover from the Pol Pot days," Sam assured me. "History," he smiles, "is hard to predict." The construction of one of the world's wonders fascinates spectators because it exemplifies the human imagination. The holocausts perpetrated by Pol Pot or Adolph Hitler reflect the other side of the human potential.

UN and some Cambodian leaders have made unsuccessful attempts to fashion a court to try Khmer Rouge leaders. A current UN-Cambodian government tribunal looms on the horizon. Meanwhile, Pol Pot cronies live in Pnom Penh; indeed, some serve in high government positions.

In Vietnam, U.S. war crimes have taken a back seat to U.S. business. But they have not been forgotten. A late March Hanoi conference explored Agent Orange's impact on Vietnamese health, and opened up possibilities for investigating U.S. officials' "imagination" at a war crimes tribunal.

Epilogue

Freedom 2007:
Buy Sex on the Internet and
Forget the Older Freedoms

ROM THE NOBLE SOUNDING FREEDOM RHETORIC USED BY BUSH and other presidents, foreigners would not have insight into the real meanings of U.S. freedom. Most of the poor people know they must struggle just to survive. Many middle class Americans, however, don't relate to the daily hardships of the majority. Instead, they indulge their consumer whims, as the mass media conditions them, in the combined and very consuming fruits of our Judeo-Christian, freedom-loving heritage.

Those 4 billion third-worlders with factory or field jobs lack the freedoms we possess. They can however, aspire to embrace the American way of finding Jesus at nearby shopping malls or even on line. Most of the world's poor cannot hope to satisfy their most minute religious and sexual urges by sitting at their computer, which they don't have; or reading an evocative e-mail, which they've never received.

Pious and lonely Americans, however, can find mates through on-line dating at Christiancafe.com, "the premier Christian singles site." They can meet devout (read repressed but horny) partners of the other sex and read salacious biblical passages to each other—before making out, above the waist only of course.

"Thank you, ChristianCafe.com," one woman wrote, "for being used by God to bring my husband and me together. Jason and I met on ChristianCafe.com in December 2003. Then in February 2004, we met face to face for the first time. We are enjoying married life immensely!"146

Or, "thirty plus Christians"—illustrated by photos of a pretty blond woman and handsome brown haired guy—can "stop wasting time on online dating sites and meet real Christian singles."

For the lewd and lonely without religious facades, and who feel the ennui of married life, the Web offers spicy sex games. "Do you have the moves to drive your man wild? The art of the striptease involves more than a revealing costume, stiletto heels, and a red feather boa. To successfully release your inner stripper, ladies, you've got to have the moves (of course!), but most important you have to exude self-confidence. Bedroom Games Book is your key to turning your (and his!) most secret sexual fantasies into reality and giving the man in your life a night he won't soon forget! 186 pages. Hard Cover."

For non readers, the internet offers "Glow in the dark foreplay dice." "If your love life consists of been there...done that, then here is a way to spice it up!

If you just don't feel that "sense" of excitement, one company offers a game to "awaken all five senses. *Sensations* puts everything together to ensure that the mood is set for soft caresses, quivers of sensual delight, communication, passion and humor! All your senses will come alive. Includes: 2 tokens, die, hourglass, blindfold, board, 2 spinners, 30 challenge cards, 30 favor coupons, stimulator (one AA battery required, not included), bottle of massage oil and instruction booklet."

For the less sexually obsessed who still focus on the Bill of Rights, events at the Santa Cruz campus of the University of California caused serious concern. The Pentagon dispatched a snoop unit to collect data on anti-war activists on campus. On April 5, 2005, some 200 students vigorously protested the presence of military recruiters at a job fair. The protesters' enthusiasm not only drove out the recruiters, but led the university to temporarily close the job fair.

When Senator Dianne Feinstein (D-CA) learned of the Pentagon spy squad, she wrote Secretary of Defense Donald Rumsfeld: "What Department of Defense components are authorized to collect or maintain information on U.S. Persons on U.S. territory without court approval? Under what circumstances are Department of Defense components authorized to collect, report, maintain, database, analyze, fuse or otherwise handle information concerning U.S. Persons engaged in activities protected by the First Amendment?"

The Bush Administration countered by claiming the Authorization to Use Military Force (AUMF) implicitly authorized domestic spying and prohibiting warrant-less domestic spying impinges upon the president's authority as commander-in-chief. Harvard Law School Professors argued that such spying could violate the Fourth Amendment's prohibition on unreasonable searches and seizures.

Two other incidents should alert people about the precarious state of that "other freedom" that lots of Americans once treasured almost as much as shopping. Hector Carreon in the January 12, 2006 *La Voz de Aztlan* reported that a Homeland Security agent left a business card under his door with a note that said "Please call."

The DHS agent wanted to interrogate him about *La Voz de Aztlan*, which Carreon says, is "an internet news service for Mexican and Mexican-Americans in the U.S. Southwest and in Mexico."

Subsequently, in Carreon's home, one agent said "La Voz de Aztlan has raised eyebrows in Washington." Another agent asked about "Aztlan being a separatist organization, and whether I believed that the Southwest should separate from Washington and become part of Mexico." Did Carreon believe "in the armed and violent overthrow of the U.S. government." They asked him for the names of his associates and the location of his weapons.

Carreon replied that he "believed in making social and political changes through the ballot box."

Carreon signed a document permitting them to examine his computer. "I decided that it would be the best course to continue to fully cooperate with the federal agents.... Right after I signed, the lead agent radioed someone and within five minutes two more special agents arrived to my home with suitcases of electronic equipment. The lead agent asked me to escort them to my computer room where they spent two hours copying the hard disk of my computer."

Another indication of the wobbly state of our other freedoms comes from James Moore, former television news correspondent and co-author of *Bush's Brain: How Karl Rove Made George W. Bush Presidential*.[147] Moore confirmed his flight reservation before leaving home, "went to the electronic kiosk" and got an error message when he tried to print his boarding pass. "Please see agent," the screen read.

After the agent entered his driver's license number into the computer system, she said: "I'm sorry, sir. There seems to be a problem. You've been placed on the No Fly Watch List." That's the one the Transportation Security Administration (TSA) created "or people who might have terrorist connections."

Moore called TSA in Washington to find out how he "got on the No Fly Watch List." "I'm not really authorized to tell you that, sir," the TSA bureaucrat said. She did offer, however, that there was "something in your background that in some way is similar to someone they are looking for."

Moore, whose name has appeared on the No Fly Watch List for a year, concluded that "I will never be told the official reason. No one ever is. You cannot sue to get the information. Nothing I have done has moved me any closer to getting off the list. There were 35,000 Americans in that database last year. According to a European government that screens hundreds of thousands of

American travelers every year, the list they have been given to work from has since grown to 80,000."

While TSA punishes people by not letting them on airplanes, NSA spies on them—not only by eavesdropping on their telephones and e-mails. NSA used local police in New York City and Baltimore to monitor anti-war protestors. Members of the Baltimore Pledge of Resistance, loosely connected to the local American Friends Service Committee, have a history of nonviolent civil disobedience.

An NSA e-mail proves the "Baltimore Intel Unit" of the Police Department gave NSA all the details of a July 3, 2004, protest at Fort Meade. An attorney for the Baltimore Pledge people obtained the e-mail through the discovery process from NSA.[148]

If you want freedom to have virtual sex—even with pious Christians running all three branches of government—the U.S. is the place to be. In 1944, Franklin Roosevelt proclaimed: those old-fashioned freedoms: of speech, expression and worship; and freedom from want and fear. Well, that's history—at least for now.

We don't need more documents to know that the once inviolable rights not to be abused or tortured have eroded. Indeed, despite denials from the White House, Human Rights Watch (HRW) declared that the Bush administration's strategy depends on abusing terror suspects during interrogations.[149]

HRW drew this conclusion from solid evidence, including statements by senior Bush officials. The report stated that Bush's declaration that the United States does not torture suspects rang hollow.

Enjoy the freedom to shop and play sex games, but don't foolishly endanger national security with those other, once sacred freedoms?

History, the unfolding of freedom, as Hegel and Marx saw it, will offer something more profound. Indeed, millions of young people have already understood, instinctively or intellectually, that they have the task of making their own history—not of wasting their lives on virtual pleasure or shopping for the latest gadgets. My children and my students have shown me that they transcend such a banal, consumer world. It provides me with living fact for my living hope.

Notes

1   See http://www.botoxcosmetic.com

2   Ibid.

3   Ibid.

4   Ibid.

5   Ibid.

6   URL: http://www.weeklystandard.com/Content/Public/Articles/
    000/000/003/834llyrg.asp

7   See http://www.botoxcosmetic.com

8   Ibid.

9   URL: http://www.botoxseveresweating.com/can_botox_help/can_
    botox_help.aspx

10 URL: http://iw.rtm.com/bcbc/register.asp?source=&sitecode=bcbc

11 *Melbourne Morning Herald*, July 28, 2004

12 Bush sold the Texas Rangers in 1998

13 URL: http://transcripts.cnn.com/TRANSCRIPTS/0407/12/se.01.html

14 *Tallahassee Democrat*, June 12, 2004

15 The Pentagon's March 15, 2005 "Doctrine for Joint Nuclear
    Operations," reported by the September 11, 2005 *Washington Post*

16 Counting Afghanistan and Iraq

17 Lt. Col. Anthony Shaffer, a former member of a Pentagon task force
    that supported Able Danger, an intelligence unit searching for Al
    Qaeda terrorists, told CNN on August 16, 2005 that "Able Danger
    uncovered information in 2000 about lead hijacker Mohamed
    Atta by searching through public databases and looking for pat-
    terns." His meetings set up with FBI officials in 2000 were canceled
    because "lawyers for the Special Forces unit—of which Able Danger
    was a member—allegedly were concerned military authorities could
    not legally share information with domestic law enforcement about

potential terror suspects in the United States." URL: http://www.
cnn.com/2005/POLITICS/08/17/sept.11.hijackers/

18 In one instance of war profiteering, David H. Brooks, CEO of bul-
letproof vest maker DHB Industries, "has seen his fortunes soar
since the 9/11 terrorist attacks," writes Sarah Anderson, a fellow of
the Institute for Policy Studies. "Last year, he earned $70 million,
most of it from stock options. That represented an increase of 13,349
percent over his pre-9/11 compensation, according to *Executive
Excess*, co-published by the Institute for Policy Studies and United
for a Fair Economy." Even more troublesome, Anderson further
notes, is that "In May 2005, the Marines recalled more than 5,000
DHB armored vests after questions were raised about their effective-
ness in stopping 9 mm bullets." See Anderson, "Put an End to CEO
Excess," *Alternet*, December 17, 2005. URL: http://www.alternet.
org/story/29709/

19 In a November 22, 1982 speech, Reagan called for the United States
to "proceed with the production and deployment of the new ICBM
known as the MX." Reagan called the MX the "Peacekeeper," which
was "the most powerful intercontinental ballistic missile system the
world ever had seen," according to the September 19, 2005 *Associated
Press*. "Each 71-foot-tall, 8-foot-diameter missile, deployed in the
1980s, carried 10 warheads." URL: http://www.billingsgazette.
com/newdex.php?display=rednews/2005/09/19/build/wyoming/50-
missle-system.inc

20 In justifying why he took five draft deferments to avoid serving in
Vietnam, Cheney explained in the April 5, 1989 *Washington Post*, "I
had other priorities in the '60s than military service."

21 On October 6, 2004 the Iraq Survey Group headed by Charles
Duelfer released its final report, confirming that it had "not found
evidence that Saddam possessed WMD stocks in 2003." Previously,
on January 25, 2004, former Bush administration weapons inspector David Kay told National Public Radio's "Weekend Edition," "My
summary view, based on what I've seen, is we're very unlikely to
find large stockpiles of weapons." URL: http://www.cnn.com/2004/
WORLD/meast/01/25/sprj.nirq.kay/

22 *Business Report*, June 6, 2004

23 Halliburton received the first contract to rebuild US military facilities in Louisiana following Hurricane Katrina in September 2005

24 See Francis Harris, "Powell Admits his Iraq WMD Claim is 'Painful
Blot,'" *The Telegraph*, September 10, 2005

25 In February 2002, President Bush appointed retired Admiral John
Poindexter, President Reagan's National Security Adviser, to head

the Information Awareness Office, an offshoot of the Pentagon's ultra secret Defense Advanced Research Projects Agency. In the late 1980s, Poindexter lied to Congress and secretly plotted to circumvent the law prohibiting the sale of missiles to the US-hating fanatics in Iran. Poindexter colluded with other officials, including Elliot Abrams, to use the proceeds to buy weapons for the CIA's contra rebels. In April 1990, the judge gave him six months in prison, but an appellate court reversed the sentence because Congress had granted him immunity. In December 2002, Bush appointed Reagan's Deputy Assistant Secretary of State to Central America, Elliot Abrams, as Special Assistant to the President and Senior Director for Near East and North African Affairs, and later in February 2005, as Deputy Assistant to the President and Deputy National Security Advisor for Global Democracy Strategy. Back in October 1991, Abrams pled guilty to withholding information from Congress in the Iran-Contra scandal and received two years probation and 100 hours of community work. See Landau's December 5, 2002 and January 4, 2003 *Counterpunch* essays on Abrams and Poindexter, http://www.counterpunch.org/landau1205.html and http://www.counterpunch.org/landau01042003.html

26 The government's behavior in the aftermath of Hurricane Katrina gave Louisiana and Mississippi citizens good reason to hate government agencies and officials who ran them. Michael Brown, head of FEMA at the time said to CNN's Paula Zahn on September 1, 2005 that "the federal government did not even know about the convention center people until today."

27 URL: http://politicalhumor.about.com/cs/quotethis/a/reagan-quotes.htm

28 President Bush's "Address to a Joint Session of Congress and the American People," September 20, 2001. URL: http://www.whitehouse.gov/news/releases/2001/09/20010920-8.html

29 *Associated Press*, August 30, 2005

30 *Times-Union News*, June 29, 2004

31 *Boston Globe*, April 27, 2004

32 Reagan cited in *OneWorld US*, January 27, 2004. URL: http://www.globalpolicy.org/finance/docs/2004/0127usagencydues.htm

33 On January 4, 2006 Israeli Prime Minister Ariel Sharon suffered a "significant" stroke and brain hemorrhage. He remains in a drug-induced coma. His powers were transferred to Deputy Prime Minister Ehud Olmert, who together with Sharon, quit the right-wing Likud Party in November 2005 and formed the new centrist party, Kadima.

34 In Reagan's June 12, 1987 remarks at Brandenburg Gate, West Berlin, Germany, he implored, "Mr. Gorbachev, tear down this wall!" URL: http://www.reaganlibrary.com/reagan/speeches/wall. asp

35 During the Spring of 1954, McCarthy had alleged that the U.S. Army failed to provide adequate security at a secret army facility. In response, the Army hired Boston attorney Joseph Welch and at the June 9 hearing, McCarthy accused a Welch attorney of having Communist ties. "Until this moment, Senator," Welch responded, "I think I never really gauged your cruelty or your recklessness." Before McCarthy could continue on with his tirade, Welch interrupted, "Let us not assassinate this lad further, senator. You have done enough. Have you no sense of decency?" See http://www. senate.gov/artandhistory/history/minute/Have_you_no_sense_of_ decency.htm

36 *Washington Post*, February 13, 2005

37 URL: http://americablog.blogspot.com/screencapture2x.jpg

38 *New York Times*, February 14, 2005

39 David F. Krugler, "God, Monogamy, and the Newsroom? The 1953 McCarthy Investigation of the Voice of America," Organization of American Historians April 2-5, 1998, Indianapolis, Indiana

40 *Daily Kos*, February 18, 2005

41 On February 2, 2004 Jackson apologized to those television viewers offended by seeing her exposed breast. The Federal Communications Commission on September 22, 2004 fined CBS a record total of $550,000 for broadcasting the incident. URL: http:// www.cbsnews.com/stories/2004/07/01/entertainment/main626925. shtml

42 Limbaugh made this statement on October 5, 1995. See "Limbaugh on Drugs," Fairness and Accuracy in Reporting (FAIR) *Extra!*, November/December 2003. URL: http://www.fair.org/index. php?page=1159

43 On October 10, 2003, Limbaugh publicly confessed to taking Oxycontin. "I take full responsibility for my problem," he said to his listeners. See radio transcript of his confession. URL: http://radio. about.com/library/bllimbaughstatement.htm

44 "O'Reilly Hit with Sex Harass Suit," *The Smoking Gun*, October 13, 2004. Legal complaint available online at http://www.thesmoking-gun.com/archive/1013043mackris1.html

45 According to the Council on American-Islamic Relation's (CAIR) 2005 report, "Unequal Protection," the organization found a "49 percent increase in the reported cases of harassment, violence and discriminatory treatment of Muslim-Americans from 2003" and "received 141 reports of actual and potential violent anti-Muslim hate crimes, a 52 percent increase from the 93 reports received in 2003." Executive Summary, URL: http://www.cair-net.org/asp/execsum2005.asp

46 Fitzgerald indictment, Page 5

47 *The Price of Loyalty*

48 Pat Robertson, "The 700 Club," October 29, 1982

49 "The 700 Club," January 21, 1993

50 *The Independent*, July 24, 2005

51 Friedman's quote cited in Scott Whitney's Salon.com review of *The Lexus and the Olive Tree*, April 19, 1999

52 Steve Conner, *The Independent*, July 24, 2005

53 *The Lexus and the Olive Tree*, page 378, Farrar, Straus and Giroux

54 "In Defense of Government," Commencement Address to the graduating class of Roosevelt University, May 21, 1995

55 *NY Times* op-ed, August 1, 2005

56 *Bush on the Couch*, 2004

57 Judy Keen, *USA Today*, April 2, 2003

58 *The Observer*, November 2, 2003

59 Barbara Bush, after touring the devastated areas, NPR "Marketplace," September 5, 2005

60 UPI, April 11, 2003. Rumsfeld resigned in November 2006. Robert Gates replaced him.

61 Landrieu, September 3, 2005 press release

62 Ibid.

63 CNN, September 1, 2005

64 April 20, 2004

65 Doug Thompson, *Capitol Hill Blue*, December 8, 2005

66 December, 17, 2005. URL: http://www.cnn.com

67 *Alternet*, December 17, 2005

68 *Washington Post*, November 2, 2005

69 Ibid.

70 See http://www.cnn.com

71 August 12, 1945

72 BBC, November 11, 2004

73 *Reuters*, November 12, 2004

74 Israeli journalist Uri Avnery used this expression in his essay, "A Crooked Mirror: Presstitution and the Theater of Operations," *Counterpunch*, April 3, 2003. URL: http://www.counterpunch.org/avnery04032003.html

75 *Associated Press*, "Audit: Funds for Iraq Rebuilding Squandered," January 29, 2006. According to the AP, "A U.S. government audit found American-led occupation authorities squandered tens of millions of dollars that were supposed to be used to rebuild Iraq through undocumented spending and outright fraud." Among the examples of corruption cited in a report issued by the Special Inspector General for Iraq Reconstruction, "Only a quarter of $23 million entrusted to civilian and military project and contracting officers to pay contractors ever found its way to those contractors" and that of the "$7.3 million spent on a police academy near Hillah, auditors could account for just $4 million...$1.3 million was wasted on overpriced or duplicate construction or equipment not delivered. More than $2 million was missing."

76 1935

77 *Chicago Sun Times*, November 12, 2004

78 General James Rusling, "Interview with President William McKinley," *The Christian Advocate* 22 January 1903, 17. Reprinted in Daniel Schirmer and Stephen Rosskamm Shalom, eds., *The Philippines Reader* (South End Press, 1987), 22–23.

79 Daphna Berman, *Ha'aretz*, October 4, 2004

80 *The Washington Star*, July 3, 1980

81 April 18, 2002

82 Daphna Berman *Ha'aretz*, October 4, 2004

83 Kingsport, Tennessee Conference. URL: http://www.j-cinstitute.org/Articles/Blewett_Antichrist.htm

84 Maura Jane Farrelly, April 28, 2005

85 Michael A. Fuoco, *Pittsburgh Post-Gazette*, April 28, 2005

86 Gabriel Kolko, *Anatomy of War: Vietnam, the US and the Modern Historical Experience."* See *Counterpunch*, April 30, 2005

87 *New York Times*, May 1, 2005

88 *Counterpunch*, April 30, 2005

89 See John Ross, *Counterpunch* February 21, 2005

90 *Christian Science Monitor*, March 3, 2005

91 John Ross, *Counterpunch*, February 21, 2005

92 August 26, 2005

93 *Al Jazeera*, "Global News Monday," December 13, 2004

94 *Associated Press*, Dec. 17, 2005

95 MSNBC, January 6, 2006

96 "The Wiretappers That Couldn't Shoot Straight," *New York Times*, January 8, 2006

97 UPI, August 1, 2004

98 Ibid.

99 Michael Manley defined it as "mashing up the good order of society." See Landau's 1980 film, "Steppin'"

100 In 2005 and 2006, Chilean judges stripped Pinochet of his immunity and charged him with kidnapping, torture and assassination, as well as tax evasion and money laundering. On December 10, 2006, International Human Rights Day, Pinochet died at age 91.

101 Jamail testimony at the World Tribunal on Iraq, June 25, 2005, Istanbul

102 Fasy testimony at the World Tribunal on Iraq, June 26, 2005, Istanbul

103 *The Nation*, April 28, 2003

104 Naomi Klein, speech at Cal Poly Pomona University, November 2004

105 *The Nation*, February 11, 2005

106 *Commentary*, 1979

107 Andrea Chaparro, *La Nacion*, July 30, 2005

108 Alicia Herrera, *We Placed the Bomb and So What*

109 In March 2004, the Massachusetts Senator was stopped by Homeland Security five times on the East Coast, including at Boston's Logan International Airport. His name had appeared on the government's "No-Fly" list.

110 "Bush's Booze Crisis," September 21, 2005

111 "Limbaugh Caught in Drug Ring," October 2, 2003

112 See http://www.whitehouse.gov, September 12, 2005

113 *Counterpunch*, January 22, 2003

114 *Counterpunch*, October 11, 2002

115 Speech to the National Endowment for Democracy, October 6, 2005

116 Jim Lobe, Inter Press Service, September 29, 2005

117 On September 28, 2005 DeLay was forced to resign as House Majority leader after a Texas Grand Jury charged him and two associates with one count of criminal conspiracy for "improperly funneling corporate donations to Republican candidates for the Texas legislature," reported CNN on September 29, 2005. He quit his leadership post on January 8, 2006. On February 2, 2006, House Republicans elected Ohio Representative John Boehner as House Majority leader.

118 *Bush On The Couch: Inside The Mind Of The President*

119 *The National Enquirer*, September 21, 2005

120 As of February 20, 2006 the Justice Department had not decided whether it would free Posada or deport him. Cuba and Venezuela both want him extradited. No other country, thus far, will accept him. The US government must file charges by February 2007, or a judge will free Posada.

121 One website called "The Che Guevara Store...For All Your Revolutionary Needs," sells an array of Che-inspired t-shirts, berets, posters and collectibles. URL: http://www.thechestore.com/

122 *Al Jazeera*, August 25, 2005

123 pg. 31

124 Norman Finkelstein, *Beyond Chutzpah: On the Misuse of Anti-Semitism and the Abuse of History*, pg. 52, University of California Press, 2005

125 *The New Yorker,* May 31, 2005

126 *The New Yorker,* May 31, 2005

127 "On This Earth," *Unfortunately, It Was Paradise,* University of California Press, 2003, pg. 6

128 According to the January 26, 2006 official election results, Hamas won 76 of the 132 parliamentary seats.

129 Robert Fisk, *The Independent,* January 21, 2006

130 Max Blumenthal, "Her Kinsey Obsession," *Alternet,* December 15, 2004. URL: http://www.alternet.org/election04/20744/

131 Ibid.

132 *Sydney Morning Herald,* July 16, 2004

133 http://www.rotten.com/library/bio/business/william-randolph-hearst/

134 Randy Davis, "Nazis in the Attic: Part I." URL: http://www.emperors-clothes.com/articles/randy/swas1.htm

135 Ibid.

136 "Lines Composed a Few Miles Above Tintern Abbey"

137 May 9, 2005

138 *Los Angeles Times,* June 4, 2005

139 June 4, 2005

140 Bergman, *Columbia Journalism Review,* May/June 2000

141 *Reuters,* February 19, 1999

142 *Capitol Hill Blue,* August 17, 1999

143 On February 16, 2006 the Senate voted 96-3 to a compromise in renewing the Patriot Act. It added provisions designed to protect civil liberties. Those new provisions include allowing "recipients of secret national-security letters...to appeal gag orders," removing "the requirement that recipients of national security letters must notify the FBI of the identity of any attorneys consulted on the matter" and exempting "libraries that provide only traditional services such as book lending and Internet access from receiving national security letters." Source: James Kuhnhenn, "Patriot Act Renewal Clears Hurdle in Senate," *Knight Ridder,* February 16, 2006. Wisconsin Democratic Senator Russell Feingold, the only Senator who had voted against the original 2001 version of the Patriot Act, was one of three senators who objected to the compromise bill. In

his February 15, 2006 remarks on the Senate floor, Feingold called the negotiated deal "a capitulation to the intransigent and misleading rhetoric of a White House that sees any effort to protect civil liberties as a sign of weakness... We've come too far and fought too hard to agree to reauthorize the Patriot Act without fixing any of the major problems with the Act." See Feingold's statement, http://www.truthout.org/docs_2006/021506R.shtml

144 URL: http://www.kff.org

145 Ibid.

146 URL: http://www.christiancafe.com/guests/join/ad/index.jsp?id=16318

147 URL: http://www.huffingtonpost.com/jim-moore/branded_b_13272.html, January 4, 2006

148 URL: http://www.commondreams.org/cgi-bin/print.cgi?file=/headlines06/0113-09.htm

149 Human Rights Watch Annual Report, released on January 18, 2006

Index

AK Press

ORDERING INFORMATION

AK Press
674-A 23rd Street
Oakland, CA 94612 1163
U.S.A
(510) 208-1700
www.akpress.org
akpress@akpress.org

AK Press
PO Box 12766
Edinburgh, EH8 9YE
Scotland
(0131) 555-5165
www.akuk.com
ak@akedin.demon.uk

The addresses above would be delighted to provide you with the latest complete AK catalog, featuring several thousand books, pamphlets, zines, audio products, video products, and stylish apparel published & distributed by AK-Press. Alternatively, check out our websites for the complete catalog, latest news and updates, events, and secure ordering.

Also Available from AK Press

The first audio collection from Alexander Cockburn on compact disc.

Beating the Devil

Alexander Cockburn, ISBN: 1 902593 49 9 • CD • $14.98

In this collection of recent talks, maverick commentator Alexander Cockburn defiles subjects ranging from Colombia to the American presidency to the Missile Defense System. Whether he's skewering the fallacies of the war on drugs or illuminating the dark crevices of secret government, his erudite and extemporaneous style warms the hearts of even the stodgiest cynics of the left.

Available from CounterPunch/AK Press

Call 1-800-840-3683 or order online from
www.counterpunch.org or www.akpress.org

The Case Against Israel
by Michael Neumann

Wielding a buzzsaw of logic, Professor Neumann dismantles plank-by-plank the Zionist rationale for Israel as religious state entitled to trample upon the basic human rights of non-Jews. Along the way, Neumann also offers a passionate amicus brief for the plight of the Palestinian people.

Other Lands Have Dreams: From Baghdad to Pekin Prison
by Kathy Kelly

At a moment when so many despairing peace activists have thrown in the towel, Kathy Kelly, a witness to some of history's worst crimes, never relinquishes hope. Other Lands Have Dreams is literary testimony of the highest order, vividly recording the secret casualties of our era, from the hundreds of thousands of Iraqi children inhumanely denied basic medical care, clean water and food by the US overlords to young mothers sealed inside the sterile dungeons of American prisons in the name of the merciless war on drugs.

Dime's Worth of Difference: Beyond the Lesser of Two Evils
Edited by Alexander Cockburn and Jeffrey St. Clair

Everything you wanted to know about one-party rule in America.

Whiteout: the CIA, Drugs and the Press
by Alexander Cockburn and Jeffrey St. Clair, Verso.

The involvement of the CIA with drug traffickers is a story that has slouched into the limelight every decade or so since the creation of the Agency. In Whiteout, here at last is the full saga.

Been Brown So Long It Looked Like Green to Me: the Politics of Nature
by Jeffrey St. Clair, Common Courage Press.

Covering everything from toxics to electric power plays, St. Clair draws a savage profile of how money and power determine the state of our environment, gives a vivid account of where the environment stands today and what to do about it.

Imperial Crusades: Iraq, Afghanistan and Yugoslavia
by Alexander Cockburn and Jeffrey St. Clair, Verso.

A chronicle of the lies that are now returning each and every day to haunt the deceivers in Washington and London, the secret agendas and the underreported carnage of these wars. We were right and they were wrong, and this book proves the case. Never leave home without it.

Why We Publish CounterPunch
By Alexander Cockburn and Jeffrey St. Clair

Ten years ago we felt unhappy about the state of radical journalism. It didn't have much edge. It didn't have many facts. It was politically timid. It was dull. CounterPunch was founded. We wanted it to be the best muckraking newsletter in the country. We wanted it to take aim at the consensus of received wisdom about what can and cannot be reported. We wanted to give our readers a political roadmap they could trust.

A decade later we stand firm on these same beliefs and hopes. We think we've restored honor to muckraking journalism in the tradition of our favorite radical pamphleteers: Edward Abbey, Peter Maurin and Ammon Hennacy, Appeal to Reason, Jacques René Hébert, Tom Paine and John Lilburne.

Every two weeks CounterPunch gives you jaw-dropping exposés on: Congress and lobbyists; the environment; labor; the National Security State.

"CounterPunch kicks through the floorboards of lies and gets to the foundation of what is really going on in this country", says Michael Ratner, attorney at the Center for Constitutional Rights. "At our house, we fight over who gets to read CounterPunch first. Each issue is like spring after a cold, dark winter."

The Secret Language of the Crossroads

How the Irish Invented Slang

By Daniel Cassidy

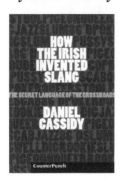

In *The Secret Language of the Crossroad: How the Irish Invented Slang*, Daniel Cassidy co-director and founder of the Irish Studies Program at New College of California cuts through two hundred years worth of Anglo academic "baloney" and reveals the massive, hidden influence of the Irish language on the American language.

Irish words and phrases are scattered all across the American language, regional and class dialects, colloquialism, slang, and specialized jargons like gambling, in the same way Irish-Americans have been scattered across the crossroads of North America for five hundred years.

In a series of essays, including: *"Decoding the Gangs of New York," "How the Irish Invented Poker and American Gambling Slang," "The Sanas (Etymology) of Jazz," "Boliver of Brooklyn,"* and in a *First Dictionary of Irish-American Vernacular*, Cassidy provides the hidden histories and etymologies of hundreds of so-called slang words that have defined the American language and culture like *dude, sucker, swell, poker, faro, cop, scab, fink, moolah, fluke, knack, ballyhoo, baloney*, as well as the hottest word of the 20th century, *jazz*.